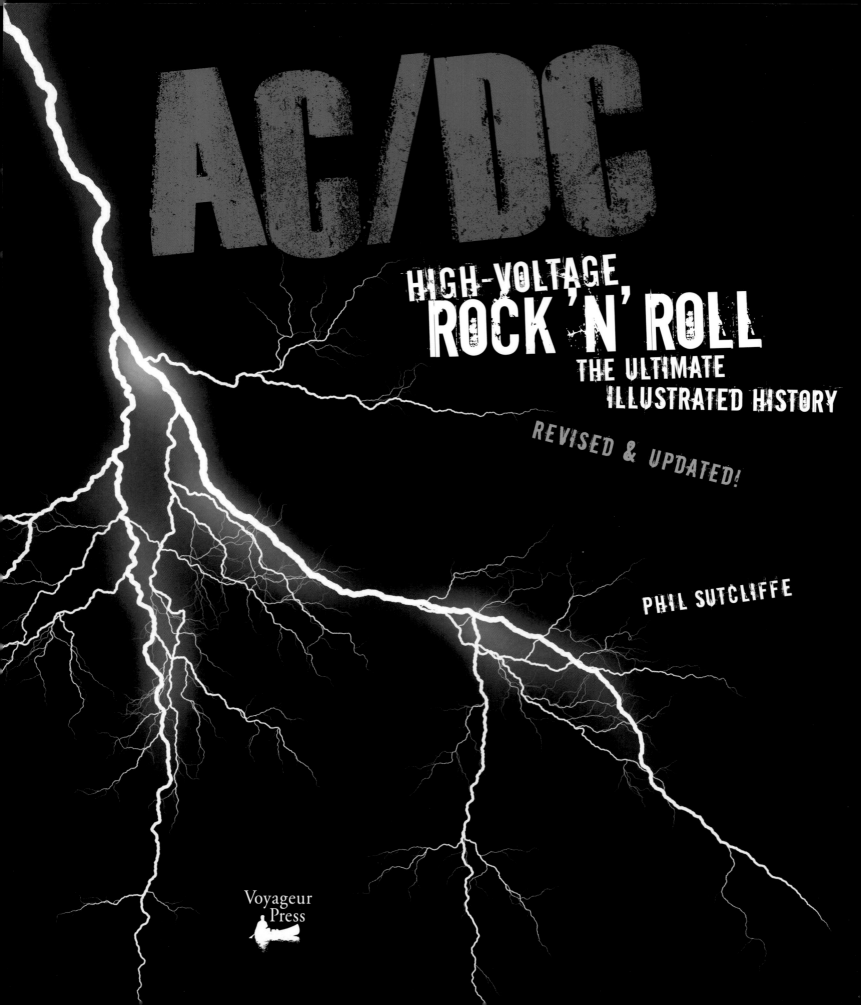

AC/DC

HIGH-VOLTAGE, ROCK 'N' ROLL
THE ULTIMATE ILLUSTRATED HISTORY

REVISED & UPDATED!

PHIL SUTCLIFFE

Voyageur
Press

By

Phil Sutcliffe

⚡ with ⚡

Robert Alford
Joe Bonomo
Anthony Bozza
Jen Jewel Brown
Daniel Bukszpan
Garth Cartwright
Ian Christe
David Dunlap Jr.
Andrew Earles
Robert Ellis
Robert Francos
Gary Graff
Dave Hunter
Bob King
Jenny Lens
James McNair
Philip Morris
Graeme Plenter
Martin Popoff
Sylvie Simmons
Bill Voccia

First published in 2010 by Voyageur Press, an imprint of Quarto Publishing Group USA Inc., 400 First Avenue North, Suite 400, Minneapolis, MN 55401 USA. This revised edition published 2015.

The information in this book is true and complete to the best of our knowledge. All recommendations are made without any guarantee on the part of the author or Publisher, who also disclaims any liability incurred in connection with the use of this data or specific details.

We recognize, further, that some words, model names, and designations mentioned herein are the property of the trademark holder. We use them for identification purposes only. This is not an official publication.

This book has not been licensed or approved by AC/DC, its members, or affiliated partners. This is not an official publication.

Voyageur Press titles are also available at discounts in bulk quantity for industrial or sales-promotional use. For details write to Special Sales Manager at Quarto Publishing Group USA Inc., 400 First Avenue North, Suite 400, Minneapolis, MN 55401 USA.

To find out more about our books, visit us online at www.voyageurpress.com.

ISBN: 978-0-7603-4946-5

The Library of Congress has cataloged the hardcover edition as follows:

Sutcliffe, Phil.
AC/DC : the ultimate illustrated history / Phil Sutcliffe.
   p. cm.
Includes index.
ISBN 978-0-7603-3832-2 (hb w/jkt)
1. AC/DC (Musical group) 2. Rock musicians–Australia–Biography. I. Title.
ML421.A28S87 2010
782.42166092'2–dc22
[B]   2010003185

Front cover © *Robert Alford*
Page 1: *Fin Costello/Redferns/Getty Images*
Pages 2–3: © *Robert Alford*
Page 4: *Plavusa87/Shutterstock*
Pages 6–7: *Michael Putland/Hulton Archive/Getty Images*

AC/DC: Maximum Rock & Roll, copyright © 2006 by Murray Engleheart and Arnaud Durieux, published by HarperCollins Australia, 2006. All rights reserved. Used with permission.

Editor: Dennis Pernu
Design Manager: LeAnn Kuhlmann
Design: Mighty Media
Layout: Chris Long, Anders Hanson
Cover Design: Chris Long & Brad Norr

Printed in China

Contents

Chapter 1

Head-on Rock 'n' Roll Down Under

AC/DC. Just think about that name and you start to sweat—whether you first saw them in 2010 on the *Black Ice* tour in a modern arena with 20,000 souls from every drenched, exalted generation or, like this writer, at The Marquee in London in 1976, jammed into a dank and dripping cave of a club.

Good rockin' tonight. And every night.

That's what AC/DC have always stood for. Pure and simple. Dirty and simple. Ablaze with the original spirit of rock 'n' roll. They mingled the teenage joys of groin-stirring riffs, blood-stirring rhythm, and belly-laugh or sometimes gut-level-blue lyrics into an elixir of eternal youth promising age cannot wither us nor custom stale our infinite . . . sweatiness at least—as the late bards William Shakespeare and Bon Scott might have agreed.

AC/DC play rock 'n' roll as life met head-on. Scruffy reality, good times and bad.

Logic won't explain the minor miracles that create such a band. But

> **We are going to be one of the greatest bands in the world. . . . It's a shame Hendrix is dead: I wanted to blow him off stage.**
>
> —Angus Young, quoted by early AC/DC bassist Neil Smith

exploring AC/DC's story, it's striking that this enduring force sprang from a great European migration to the New World—the Australasian New World, that is. Driven by poverty, desperation, ambition, and high hope against all odds . . .

⚡ ⚡ ⚡

The Young family was numerous and loving, George Redburn (born November 6, 1947), Malcolm John (January 6, 1953), and Angus McKinnon (March 31, 1955) being the last three of eight children spread over twenty-two years. Their mother, Margaret, born 1915 (maiden name Young, too), and father William (1910), who worked as a spray painter, valve grinder, and, during World War II, a Royal Air Force mechanic, brought them up in Cranhill, Glasgow, a Scottish shipbuilding city in decline.

By the 1950s, the city council had moved many slum dwellers from tenements in the city's center to new tenements in suburbs like Cranhill, and

it was getting tough. With few residents owning cars, and few shops in walking distance, a succession of delivery vans circulated selling groceries, paraffin, fish and chips, and ice cream.

Like other kids, the Youngs played football on the streets, but they always had their music too. The only girl in the family, Margaret (born in 1936), introduced the household to black rock 'n' roll from Fats Domino, Little Richard, and Chuck Berry, along with some Dixieland jazz. In 1991, talking to *Musician*'s Charles M. Young (no relation), Angus recalled her taking him to see Louis Armstrong (this was probably in Australia): "I liked the way he smiled. Some people, you get goose bumps when they perform, and he was one. You could tell he was honest, a good man and a happy man." The Youngs made their own entertainment via a parlor band comprising brothers Steven (born in 1933) on accordion, John (1938) and Alex (1938) on guitars, and the kids singing along.

The Easybeats, November 1966, from left: Dick Diamonde, Harrry Vanda, George Young, Gordon "Snowy" Fleet, and Stevie Wright (seated). *Caroline Gillies/BIPs/Getty Images*

The Easybeats, "She's So Fine" w/ "Say That You're Mine," "For My Woman," and "The Old Oak Tree," 7-inch EP, Australia, 1965.

The Easybeats, "Friday on My Mind" b/w "Made My Bed (Gonna Lie in It)," Italy, 1966.

The Easybeats, "Friday on My Mind" w/ "Remember Sam," "Pretty Girl," and "Made My Bed (Gonna Lie in It)," 7-inch EP, France, 1967.

The Easybeats, "St. Louis," promo single, U.S., 1969.

Easybeats George Young and Harry Vanda. © Philip Morris

In 1963, the Youngs decided there had to be something better than Cranhill. As Angus said later (source unknown), "Me dad found it impossible to support a family of our size, so he decided to try his luck Down Under." Abandoning everything they knew, the Youngs joined the "£10 Poms," the million Britons who took up the Australian government's post-World War II "assisted passage" scheme (almost as big as the United States, Australia had only 8 million people in 1945).

His uniform is filthy, his knees are constantly bruised, his eyes blackened, his nose running.

—R. K. Lanning, headmaster of Ashfield Boys' High School, reporting on Angus

The family—minus Steven and Alex, the latter already playing in Hamburg, like The Beatles—flew to Sydney. Initially, they lived at Villawood migrant hostel ("Tin huts, and it rained, relentlessly; when you got up in the morning, there was two inches of water in the hut and black worms swimming through it," Malcolm told David Fricke, *Rolling Stone*, 2008). One of Angus' early migrant memories, related, unattributed, in Paul Stenning's *AC/DC: Two Sides to Every Glory*, is of young men on their way to Bondi Beach, "standing there with these wooden boards. . . . I'd never seen a surfboard in my life. I went home and said, 'Mum, I think we're on another planet.'"

In no time, though, dynamic George had organized a Villawood band with himself on rhythm, Anglo-Aussie Stevie Wright on vocals, and Dutch lead guitarist Johannes Vandenberg (who soon became "Harry Vanda"). Their band, The Easybeats, shortly signed to a new label called Albert Productions, run by Ted Albert, whose father owned a radio and music publishing company. By 1965, they had a No. 1 hit single in Australia with "She's So Fine." The following year, they set off for England.

Meanwhile, the family having set up a crowded home overrun with siblings and rock 'n' rolling mates on Burleigh Street, Burwood district, Malcolm and Angus embarked on school careers characterized by a letter to their mother from R. K. Lanning, headmaster of Ashfield Boys' High School. It accused them of "abusive language . . . obscene gestures" and "obstreperousness verging on violence." Lanning portrayed Angus as the ultimate cartoon naughty boy: "His uniform is filthy, his knees are constantly bruised, his eyes blackened, his nose running."

Although school rejected them, music offered enticing blandishments; at The Easybeats' peak with "Friday on My Mind" in October 1966 (U.K. No. 6, then U.S. No. 16 the following May), girl fans would chase big star George's kid brothers home from school. "Me and Angus thought, 'This is the way to go!'" Malcolm told *Mojo*'s Sylvie Simmons in 2000. Their mother bought them their first guitars in 1965 when they were twelve and ten. Two years later, Harry Vanda gave Malcolm a 1963 Gretsch Jet Firebird he'd bought in London (Malcolm loved its dirty sound, which Vanda detested) and handed down his Hofner to Angus. Their father discouraged his youngest sons' rock 'n' roll ambitions, but they had learned his fierce work ethic and practiced relentlessly.

They bought every record they could afford: The Rolling Stones, Bluesbreakers with Eric Clapton, Mountain, Argent, Jimi Hendrix, Cactus (an Angus favorite). They loved to read about "new" names, such as R&B greats Buddy Guy or Elmore James, in the music papers George mailed home from England and then order their albums from the Burwood record shop on import.

This ardor even brought out the Scottish working-class self-educator in Angus (Stenning, unattributed): "If I wanted to learn something, my old man used to say, 'Angus, do yourself a favour. There's a library down the road, go in there.' When I'd truant that was the first place I'd head to. It was great . . . racks of *Down Beat* magazine from America with articles on people like Muddy Waters." He played snatches of magic tracks over and over to analyze what made them so explosive—Little Richard's "Keep A Knockin'" for instance: "I'd take the needle and keep putting it back on the same spot . . . the blues bit."

The two brothers loved live bands too. They'd join the crowd of kids gathered at Burwood railway station on a Saturday night to travel in to city-center gigs. Some shows they remembered like master classes: The Yardbirds (with Jimmy Page) at Sydney Stadium, January 21 and/or 23, 1967 ("wild and exciting," Angus reckoned); The Who and The Small Faces at the same venue, January 22, 1968 (they liked the guitar smashing).

And Malcolm would dish out fairly rudimentary, sometimes pugilistic, tutorials. Angus recalled: "He would always tell me, 'Don't tickle the guitar, hit the bugger.'" Whenever The Easybeats came home, George proved more constructive: "He would pick up a bass and hand you the guitar. You'd think you were incompetent, but before you knew it you were playing. He would go, 'G . . . A . . .' and you were away. . . . He was into some crazy things too. He'd tell me the D string annoyed him. The G too. . . . The last time I saw him

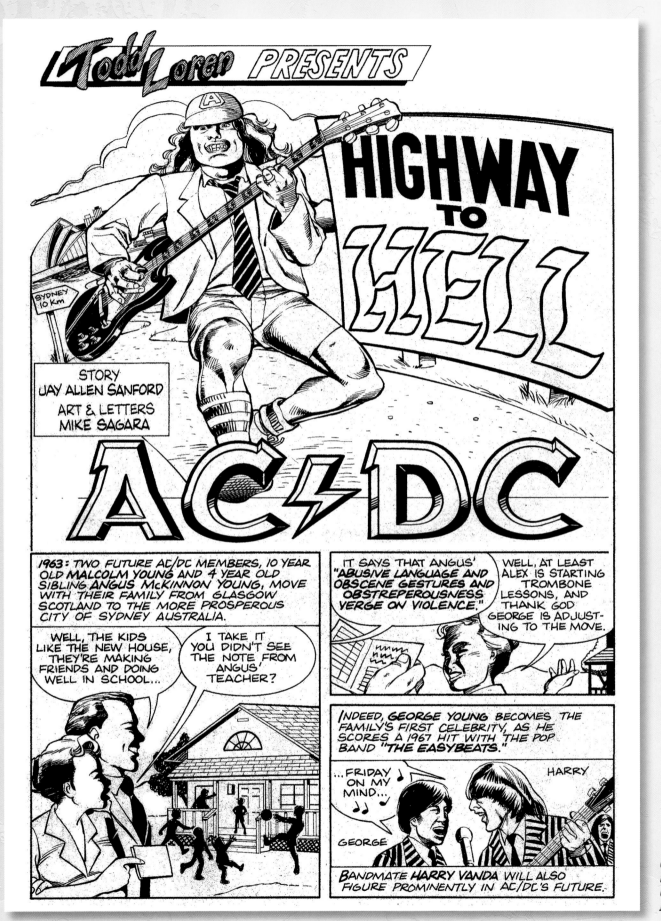

with The Easybeats he had four strings on that guitar!"

Both brothers left school the moment they legally could, at age fourteen years nine months, in October 1967 and December 1969, respectively. Malcolm found work at the Hestia bra factory servicing sewing machines. But on the weekend he played local gigs with a series of bands: Beelzebub Blues, Red House, and Rubberband. Although he began writing songs with a friend, mostly they covered '60s pop, Beatles to early Cream. Already a strong lead guitarist, Malcolm tended toward bandleader, too, because of his purposeful thinking.

By July 1971, though, when Stevie Wright recommended him to the (Australian) Velvet Underground, a West Coast covers combo, he grabbed at the chance and quit the day job. A touring band, it took him outside Sydney (for the first time since his family flew in from Glasgow) and introduced him to groupies, pot, and other deviations from the true path, such as "jazz chords and progressive music," Malcolm told Anthony O'Grady of Australian magazine *RAM* in 1975. Velvet Underground, later renamed Pony, broke up in February 1973, leaving Malcolm at a loose end.

Meanwhile, school-leaver Angus made fruitless inquiries about openings for songwriters and then trained to be a printer. Saving up, he had bought a Gibson SG that was to become a lifelong companion—he went for it because Pete Townshend and Mountain's Leslie West played them, the neck suited his small hands, and, as some legends have it, he fell in love with its double-horned shape. He messed around with the relatively harmless Town Hall Sharps skinhead gang and followed Malcolm and Velvet Underground around, making them all cups of Ovaltine when they brought him home late at night.

Angus formed his first semiserious band, Kantuckee, at seventeen in 1972. It rehearsed in a Boy Scouts hut. His dubious degree of rock 'n' rollness might be calibrated from his conspicuous consumption of tea and biscuits. He'd smoked since he was eight, but a brief, chunder-inducing experiment with Bond 7 Australian whiskey turned him teetotal for life. Teeth turned green from a lack of diligent brushing only emphasized his glamour-free aspect. Diligently, Kantuckee (who turned into Tantrum) built a fifty-song set to fill the four hours a night required by their regular gig at decaying, though marble-staircased, Sydney club Chequers, where Frank Sinatra and Shirley Bassey had once entertained Aussie gangsters Duke Delaney and Iron Bar Miller.

If he had to proclaim himself "a dwarf" to venue managers nervous about his age, no worries. Angus could make the best of anything. When, one night, he tripped over his guitar lead, he alchemized embarrassment into a routine so crowd-pleasing it became a staple of his act to this day. As Angus related, unattributed, in Martin Huxley's *AC/DC: The World's Heaviest Rock*, "I kept rolling across the floor. I made it look like a big death scene, screaming all hell from the guitar."

Still, when he lost his drummer after a scrap, Angus dumped Tantrum just as Malcolm left Pony. The brothers remained close if abrasive. They still went to gigs together—landmarks included Led Zeppelin (February 27, 1972, Sydney Showground; Angus scoffed that Robert Plant sang "like he was picking his nose"); The Rolling Stones (Royal Randwick Racecourse, February 26 and/or 27, 1973; Malcolm loved their entrance in a white horse-drawn carriage); and probably Muddy Waters (Sydney Auditorium, May 3, 1973).

Malcolm put a new band together. First he acquired a rhythm section—well-known local drummer Colin Burgess and San Francisco-born bassist and Villawood graduate Larry Van Kriedt—and singer, Dave Evans, who'd briefly overlapped with Malcolm in Pony (born in Wales, he'd come to Australia in 1958, at age five).

Chequers, Sydney, May 18, 1974. © *Philip Morris*

Despite natural concerns that two fiery brothers in one band could prove disastrous, when Malcolm asked Angus to join his outfit, as he told *Mojo*'s Simmons, "Angus said, 'I don't know, the [rest of the band] may not like me.' I said, 'Screw them.'" Evans did immediately test Malcolm's loyalty, saying, "We can't have this guy, he doesn't look like a rock star." Malcolm replied, "If you don't like it, you can move on."

They rehearsed at a derelict office building in Newtown district, Malcolm and Angus readily alternating rhythm and lead roles at first. The usual puzzling over what to call themselves ended when sister Margaret suggested AC/DC. She'd spotted it on her sewing machine; the brothers got the sexual ambiguity angle, shrugged, and went with it (in a belated deviation from the usually accepted account of the band's christening, Angus told Paul Cashmere of *undercover. com.au* in 2008 that the name came from George's wife Sandra).

They played that December at a club called The Last Picture Show, but Chequers' New Year's Eve party is usually

CHEQUERS
5–11TH JUN

WED	BAND OF LIGHT, AC-DC
THUR	BAND OF LIGHT, AC-DC
FRI	SIREN, HOT CITY BUMP BAND
SAT	AC-DC, STEVIE WRIGHT BAND
MON	BUSTER BROWN, CHAIN
TUES	BUSTER BROWN, CHAIN

15

cited as their debut. Five hours of covers and the occasional Malcolm original certainly matched his credo. "If we don't come off stage really sweating and absolutely stuffed [exhausted], we don't reckon it's been worthwhile out there," he told O'Grady in *RAM*.

The name snagged them a few gay club bookings, which Malcolm enjoyed in his irredeemably macho way (Stenning, unattributed): "Upfront bisexual women had T-shirts with holes in the front and their boobs poking out. It was great!" AC/DC were up for anything—if the revellers at a Greek wedding wanted "Zorba the Greek," they got it. With that kind of gamecock attitude, the band probably deserved a little outside help.

After The Easybeats broke up in 1969, Harry Vanda and George Young spent three years in London developing their studio skills and returned to Australia a renowned production team. In January 1974, they took AC/DC to EMI's Sydney studios to demo a batch of Malcolm/Angus and Malcolm/Evans originals: "Can I Sit Next to You Girl," "Rockin' in the

Above and opposite: Chequers, Sydney, May 18, 1974.
Both © Philip Morris

If we don't come off stage really sweating and absolutely stuffed [exhausted], we don't reckon it's been worthwhile out there.

—Malcolm Young, *RAM*, 1975

"Rockin' in the Parlour," B-side to "Can I Sit Next to You Girl," featuring lead singer Dave Evans, Australia, 1974. *Bill Voccia Collection*

somewhat soiling residency at the Hampton Court Hotel, Kings Cross, playing to "drunks and prostitutes having a break," Taylor told Voccia. Then they pitched into Malcolm's experiment with Marc Bolan-influenced glam-rock costumes. At an April gig, variously recalled as a school dance or an open-air show in Sydney's Victoria Park, Smith posed as a motorbike patrolman, Taylor wore a harlequin clown suit and a top hat, Evans tarted himself up with bright red boots, Malcolm opted for a white jumpsuit, and, probably for the first time, Angus donned his school blazer, satchel, and shorts. "[Angus] stole the show," Taylor told Voccia.

AC/DC did toy with different costumes after that—Angus tried out as a gorilla, Zorro, and his childhood hero, Superman (he once jumped off the garage roof at home thinking the costume would enable him to fly). But the Victoria Park gig framed stage gear policy for the duration: glam out, shorts and satchel in. As Angus once said (Stenning, unattributed), "When I put that school suit on . . . it takes over. Malcolm says, 'It's like he's possessed.'" In their authoritative band biography, *AC/DC: Maximum Rock & Roll*, Murray Engleheart and Arnaud Durieux suggest more sophisticated sister Margaret suggested the uniform with the idea of "freezing Angus in time"—thirty-five years on, that doesn't seem such a fanciful notion, although Angus avers it began accidentally because he went to his early bands' rehearsals straight from school. The costume also triggered one of AC/DC's showbiz-instinctive lies: they decided Angus could pass for sixteen, and that's what they told their first wave of interviewers in Australia and the U.K. (after they'd stopped playing bars, that is).

Smith and Taylor departed after the glam-rock digression. Further short-lived replacements followed. Although they signed to Albert's, the same label as The Easybeats, that June, their first single "Can I Sit Next to You Girl" hit only the Sydney charts—in vast, empty Australia record sales followed very localized trends—but, via Albert's influence, they landed the support spot on Lou Reed's August tour. "People said, 'Oh, AC/DC and Lou Reed. This is gonna be a big bisexual show,'" Angus deadpanned to *New York Rocker*'s Howie Klein in 1977. When Reed's crew threatened to hold back part of the PA for AC/DC's set in Melbourne, the small yet formidable George Young took the hour's flight down to (successfully) urge them to "give these boys the fucking lot!"

But a more significant event for AC/DC's future had occurred before the tour's first night, in Adelaide on August 17, 1974. To welcome the support band, the local promoter kindly offered AC/DC use of a battered "limo" and its battered owner. Angus vividly remembered what happened when they emerged from the airport building (Stenning, unattributed): "The driver's first words when he got out of the car were, 'I'm Bon.' Then he looked down and went, 'Aaah, I've put on my wife's underwear.'" ⚡

Parlour," and "Soul Stripper" made their way onto early singles and/or albums; on the Australian version of *High Voltage*, they revamped "Sunset Strip" as "Show Business." Years later, Evans described the experience to Bill Voccia: "A dream come true . . . to be working with George Young and Harry Vanda."

Their two relentless characters combined, the Young brothers demanded everything of their band mates. In an interview with Voccia, Neil Smith (bassist from February to April 1974) recalled Angus preachifying, "We are going to be one of the greatest bands in the world. . . . It's a shame Hendrix is dead: I wanted to blow him off stage."

Ruthlessly, Malcolm fired and hired rhythm sections throughout their first nine months. One moment they'd be rehearsing in the brothers' bedroom at home—all-acoustic out of consideration for the parents, with sister Margaret proffering giant bowls of soup—the next they were out. Burgess fell off his drumstool mid-gig, Van Kriedt played too jazzy. Smith and drummer Noel Taylor replaced them and endured a

IN 1973, BROTHER MALCOLM FORMS HIS OWN ROCK BAND WITH TWO DISINTERESTED SCHOOL MATES.

I DUNNO. MAYBE WE NEED TO PICK SOME NEW SONGS INSTEAD OF DOING ALL *STONES* AND *WHO* COVERS.

HOW ABOUT WE GET A KEYBOARDIST? EXPAND OUR SOUND?

WHAT WE *REALLY* NEED IS A SECOND GUITARIST. I CAN'T FILL ALL THE TIME. AND THEN MAYBE A *SINGER*...

THE LINEUP CHANGES FROM WEEK TO WEEK, THOUGH MALCOLM FINALLY FINDS A SERIOUS SINGER IN SCHOOLMATE *DAVE EVANS*. THEY MAKE A MINOR SPLASH IN THE UNCOMPETITIVE SCHOOL DANCE CIRCUIT.

MALCOLM FINDS HIS SECOND GUITARIST IN THE BEDROOM DOWN THE HALL.

HEY, ANGUS, I HEARD YOU PLAYING IN YOUR ROOM YESTERDAY. YOU'RE GETTIN' PRETTY GOOD!

WANNA JAM WITH US ON THURSDAY AT 3 O'CLOCK?

BUT I DON'T GET OUTTA SCHOOL 'TILL 2:30... I WON'T EVEN HAVE TIME TO CHANGE MY SCHOOL CLOTHES!

UNDAUNTED, THE 14 YEAR OLD ANGUS, A FIVE-FOOT-THREE DYNAMO OF PERFORMING ENERGY, SHOWS UP IN FULL ACADEMIC REGALIA. THE BAND LOVES IT, AND HIRES THE "BABY GUITARIST" ON THE SPOT. AT THEIR FIRST GIG, AT A YOUTH CLUB IN DECEMBER 1973, HE COMES DIRECT FROM SCHOOL AND PERFORMS IN HIS UNIFORM; THE ANTITHESIS OF THE CURRENT SPANDEX-GLAM FAD.

AT SCHOOL, ANGUS BRAGS OF HIS NEWFOUND "CELEBRITY" STATUS.

I'M GONNA BE RICHER THAN HUGH HEFNER...AND PLOOK MORE BOSSY!

MEANWHILE, ANOTHER SCOTTISH IMMIGRANT, 27 YEAR OLD *BON SCOTT*, IS RECUPERATING FROM A MAJOR CAR ACCIDENT AND LOOKING FOR AN EASYGOING JOB.

I USED TO PLAY PIPE IN MY DAD'S GROUP, BUT MY HANDS ARE PRETTY STIFF FROM THE CRASH. YOU GUYS MAYBE NEED A ROADIE?

WELL, YOU COULD DRIVE THE TRUCK, I GUESS.

Let There Be Guitar

The Gear of Malcolm and Angus

By Dave Hunter

Heavy rock guitar tones existed before AC/DC, and plenty of new ones have been crafted after their emergence, but in the minds of players and fans, few artists embody that "huge rock-guitar tone" quite like Malcolm and Angus Young. Plenty of other guitarists have sounded filthier, and many have sounded hotter, but you'd be hard-pressed to claim any have ever sounded *bigger*. The impressive thing is that each of the Young brothers has managed this feat with relatively simple ingredients, which might have varied some over the years, but never strayed far from the basic building blocks. In doing so, the Youngs have maintained a virtue and a purity of tone that is almost contradictory to the genre. When we think of "heavy rock," most of us conjure a dirty, high-gain guitar tone with a scooped EQ curve that runs from heavy crunch to sizzling, saturated overdrive. Revisit any of AC/DC's standout recordings, however, and as often as not you hear size, punch, and presence far more than sheer distortion. In rock terms, their rhythm tone is right on the edge of being clean—while ramping up into searing, eviscerating overdrive for leads, of course—but it carries a bone-crushing weight that makes a huge impact on the listener. If anything, it's almost more of a blues-rock tone than a heavy rock tone, accompanying what are essentially blues-based riffs. But it's blues rock done large. *Very* large. As Angus Young told *Guitar Player* magazine's Jas Obrecht in 1984, "Most people hear distortion and they think it's loud. We keep it as clean as possible. The cleaner you do it, the louder it will sound when they do the cutting of [the record]." For all their straight-on, no-nonsense simplicity, both Malcolm and Angus possess guitar tones that are utterly distinctive and unmistakable, and this in itself has played a big part in the band's honored place amid a crowded rock field.

Electric Guitars

As lead man in this rhythm/lead brother duo, Angus Young has perhaps garnered more attention than his older brother. And like most guitar stars, Angus owns a number of classic electrics—a Gibson Firebird and ES-335 and a Fender Telecaster among them—but he has rarely been seen on stage without his lifelong model of choice: the Gibson SG Standard. Angus' number-one SG is a 1968 model that he acquired second-hand in 1970 after, legend has it, he fell in love with its double-horned image after seeing it in a friend's catalog. It has remained his go-to guitar since the band's formation in 1973, although it occasionally has been laid-up for live use and/or repair, given its age and value.

Angus has often declared his love of this particular SG's ultra-thin neck, found to be slimmer than other SGs from the era when examined by the Gibson factory in the late '70s or early '80s. His guitar's neck also has a narrow 1 5/8-inch width at the nut. Given Angus' small hands and short reach, these dimensions certainly must have aided his playing style. His '68 was originally equipped with the Maestro "lyre" vibrato tailpiece that many SGs featured in the '60s, but Angus removed this and replaced it with a standard stop-bar stud tailpiece to accompany the Tune-O-Matic bridge. Other than this, his favorite guitar was and remains largely original, down to its original Gibson "T-top" humbucking pickups.

Gibson first introduced the SG in 1961 as the replacement for the Les Paul Standard in the wake of that guitar's declining sales. Upon its release, the new design still wore the Les Paul name, but the model was changed to "SG" (for Solid Guitar) in 1963 when Les Paul's endorsement deal with Gibson expired. Whatever it said on the headstock, this new design was extremely different from the Les Paul version of the '50s. The new Les Paul/SG had the same PAF humbucking pickups (later "Patent Number" and then "T-top" humbucking pickups), the same bound neck with jumbo frets, and the same Tune-O-Matic bridge that the Les Paul featured in 1960, but it's thin, all-mahogany body contributed to a very different tone right off the blocks. Where the Les Paul was thick, dark, and meaty,

Don't tickle the guitar, hit the bugger.

—Early advice from Malcolm Young to younger brother Angus

the SG was slightly snappier and marginally thinner (though still big and bold), with a bit of a metallic, percussive edge to the notes. Put it all together, and this voice gives the SG excellent clarity and note definition, but still with a slight furring of the edges to help thicken the overall tone. The thinner-bodied guitar's weight, usually somewhat less than that of a Les Paul, is also considered by many to be a boon, and Angus has commented several times that this particularly light example from 1968 (along with a wireless transmitter) helps him get through his vigorous stage antics during the course of AC/DC's notoriously arduous sets.

Unsurprisingly, Angus has owned and played several other SGs, and he often plays a backup on stage to augment his beloved '68. An original 1964 SG is notable among these (which Angus played on 1995's *Ballbreaker* album), as is an SG copy made for him by Jaydee and, in a rather ironic twist, a custom-made Gibson SG that replicates the Jaydee's "lightning bolt" position marker inlays. Also, Gibson has released an Angus Young Signature SG, which is based on the proportions of the '68 but carries the long-removed vibrato tailpiece and features a "little devil" graphic on the headstock.

Angus uses light, bend-friendly .009 to .042 gauge strings on his thin-necked '68 SG and .010 to .048 strings on most of his other guitars.

Malcolm Young's lonely guitar arsenal displays even more slavish devotion to a single instrument than does his younger brother's. Throughout his career with AC/DC, Malcolm has used a 1963 Gretsch Jet Firebird that was given to him by Harry Vanda, one of his older brother George's band mates in The Easybeats, a popular Australian rock 'n' roll band of the mid-1960s. In addition to the red finish that gave it its name (and which Malcolm stripped from the maple top), Malcolm's Gretsch would have left the factory with a Burns vibrato tailpiece, a floating bridge, and two Filter'Tron humbucking pickups, but over the years, Young modified the guitar to suit his austere tastes. First, Malcolm "upgraded" the Jet Firebird with the addition of a Gibson humbucking pickup

Angus is in a self-induced hypnotic guitar trance when he plays. He is completely and utterly possessed by the music and his guitar playing, and that's why he is so effective.

—Steve Vai

Angus' original SG with its lyre tailpiece intact and its T-top humbuckers. Cleveland Municipal Stadium, Cleveland, Ohio, July 28, 1979. © Robert Alford

Backstage at Hordern Pavilion, Sydney, December 12, 1976. © Bob King/bobking.com.au

and replaced it with a stationary Badass wraparound bridge. This is much the way the guitar remained for twenty-five years or so, although Malcolm did reinstate the Burns vibrato around 2000.

The Gretsch Filter'Tron humbucker is a brighter, tighter-sounding unit than the humbuckers on Angus' SG, with less output as well. Engineered to maintain Gretsch's twangy, jangly sound when it replaced the DeArmond-made Dynasonic single-coil pickups on many Gretsch models in 1958, the Filter'Tron is also known for its firm, full tone when injected into a cranked tube amp and is clearly one of the key ingredients in Malcolm's AC/DC sound.

Malcolm's strings of choice are another notable component of his tone. Since the mid-'70s he has used heavy .012 to .056 gauge, pure-nickel-wound strings, which serve to augment the firm, punchy power of his rhythm playing. Both brothers use heavy picks (often Fenders) for a firm, bright attack.

Malcolm has owned several other guitars, including many Gretsch reproductions of his Jet Firebird, but throughout AC/DC's golden period he was only known to have recorded a single song with a different guitar, 1975's "High Voltage," on which he played a Gibson L5S. He also used a Gretsch White Falcon for some live performances in the early '80s, and played it, notably, in the "Back in Black" video, but is not believed to ever have recorded with the guitar.

in the middle position, hence its appearance as a three-pickup guitar (the Jet Firebird was only ever made with two pickups), but by the mid-'70s he had removed this additional pickup, along with the Filter'Tron

in the neck position, giving his Gretsch the single-pickup status that it has maintained every since. The switches and controls that had been rendered irrelevant came out too, and Malcolm also removed the vibrato

I like the way they layer the power chords—they've always had great guitar sounds. I think with them it's all about the guitars and the songs.

—Ace Frehley

Malcolm's stripped-down Jet Fire Bird, Roseland Ballroom, New York City, March 11, 2003. Contrast it with the photo from almost three decades earlier (above). Ian Wilson/Capital Pictures/Retna Ltd.

Amplifiers

For both Young brothers, the choice in amplification for some thirty-five years can be summed up in one word: Marshall. Angus has frequently recalled the use of a 100-watt late-'60s Marshall JMP100 Super Lead amp with EL34 output tubes in the early days of the band, while Malcolm often played through a slightly earlier JTM100 Super Amp with KT66 output tubes, a late-'60s Super Bass with EL34 output tubes, or a 100-watt Plexi Super Lead much like his brother's.

Malcolm's tighter, punchier rhythm tone is consistent with the use of any of these big 100-watters (a Marshall Super Bass would be particularly bold in this department), and this was clearly another key ingredient—partnered with his Filter'Tron-loaded Gretsch—in the unparalleled chunk of the AC/DC rhythm assault. While Angus also often records through the 100-watters, he has been known to use any of a range of several JTM45s, a JTM50, and a later JMP50 in the studio (the former with KT66s, the latter two amps with EL34s). These lower-output Marshalls are often employed for solos, where they can be cranked up a little more easily, to give a fatter, juicier, more pliant sound and feel to Angus' riffs.

The Young brothers' live rigs have run the gamut of the bigger Marshall models over the years. Both Malcolm and Angus are pictured using Marshall JCM800-2203s live in the late '70s, while in the early '80s Angus purportedly used high-powered custom-made Marshall stacks. The trusty 100-watt Plexi and metal-panel Super Leads often got the call for later tours, often with eight full stacks on stage for each guitarist—four on at once, four more for backup. For many years, Angus has also taken to replicating his recorded lead tone live with a JTM45, which is sometimes miked through an isolation cab under the stage.

The Youngs' Marshall 4x12 cabinets have featured a range of Celestion speakers. Early on they were loaded with original G12M Greenbacks or, very often, the firmer, bolder, more efficient G12H-30s. Throughout the '90s, the brothers tended to use Celestion's more contemporary Vintage 30 speaker, first in evidence on the 1990 album *Stiff Upper*

Angus has that kind of blues/boogie thing going, very Chuck Berry-ish with a little more modern influence—but it's all feel. He's got good fingers and isn't worried about being too flashy. He just gets up there and jams.

—Paul Phillips, Puddle of Mudd

© *Rock 'N' Roll Comics No. 22, Revolutionary Comics, 1990. Courtesy Jay Allen Sanford*

Lip, although both have often returned to reissues of the G12H-30 and the Greenback in more recent years.

Even more significant than all of these ingredients, perhaps, is the way in which Malcolm and Angus use them. Put simply, they do it the good old-fashioned way: guitar straight into amp, with no effects pedals to get in the way. Angus, in particular, is known to use his guitar's volume control to manipulate his distortion levels for rhythm and lead sounds, while a guitar tech has often kicked in the smaller under-stage amp for solos. ⚡

On tour somewhere in Australia, 1976. © *Newspix/Gary Graham*

Chapter 2

Rockin' Rollin' Man

Unforgettable Ronald Belford Scott was born on July 9, 1946, in Kirriemuir, County Angus, Scotland, a small market town. After war service in the army, his father, Chick, worked at the family's bakery. His mother, Isa, was a housewife, and he had three younger brothers. Stable yet sharing their generation's restlessness, the Scotts and their children sailed for Australia when Ronald was six, settling in Melbourne initially. After four years, they moved 2,000 miles west to Fremantle, a coastal conurbation with Perth, combined population around 440,000, in 1956.

In Australia, the eldest Scott brother was naturally nicknamed "Bonny" (as in "Bonny Scotland," later shortened to Bon). At school, he got over hostility to his accent by changing it and passed through school unnoticed. Music was his extracurricular consolation, from Elvis Presley, Jerry Lee Lewis, and Chuck Berry to playing side drum with his father in a proper marching, kilt-wearing, Scottish pipe band. At fifteen, he left school and worked as a postman and then on the crayfishing boats. He acquired his first tattoos and earrings and joined a rocker gang.

Later, he talked vaguely about spending some months at reform school. Clinton Walker, author of Scott biography *Highway to Hell The Life and Death of AC/DC Legend Bon Scott*, discovered that his term at Riverbank Juvenile Institution when he was sixteen followed a conviction for "giving a false name and address to the police, having escaped legal custody,

> I was getting old . . . then these guys come along and took ten years off my age.
>
> —Bon Scott, *RAM*, 1975

The Valentines, "My Old Man's a Groovy Old Man" w/ "Nick Nack Paddy Whack," "Ebeneezer," and "Getting Better," 7-inch EP, Australia, 1969. *Bill Voccia Collection*

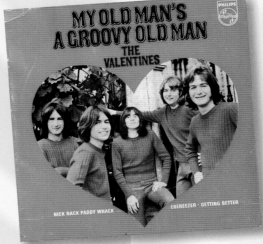

Fraternity, clockwise from lower left: Bon Scott, John Bisset, Bruce Howe, Mick Jurd, and John Freeman. © *Philip Morris*

Fraternity, "If You Got It" w/ "Raglan's Folly" and "You Have a God" (Australia's first maxi single), 1971. *Bill Voccia Collection*

having unlawful carnal knowledge, and having stolen 12 gallons of petrol." This arose from Scott fighting off a gang of boys who intended to rape his (underage) girlfriend and a consequent police car chase. Nonetheless, young Scott felt deep remorse for the shame he'd brought to his beloved parents. Fortunately, he came upon an unlikely path to redemption: rock 'n' roll.

By early 1965, he'd started playing drums with The Spektors and then The Valentines, a decent soul band fronted by school friend Vince Lovegrove. They recorded a single, did well in a national bands competition, and, in October 1967, moved to Melbourne. Significantly, on tour they met The Easybeats—George Young befriended Scott and The Valentines recorded several Vanda and Young songs, including a single, "Peculiar Hole in the Sky," in June 1968.

Gradually finding himself, Scott took some lead vocals and co-wrote with Lovegrove. Their first attempts were formula love songs, but he began jotting and keeping ideas in school exercise books. Writing at *adelaidenow.com.au* in 2008, Lovegrove, who later turned journalist, recalled their sleeping-in-the-van days: "We were very poor,

Bon and fraternity bandmade Bruce Howe. © *Philip Morris*

almost starving, driving down the highways, absorbed with rock 'n' roll, stealing people's front door milk money . . . living on boiled potatoes, the dreams of success our mantra." However, Lovegrove added, "When he sang, Bon took off into charisma-land."

After The Valentines broke up in August 1970, having perversely both gone bubblegum and been busted for pot possession, Scott became sole frontman with a Band-loving outfit called Fraternity. Sponsored by hippie entrepreneur Hamish Henry, they lived communally in the hills outside Adelaide. Although they did a lot of booze, magic mushrooms, and girls, they rehearsed fanatically enough to come to blows over a chord change. "The dollar sign is not the ultimate," Scott advised Lovegrove for Australian magazine *Go-Set* at the time. "We want to try and help each other develop and live."

Fraternity quickly produced two albums, *Livestock* (1971) and *Flaming Galah* (Australian for "idiot," 1972). But its next move suggested that both the band and Scott were lacking as career and life strategists. They group made the classic Australian immigrant move: try your luck in the old country.

We were very poor, almost starving, driving down the highways, absorbed with rock 'n' roll, stealing people's front door milk money.

—Fraternity bassist Vince Lovegrove, 2008

Henry paid for the band, partners, crew, and, strangely, a tour bus to fly over. But they left before they had time to promote *Flaming Galah* and just after Scott married longtime girlfriend Irene Thornton on January 24, 1972. She traveled with them, but band and personal relationships suffered two years of testing by failure and poverty.

Retrospectively notable was their April 1973 encounter with a band called Geordie, whom they supported in Torquay and Plymouth. Scott admired their singer, Brian Johnson. But Fraternity bassist Bruce Howe told Walker the gloomy U.K. experience brought out Scott's "fatalistic side" and led him to take risks with drugs: "You were dealing with a person who didn't care if he lived or died."

Fraternity became Fang and then broke up. Scott and Irene got home in December 1973 and separated immediately, although their volatile relationship never ended. Scott stayed with Howe and his wife and earned a wage scraping barnacles off boats at an Adelaide dry dock while singing and writing with a loose lineup called The Mount Lofty Rangers.

On May 3, 1974, Scott came to rehearsal drunk, raging about a row with Irene, stormed out, jumped on his 500cc motorbike, roared away, and crashed into an oncoming car. In a coma for three days, his jaw, collarbone, and several ribs broken, Scott suffered pain from his injuries for the rest of his life. But the tender care of Irene and his mother, who flew over from Fremantle, saw him through the worst.

Lovegrove assessed his old friend that summer (*adelaidenow.com.au*): "[Bon] was desperate for success . . . he felt trapped, frustrated, almost too old, and without direction."

⚡ ⚡ ⚡

Mirthful myth fogs the story of Bon Scott joining AC/DC. But, according to George Young in French fanzine *Let There Be Light* (1993), after the Lou Reed gig in Melbourne, Scott saw them play again at the Pooraka Hotel in Adelaide, in late August 1974, and told the brothers, "I love the group, but the singer's really shitty." They jammed back at Bruce Howe's house later that night. Nothing more was said, but the Youngs were already unhappy with Dave Evans' vocal power and his onstage style—one reviewer had compared him to David Cassidy.

AC/DC drove to Perth for a weird six-week residency supporting drag artist Carlotta at Beethoven's Disco. Given time for reflection, the brothers decided to separate their previously mixed guitar roles, assigning Malcolm strictly to rhythm, Angus to lead. Further, with Evans both complaining about money to Dennis Laughlin, the band's first manager, and missing gigs (he said sore throat, they said hung-over), the brothers rang Scott and offered him the job. He jumped at it.

Evans sang with them once more, at the Esplanade Hotel in St. Kilda, Melbourne, in late September. Then, as Evans recalled for Phil Lageat at *highwaytoacdc.com* some thirty years later, Malcolm told him, "OK Dave, you're out." A week or so later, Scott debuted at Brighton-le-Sands Masonic Hall in Sydney, a lively affair. Angus once recalled (Stenning, unattributed), "Bon downed about two bottles of bourbon with dope, coke, speed and says 'Right, I'm ready'. . . . He got out there and this huge, hurricane yell came out. The whole place went, 'What the fuck is this?'" Quoted in the liner notes to the *Bonfire* box set (1997), Malcolm remembered, "He strides on . . . and announces, 'Anyone that come to see Dave Evans sing with AC/DC ain't gonna see it tonight!' Bon took command." Angus treasured the memory of the T-shirt Scott wore that night "with a drawing of his cock on it" and also recalled (in Stenning, unattributed) that "[Bon] said to Malcolm, 'Do you want me to sing like someone?' Malcolm said 'We want you and what you are.' Bon loved the fact that he could get on and be himself."

Indeed, Scott felt reborn: "I was getting old . . . then these guys come along and took ten years off my age," he told Anthony O'Grady of *RAM* in 1975.

AC/DC promptly slipped into overdrive. When Melbourne Hard Rock Café promoter Michael Browning offered to take over their management, the Youngs scrutinized Laughlin's unambitious scuffling approach and accepted. Early that November, Albert's had them record an album, albeit during downtime late at night after gigs, at their King Street, Sydney, studio with Vanda and Young producing. Apart from Big Joe Williams' "Baby, Please Don't Go" and Malcolm and Angus' "Soul Stripper," all tracks carried Young/Scott/Young credits, with the singer taking the lead on writing lyrics. That included "She's Got Balls," Scott's fruity tribute to Irene, his enduring love.

"Love Song (Oh Jene)," A-label promo, AC/DC's first official single with Bon Scott and first single in Australia, 1975. The B-side, "Baby Please Don't Go," ended up getting picked up by radio stations and receiving airplay instead of the A-side. *Bill Voccia Collection*

After supporting Black Sabbath at Hordern Pavilion in Sydney on November 10, they moved down to Melbourne, Angus and Malcolm finally leaving the family home. Browning insisted it was the only Australian city with the "support system" to carry a band beyond parochial success. He quickly proved his point. On November 29, AC/DC made their TV debut on *Countdown*, a new ABC (Australian Broadcasting Corporation) weekly pop show that virtually adopted AC/DC—they made thirty-eight appearances through December 1976.

Melbourne also gave them free rein. Band headquarters shifted from the Octagon Motel in Prahran suburb to a house in Lansdowne Road in St. Kilda, and, from June 1975, to the Freeway Gardens Motel in Parkville. As Malcolm told Sylvie Simmons for *Mojo*, 2000, "There'd be a knock on the door at three in the morning, and a bunch of waitresses just off work would be there with bottles of booze, a bag of dope, and everything else. Never a dull moment." (Amid the chaos, Angus stuck to his tea and resolutely practiced his guitar licks).

January 1975 saw the recruitment of drummer Phil Rudd, AC/DC's only native Australian long-termer. Born Philip Hugh Norman Witschke Rudzevecuis, on May 19, 1954, in Melbourne, he told *Rock Hard* magazine in 2001 that he chose his drum heroes—Free's Simon Kirke, The Beatles' Ringo Starr, The Small Faces' Kenney Jones—for "their ability to keep time while kicking like mules." An apprentice electrician in an air-conditioner factory after leaving

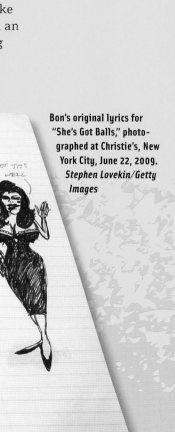

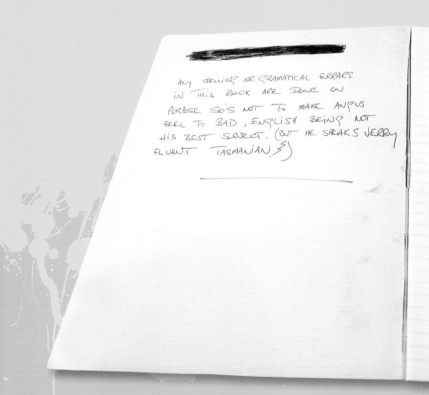

Bon's original lyrics for "She's Got Balls," photographed at Christie's, New York City, June 22, 2009. *Stephen Lovekin/Getty Images*

school, he'd flogged through pub bands Charlemagne, Mad Mole, and Smack. With Buster Brown, he recorded an album, *Something to Say* (1974), before they sacked him over a money row. He was washing cars at his father's garage when he heard AC/DC needed another drummer—the latest aspirant, Peter Clack, had fallen seriously ill, George Young later recalled in *Let There Be Light*.

At Lansdowne Road, Rudd caught the band members in their underwear—because of the heat. After running through a few covers plus AC/DC originals, he was in as drummer and housemate. He found them surprisingly professional. They even paid regular wages; the booking agency manager Michael Browning had put them on to Joseph's Premier Artists, which offered $60 Australian a week each plus a sound system *and* free vehicle repairs. Rudd told *Rock Hard* this all helped to make him "better organised, with a clear head. I finally knew where I was going."

His "debut" rather fizzled. On January 25, instead of playing at the Sunbury Festival—a.k.a. Melbourne's Woodstock—the band, its roadies, Browning, and George Young fought a pitched battle against Deep Purple's crew onstage in front of 20,000 people. When the headliners finished their set, they wanted to take down their gear, which meant AC/DC wouldn't be able to play. AC/DC won the fight and then walked out anyway.

Over the next few weeks, they worked the typical pubs and clubs, sometimes three a night, which Malcolm described to me for U.K. weekly *Sounds* in 1976: "The blokes stand at the bar drinking until 'time' is called then race across and grab one of the women sat by the opposite wall. Any guy who spends the whole evening with a woman has got to be a poofter!"

On February 17, 1975, Albert's released AC/DC's first album, *High Voltage* (the tracklist very different from later U.K. and U.S. versions with the same name) and the single "Love Song"/"Baby, Please Don't Go" hit No. 10 on the national chart.

Even so, the brothers Young kept firing bassists, the latest departees being Rob Bailey and Paul Matters. George or

"Baby Please Don't Go" sheet music, Leeds Music, Australia, 1975. *Bill Voccia Collection*

Phil Rudd's pre-AC/DC band, Buster Brown, "Buster Brown" b/w "Rock 'N' Roll Lady," Australia, 1974. *Bill Voccia Collection*

With George Young, Harry Vanda, and Paul Matters (top), AC/DC's bassist for a few weeks in February and March 1975.
© *Philip Morris*

We used to finish a gig at about two in the morning [and] then drive down to the studio. George and Harry would have a couple of dozen cans in and a few bottles of Jack Daniel's, and we'd all have a party and rip it up . . . so it was the same loose feeling like we were onstage still. The studio was just like an extension of the gig back then.

—Malcolm Young, *Mojo*, 2000

Malcolm filled in until they found Mark Evans. Born in Prahran, Melbourne, on March 2, 1956, until then he'd only "mucked around" on bass while working respectably as a junior civil servant. He got through the Lansdowne Road mayhem and found himself onstage at the Station Hotel in Prahran two days later (March 18) and then on a notorious edition of *Countdown* when Scott horrified presenter Ian "Molly" Meldrum by appearing in a dress and pigtailed wig.

Oddly, the tallest guy around at just five feet seven inches—Angus was five-two, Scott maybe five-six, with the others between the two—but also the youngest, Evans accepted whatever occurred with good humor, even Angus' laundry habits. "The school suit used to stink," he told Volker Janssen of German fanzine *Daily Dirt* in 1998. "He used to sweat so much . . . [and] drink so much milk and eat so much chocolate, he'd have a lot of gunk coming out. After the gig, he would put it into a suit bag and forget about it for the week."

In June a one-off single, "High Voltage" (Rudd's first AC/DC recording), reached No. 6 in Australia, boosting album sales toward 125,000, even though it missed inclusion on the LP of the same name. The following month, the band returned to Sydney and Albert Studios where Vanda and Young produced the follow-up, *T.N.T.*

AC/DC's on-the-hoof compositional process intrigued Evans. "Malcolm and Angus would have the bare ideas and sit down with George at the piano—the three of them would fit on the same piano stool because they are so tiny," Evans told Janssen. "George would . . . take the material and get the best out of those ideas. . . . The guy is . . . the most astute, the most intelligent musical person I've ever met."

Writing the lyrics, Scott sat in the kitchen at Albert's with a pen, pad, and a bottle of Stone's Ginger Wine, a traditional Scottish granny's winter warmer. If he hit problems, George would scan through Scott's notebooks

Above and opposite: Filming the "High Voltage" video, July 7, 1975. *Both © Philip Morris*

"T.N.T." b/w "I'm a Rocker," Australia, 1975.

"Baby Please Don't Go"
and "Jail Break" [sic] b/w "Soul Stripper," three-track
promo single, Germany, 1975.

This page and opposite: Victoria Park, Sydney, September 7, 1975. *All © Philip Morris*

with him looking for gems of "toilet poetry" (Scott's own phrase).

They emerged from Albert's inside two weeks with the first cluster of AC/DC classics in their hands. *T.N.T.* rocked, telling the roughest stories ever to appear on a hard rock album, all drawn from real life. The following year for *Sounds*, Scott and Angus told me the story that became "The Jack": "We were living with this houseful of ladies [in Lansdowne Road] who were all very friendly and everyone in the band got the jack. The first time we did the song on stage those girls were all in the front row with no idea what was goin' to happen. When it came to repeatin' 'She's got the jack,' I pointed at them one after another."

Gigging continued, riotously. When the Myer department store in Melbourne, booked them for a week of school-holiday lunchtime shows in August 1975, screaming girls wrecked the teen clothes section and left Scott scratched raw and near naked. The following month, onstage at Matthew Flinders Hotel in the Chadstone district, a drunk cut Angus' hand with a glass and Phil Rudd, "punching like a madman" in the ensuing melee, broke a thumb.

Malcolm reminisced in Murray Engleheart's and Arnaud Durieux's *AC/DC: Maximum Rock & Roll* about a gig in former gold-rush town Bendigo, eighty miles north of Melbourne: "All the youth of the town were ready to beat the shit out of us . . . because somebody had got one of their girlfriends last time we were in town. . . . Phil was a maniac behind the wheel, so if any shit like that went on . . . we used to get out on the bush roads, quickly pull over, all lights out. Hide! And we'd watch these guys go screaming past, crank up and go back into town [and] then get their women!"

This page and opposite: Recording *Dirty Deeds Done Dirt Cheap*, Albert Studios, Sydney, 1976. *All © Philip Morris*

Despite the ongoing "Dodge a bottle here, dodge a fist there" (Angus to Australian magazine *Juke*, 1988), at Victoria Park in Sydney in September, Scott probably inaugurated the signature walkabout among the crowd with Angus on his shoulders, playing a furious solo.

Given the accumulating tumult, that Australian summer Browning started thinking international. In December, "It's a Long Way to the Top"—complete with bagpipes played by Scott, but in jazz saxophone style, Angus reckoned— reached No. 5 in the domestic singles chart, while *T.N.T.* came out, selling a robust 45,000 that month. Meanwhile, in London, Browning's sister Coral showed Atlantic's U.K. boss Phil

Carson a live video of AC/DC (from Melbourne Festival Hall on June 16, 1975) and quickly secured a modest deal: a $25,000 U.S. album advance against 12 percent royalty for "the world outside Australia."

At this crucial moment, with a move to London planned for early the following year, doubts about Scott's place in the band suddenly arose, Evans told Janssen for *Daily Dirt*: "We were in a hotel in Canberra in late 1975. George came down, and there was a feeling that Bon may not be the right guy for the long term in the band because . . . he was involved in a drug thing that was a little bit too heavy. To Bon's credit, he pulled himself out of all those problems." (Other sources

suggest the unnamed drug may have been heroin or methadone.)

Whether or not the scare and Evans' interpretation were justified, Scott played his full part in recording AC/DC's third album, *Dirty Deeds Done Dirt Cheap*, in late January and February 1976 at Albert's, Vanda and Young producing as usual. Scott's dedication and loyalty could hardly be questioned; asked how he rated AC/DC he'd assert, "We're the kings of the scene, no one else fucking matters" (*Bonfire* liner notes). Nonetheless, some lyrics he'd just recorded worried those who knew his lonesome and blue side, especially "Ride On": "Got another empty bottle/And another empty bed/ . . . /I'm just another empty head/That's why I'm lonely/ . . . And I ain't too old to hurry."

All that remained, before flying halfway round the world, was a Young family party in Burwood for Angus' (real) twenty-first birthday and, before that, a farewell gig at the Bondi Lifesaver in Sydney on March 27. Of that show, Evans told Janssen: "Angus actually took everything off . . . shaking his skinny butt all over the place. He had no clothes on, just his shoes, duckwalking up and down the bar. Very unattractive." ⚡

Recording *Dirty Deeds Done Dirt Cheap*, Albert Studios, Sydney, 1976. © *Philip Morris*

Bradfield Park, Sydney, March 27, 1976, the same evening as the band's farewell gig at the Bondi Lifesaver. © *Philip Morris*

The LPs
High Voltage
(Australia only)

By Jen Jewel Brown

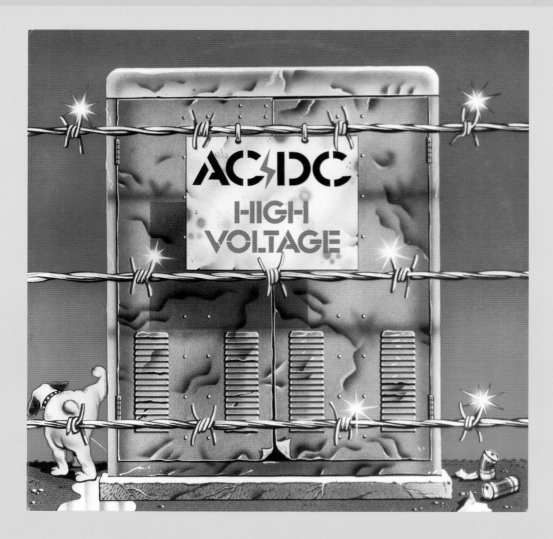

Recorded over ten nights on the midnight-to-dawn shift, after gigs and under the canny production guidance of two ex-Easybeats—Harry Vanda and George Young, Angus and Malcolm's twenty-seven-year-old big brother—AC/DC's first album was a patchy but attention-getting, Australia-only affair released February 17, 1975, to mixed reactions. The album's rhythm section tracks were stripped back, full of subtle bounce and movement with plenty of air. Drums on six of the eight tracks were played by Tony Currenti, from novelty band The 69ers, with bass and possibly some drum overdubs by George Young. George often played bass live with AC/DC around this time too, as the demanding Youngs hired and fired a succession of players before settling on the powerful Mark Evans/Phil Rudd engine room to promote *High Voltage* and record their next three studio albums.

Even now, hearing the album's opener, "Baby, Please Don't Go," is like having your carpet burns lovingly cleansed with a bottle of bourbon—you know, something to savor on your deathbed. The original version of this ramped-up Delta blues was penned and recorded in 1934 by Big Joe Williams, who added a primeval pickup and three extra strings to his guitar and then, like Angus, managed to play both rhythm and lead at the same time. "Baby, Please Don't Go" came out on the B-side of the first single

from the album. The A-side was the fey "Love Song (Oh Jene)" (it was called "Love Song" on the album). The less I say about this track the better. Let's call it a misfire. For the growing legions of Acca Dacca fans working in Australian radio and TV, the B-side killed the A stone dead.

In AC/DC's clutches, "Baby, Please Don't Go" became a strangled cry from the heart of a man on his knees. Bon Scott's absolutely wild vocal tipped its hat to Screamin' Jay Hawkins' 1956 classic "I Put a Spell on You," revealing the band's new frontman to be a brilliant improviser and an uninhibited, natural tenor with great range and expression.

Free at last after years in dubious shirts and flounces with The Valentines, then long-haired, bearded, and arty with prog rockers Fraternity, Bon was ripe to celebrate his new role as the gap-toothed, glint-eyed, newly

single ex-jailbird he was—risk-addicted, heavily drinking, and hard-wired to rock 'n' roll. He'd been recruited at twenty-eight by Angus, the increasingly impressive nineteen-year-old, five-foot-two whiz-kid guitarist, and Malcolm, his twenty-one-year-old hard-headed brother (a snifter taller in his platform boots). Bon replaced the band's original singer, Dave Evans, just two months before AC/DC entered Albert Studios in downtown Sydney in November 1974 to lay down their debut LP for Albert Productions. Now Bon was backed by a band so tight that you could tell it jammed the way other people breathed.

Bon wrote the lyrics to the album's second track, "She's Got Balls," for his newly ex-wife Irene ("She got mine for a long time," he told radio 2SM). The thudding strut of the opening riff, rough though it is, was a harbinger of "the Alberts sound," a chain-gang, rail-banging, slow boogie with the accent on the "one." The verses drip with awe at the daring and libido of this woman, who for a moment became all women, liberated by free love and the pill. Its glorious, tongue-in-cheek baritone-backing vocals turn it into a show stomper, a kind of "I Could Have Danced All Night" for the rapacious. This track is also notable for featuring the band's live drummer at the time, Peter Clack.

A third drummer, John Proud (Marcus Hook Roll Band), plays on the next track, "Little Lover," a girl-savoring, hip-swinging strip routine of a blues number. The track ends in silence then reenters in a tender, offhand saunter like a new song—a thumbing of the nose at advised radio song length and formula.

As "Stick Around" struts in with its banging cowbell and big, chiming, hole-filled riffs, Free's 1970 world chart-topper "Alright Now" jumps straight to mind. Free had swept through Australia in '71 and blew everyone away. Unfortunately, their resulting influence on parts of *High Voltage* is all too clear. Even some of Bon's vocal ad-libs smack of Free frontman Paul Rodgers. Mostly though, this band's new singer was finding out what he could do with his own style and phrasing as "The Seedies" made tentative steps toward becoming a band that sounded like no one else. Lyrically, Bon wasn't afraid to go too far (an aside to his subject of the third track entreats her to "sit on this"), but the conjoined rhythm work from Malcolm and Angus, their classic SG-meets-Gretsch guitar sounds and the pop-rock class of Vanda and Young's arrangement skills—so clever you hardly notice them—make even this one rocket through.

"Soul Stripper" is Malcolm and Angus' co-written tale of a knife-wielding femme fatale. It is fascinating to see what the brothers came up with when Bon was out of the picture (the three of them co-wrote the album's six other original tracks). "Soul Stripper" is a long, unfolding piece with a killer chorus that could have influenced White Stripes. Of course, it's also a guitar opus, the brothers trading solos and intermeshing with sensational

metal intuition and style for more than six minutes. Sharp as a spiv.

The opening guitar figure of "You Ain't Got a Hold on Me" echoes Free's "Wishing Well," with a lead solo by Malcolm. Its follower, "Show Business," is a jaunty, fairly conventional 12-bar with typically gruff AC/DC backing vocals—maybe a step along the way to the battler's hymn "It's a Long Way to the Top (If You Wanna Rock 'n' Roll)"—which would come out in December.

Despite a slowly brewing media furor arising from the dust of many public punch-ups, you could easily book AC/DC for your high school's dance or lunch hour concert in 1974 and 1975, and many did. Their new manager, Michael Browning, shared an office in the same small ground-floor terrace house in South Yarra, Melbourne, as the daily counterculture newspaper *Planet*, which I worked for in my first journalism job. This clan of small, tough geezers with an intense camaraderie had few words for strangers as they went into lengthy, serious war-planning sessions with Browning behind tightly closed doors. They were deadly serious about a world tilt at success.

However, the band's view of the music business was well summarized by the dog pissing on the electrical substation on the front cover of *High Voltage*. This mooning fox terrier (a new take on RCA's famous "His Master's Voice" trademark?) caused rows in the ranks of EMI (Albert Productions' distributors) and roused the media, who claimed AC/DC as an Australian punk band in early '75 in *RAM* and Australian *Rolling Stone* (placing them post Iggy and The Stooges and MC5 but predating The Saints, Sex Pistols, and Clash.)

I remember one gig in the regal Victoria & Albert's (Berties) rock club in Melbourne—AC/DC crammed the audience into the basement and unleashed the most intense rock 'n' roll typhoon we'd ever heard, an outrageously tight, attacking blues rock that throbbed like a post-orgasmic hard-on. There was bandleader Malcolm, hair-swinging and stomping through the whole show, burning lead lines and rhythm, rock solid as they come, and Angus, a bare arm's length away, red-faced,

fingers blurring, sweat-soaked sneakers splayed like gecko suckers across a couple of leaning Marshalls as he headbanged his whole body, dripping, transcendental, into the right state of hedonistic rock. And that weird "Super Ang" cape he wore with the "A" stitched on it flapping as he rode a jaw-dropping solo. Bon was bare-chested and tattooed in hipster jeans that left nothing to the imagination, mic jutting from the lead snaking around his wrist, climbing a stack of Marshalls that started to sway and tumble, grabbed by a roadie, his voice a trumpet call to the nine-to-five-escaping horde he sought. Their songs seemed a kind of wicked, Marshall-fried Chuck Berry–a-thon, starring the true-life adventures of the Errol Flynn of sprayed-on jeans. We loved Bon and we loved AC/DC with a passion.

We had a famous TV ad in Australia back then, where a character called Louie the Fly would sing in a Bronx accent, rough, kind of like Louis Armstrong, and then get sprayed with Mortein, a brand of household insecticide. He would then perform a radical, upside-down, spinning, thrashing dance of death. This appeared to be the model for Angus' stage act. How he could play such solid riffs and blindingly good solos while doing that stuff remains one of the great unsolved mysteries of rock.

Which brings us back to the opening track. Color TV launched in Australia on March 1, 1975, and AC/DC's notorious first appearance on *Countdown* came three weeks later with the F-111 sonic attack of "Baby, Please Don't Go." This pop culture marriage made in heaven (or was it hell?) soon had the single laying waste to the national charts, hitting No. 10.

The building intensity in "Baby, Please Don't Go" brings Bon to an unhinged orgy of blues-screaming, stagy as a Looney Tunes' Roadrunner-vs.-Wile E. Coyote battle and at the same time chillingly real. Angus' solo spins off this mayhem with a beautiful, warm repetitive blues lick in tandem with Malcolm's Gretsch Jet Firebird. In this four minutes and fifty seconds alone, AC/DC announce themselves as masters of the blues 'n' hard rock universe—even if the rest of the LP never tops the purity of the opening track's sheer rock 'n' roll orgasm. ⚡

Nashville Rooms, London, April 6, 1976. *Dick Barnatt/Redferns/Getty Images*

Chapter 3

Long Way to the Top

Uprooted back to where they came from, Scott and the Young brothers shunned sentimental delusion about the job in hand. "We were prepared to start at the bottom again," Malcolm told Australia's *Countdown* magazine in 1988. Native-born Aussie Rudd felt the same: "We had to prove ourselves whenever we landed in a new country" (*Rock Hard*, 2001).

In April 1976, they landed in London and Atlantic welcomed them with the release of their first U.K. single, "It's a Long Way to the Top"/"Can I Sit Next to You Girl." Atlantic also accommodated them in Lonsdale Road, Barnes, a genteel suburb south of the Thames—"a nice big house," Mark Evans told Volker Janssen for *Daily Dirt*, 1998. "We were all in there together, band and road crew, until Bon found an old girlfriend and moved out."

Already promotionally astute, AC/DC proffered the media glowing reviews kindly forged by their mate Lobby Loyde, guitarist with Melbourne band The Coloured Balls. But their planned first tour, a support spot with Back Street Crawler, was delayed because the band's ex-Free guitarist, Paul Kossoff, had died of a drug-related heart attack on March 19.

During this hiatus, while Angus practiced and watched *Get Smart* on TV, Scott reconnoitred the opposition. "I spent the first three weeks in England exploring the clubs and pubs," he told Australian magazine *Juke*'s Charlie Eliezer in 1978. "There wasn't one group doing what we do. They stood

> **There wasn't one group doing what we do. They stood there like jukeboxes.**
>
> —Bon Scott, *Juke*, 1978

Melody Maker, May 8, 1976.

there like jukeboxes." His wanderings took some nonmusical turns: revisiting Fraternity's North London stamping ground, Finchley, he got into a fight and suffered a dislocated jaw. (In *Highway to Hell: The Life and Death of AC/DC Legend Bon Scott*, Clinton Walker notes Scott took the opportunity to sort out the dental disarray caused by his motorbike crash; his new false teeth cost a hefty £800.)

Manager Browning, meanwhile, found the band an agent, Richard Griffiths, who lined up their first U.K. gig: April 23 at the Red Cow pub, Hammersmith Road. A "crowd" of maybe ten experienced London's introduction to "The Jack," "She's Got Balls," and even the Bon/Angus walkabout. The band gave it everything they had, and, in those pre-cell days, the early-comers raced out to street-corner pay phones to ring their friends. By the time AC/DC started their second set, the house was jammed to capacity (albeit only about a hundred). That night, says Walker, Scott celebrated by reuniting with that "old girlfriend" Evans mentioned, Australian Margaret "Silver" Smith.

Three nights later at the nearby Nashville Rooms, their first U.K. reviewer, Caroline Coon of *Melody Maker*, heard Scott rather nervously emphasize to any doubters, "We're called AC/DC, but we're not!" (not gay, he meant). Accidentally, this gig helped them by raising the "punk" debate. Were they or weren't they? In Australia, the word had been used to describe them in the pre-safety-pin era. Then the Nashville billed their show as an "Antipodean Punk

First U.K. tour, Spring 1976. *Dick Barnatt/Redferns/Getty Images*

Extravaganza," causing confusion in the very month when proper British spit-and-snarl punk got under way—The Sex Pistols supporting Clash founder Joe Strummer's 101ers at the Nashville on April 3 could be claimed as opening night for the whole movement. But here were AC/DC, loud, rough, snot flying, straight-ahead rocking. Dinosaurs? Old farts? Hardly.

The London punks checked out the Aussies too. Angus reckoned Johnny Rotten attended one of their Nashville shows on May 27 or June 3. But in AC/DC's view, proximity revealed difference. Speaking to Eliezer for *Juke*, Angus ridiculed punk's musical incompetence: "Some of these idiots wouldn't even know how to tune a guitar." In the same interview, Scott dismissed punk as "fashion": "These bastards . . . try to look hard, but musically they bring nothing, not a trace of originality." Later, Malcolm put a more fundamental argument to Murray Engleheart and Arnaud Durieux, co-authors of *AC/DC: Maximum Rock & Roll*: "The real punks were the black guys: they're the ones who had to fight from the beginning to get accepted."

On April 30, Atlantic released AC/DC's U.K. debut album *High Voltage*, a discographically bewildering eight tracks from *T.N.T.*, plus "Little Lover" and "She's Got Balls" from the Australian *High Voltage*. Through May, they interspersed London pub gigs with a national tour supporting the reconstituted Back Street Crawler. After that, weekly music paper *Sounds* sponsored a nineteen-date U.K. tour that borrowed a title they'd used in

Australia: Lock Up Your Daughters. The tour opened on June 11 in the Youngs' birthplace, Glasgow, with already knowledgeable fans waving "Welcome Home" banners. It was no-frills affair, with Rudd at the wheel of the band's Ford van, lamenting the "dives we hadn't expected to play even in our worst nightmares" (*Rock Hard*, 2001).

On June 21, BBC national pop station Radio 1's most respected DJ, John Peel, broadcast his AC/DC live session: "Live Wire," "High Voltage," "Can I Sit Next to You Girl," and "Little Lover." They had momentum. A five-day party for Scott's thirtieth birthday on July 9 seemed in order and lacked nothing except the singer's presence. He'd been away quelling his fears of instant male menopause impotence, possibly

Weekly survey, Melbourne radio station 3XY, July 30, 1976.

"High Voltage" b/w "It's a Long Way to the Top," Portugal, 1976. *Bill Voccia Collection*

"High Voltage" b/w "Soul Stripper," first German single, 1976. *Bill Voccia Collection*

"It's a Long Way to the Top" promo, first U.S. single, 1976. *Bill Voccia Collection*

"It's a Long Way to the Top" sheet music, Albert Productions, Australia, 1976. *Bill Voccia Collection*

with the assistance of Silver Smith. He returned, apparently reassured, for the band's first European tour: clubs in Sweden, Denmark, Holland, and Austria.

This writer first saw AC/DC live on the second Monday of their weekly residency at key London venue The Marquee on August 2. It proved a gloriously uncomfortable experience, amid Britain's longest, hottest summer in living memory, with temperatures in the nineties. A thousand crammed into a sweltering low-ceilinged box with no air-conditioning. "I'm raining!" I wrote as my clothes darkened and my shoes filled with my own sweat. Meanwhile,

Lyceum Ballroom, London, July 7, 1976. *Dick Barnatt/Redferns/Getty Images*

Some people got very excited about AC/DC on tour.

All communications to be addressed to the General Manager

City of Glasgow District Council

Your Reference
In reply
please quote
If telephoning or calling, please
ask for

Halls Department

Head Office

Ticket Office

CITY HALL

Robert Richards
Atlantic Records
Berners Street
London W1

16th June 1976

Dear Sir,

I have been advised by my staff that the audience in attendance at the recent concert featuring AC/DC which you produced were for most of the performance entirely out of control and were actually standing up on the seats. This has caused some damage to the upholstery and has also resulted in a back being broken off one of the seats.

The masking curtain at the rear of the stage was also removed during the course of the concert and I will have to replace it, matching the existing curtaining.

A glass section was broken in the foyer when the outer doors were first opened.

I shall be in touch with you as soon as estimates for the restoration of the damage are in hand.

Yours faithfully,

Melody Maker, July 31, 1976.

AC/DC hammered it—rhythm guitar, bass and drums on the money, lead guitar and voice ripping it like they'd been together since the cradle, endlessly rocking, the rhythm and the blues right there in the bloodstream.

You sweated. You laughed. You hollered. You couldn't believe that the little guitarist in the silly schoolboy suit—no, in his underpants after a few minutes—could thrash about and play like that. "When I'm on stage, the savage in me is released," Angus is quoted as saying in Paul Stenning's *AC/DC: Two Sides to Every Glory.* "It's like going back to being a caveman. It takes me six hours to come down after a show." To Engleheart and Durieux he mused, "Whenever I'm playing, it's like, being a little guy, where most people bend a note on a guitar, my whole body bends. . . . Other guys let their fingers do

the walking. With me, the body does the walking."

A few days after the Marquee gig, I interviewed the band "at home" for *Sounds.* They'd moved to a flat in Finborough Road, West Brompton, near London's Earl's Court Aussie colony. At 4 p.m., they ate breakfast while Coral Browning, their manager's sister, cleaned up around them. Scott went to the kitchen muttering, "Wait for these cunts to make a cuppa and you'll die of thirst." He returned with a pot of tea and Angus drank two mugs, then two more of milk. Their talk rambled, yet with a weather eye to myths and legends. Angus "confessed" the lie about his age; he wasn't sixteen, he'd just turned seventeen. I believed him. Scott, mostly living with Smith by then, talked about a teenage fight with a cop, a dope bust, the time he got dragged

"Jailbreak" original sheet music, Albert Productions, Australia, 1976. *Bill Voccia Collection*

"Jailbreak" b/w "Fling Thing," U.K., 1976. *Bill Voccia Collection*

Reading Festival, August 29, 1976. *Erica Echenberg/Redferns/Getty Images*

LOCK UP YOUR DAUGHTERS!

AC/DC ARE HERE!

Electrifying new album

K50257

THE LOW DOWN ON HIGH ENERGY FROM AUSTRALIA'S MONSTROUSLY SUCCESSFUL ROCK BAND

Powerful British Tour

MELODY MAKER May 22, 1976—Page 13

28 May	Guildford, Surrey University
29 May	Birmingham, Barbarella's
30 May	London, Victoria Palace
1 June	Newcastle, City Hall
3 June	London, Nashville Rooms
4 June	London, Marquee
5 June	Fulham, Greyhound
6 June	Croydon, Greyhound
8 June	Portsmouth, Guildhall

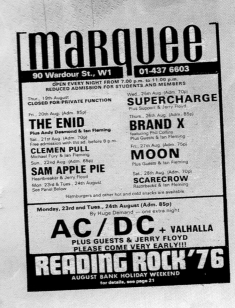

marquee

90 Wardour St., W1 01-437 6603

OPEN EVERY NIGHT FROM 7.00 p.m. to 11.00 p.m.
REDUCED ADMISSION FOR STUDENTS AND MEMBERS

Thur., 19th August
CLOSED FOR PRIVATE FUNCTION

Fri., 20th Aug. (Adm. 85p)
THE ENID
Plus Andy Desmond & Ian Fleming

Sat., 21th Aug. (Adm. 70p)
Free admission with this ad. before 8 p.m.
CLEMEN PULL
Michael Fury & Ian Fleming

Sun., 22nd Aug. (Adm. 65p)
SAM APPLE PIE
Heartbreaker & Jerry Floyd

Mon., 23rd & Tues., 24th August
See Panel Below

Wed., 25th Aug. (Adm. 70p)
SUPERCHARGE
Plus Support & Jerry Floyd

Thurs., 26th Aug. (Adm. 85p)
BRAND X
featuring Phil Collins
Plus Guests & Ian Fleming

Fri., 27th Aug. (Adm. 75p)
MOON
Plus Guests & Ian Fleming

Sat., 28th Aug. (Adm. 70p)
SCARECROW
Razorbacks & Ian Fleming

Hamburgers and other hot and cold snacks are available

Monday, 23rd and Tues., 24th August (Adm. 85p)
By Huge Demand — one extra night
AC/DC + VALHALLA
PLUS GUESTS & JERRY FLOYD
PLEASE COME VERY EARLY!!!

READING ROCK '76
AUGUST BANK HOLIDAY WEEKEND
for details, see page 21

READING ROCK '76

FRIDAY 27 AUGUST
From 3.30 p.m. to 11 p.m.

GONG
MIGHTY DIAMONDS
SUPERCHARGE
U-ROY
ROY ST. JOHN · STALLION

SPECIAL GUESTS FROM THE U.S.A.
MALLARD
.... The Original Magic Band

SATURDAY 28 AUGUST
From noon to 11.30 p.m.

RORY GALLAGHER
AND HIS BAND
MANFRED MANN'S EARTH BAND
VAN DER GRAAF GENERATOR
JON HISEMAN'S COLOSSEUM II
SADISTA SISTERS · MOON
PAT TRAVERS BAND
EDDIE AND THE HOT RODS
NICK PICKETT
SPECIAL GUESTS
CAMEL
PHIL MANZANERA
Featuring · ENO · BILL MacCORMACK
LLOYD WATSON · SIMON PHILLIPS

SUNDAY 29 AUGUST
From noon to 11.30 p.m.

BLACK OAK ARKANSAS
FEATURING: JIM DANDY and RUBY STARR

From the U.S.A
TED NUGENT
BRAND X FEATURING PHIL COLLINS

BACK DOOR · BAND CALLED 'O'
SASSAFRAS · AC/DC · THE ENID
A.F.T. · HOWARD BRAGEN

SPECIAL GUESTS:
SUTHERLAND BROTHERS & QUIVER

Advance tickets available from MARQUEE 90 WARDOUR ST. W1
All Harlequin and Virgin Record Shops and usual agencies, by personal application only

TRAVEL: Less than 40 miles West of London. 30 minutes by train from Paddington. Late trains Main station 10 mins. walk.

★ SPECIAL WEEKEND TICKETS ★
including VAT, Camping and car parking at no extra charge.
£6.95
★ IN ADVANCE ONLY ★

ADMISSIONS AT GROUNDS
Friday £2.50
Saturday £3.25
Sunday £3.25
Car Parking Camping Extra

50

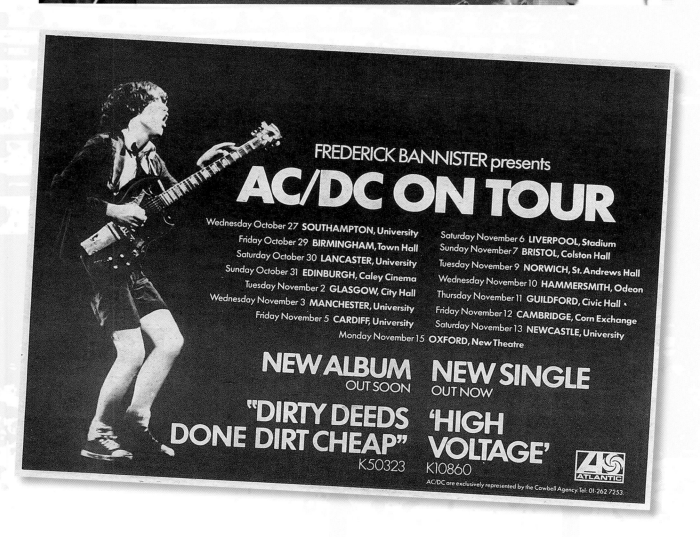

Congresgebouw, The Hague, Holland. October 18, 1976.
© Peter Mazel/Sunshine/Retna

FREDERICK BANNISTER presents

AC/DC ON TOUR

Wednesday October 27 **SOUTHAMPTON**, University
Friday October 29 **BIRMINGHAM**, Town Hall
Saturday October 30 **LANCASTER**, University
Sunday October 31 **EDINBURGH**, Caley Cinema
Tuesday November 2 **GLASGOW**, City Hall
Wednesday November 3 **MANCHESTER**, University
Friday November 5 **CARDIFF**, University
Monday November 15 **OXFORD**, New Theatre

Saturday November 6 **LIVERPOOL**, Stadium
Sunday November 7 **BRISTOL**, Colston Hall
Tuesday November 9 **NORWICH**, St. Andrews Hall
Wednesday November 10 **HAMMERSMITH**, Odeon
Thursday November 11 **GUILDFORD**, Civic Hall
Friday November 12 **CAMBRIDGE**, Corn Exchange
Saturday November 13 **NEWCASTLE**, University

NEW ALBUM OUT SOON

NEW SINGLE OUT NOW

"DIRTY DEEDS DONE DIRT CHEAP"
K50323

'HIGH VOLTAGE'
K10860

ATLANTIC

AC/DC are exclusively represented by the Cowbell Agency. Tel: 01-262 7253.

through a very thorny rose bush by an
irate father who'd caught him in bed
with his teenaged daughter, and another
naughty night that was about to become
a song. Back home, in the dressing room
after a show, two women had joined
them, one "ugly but not that bad," the
other a majestic female he called "Big
Bertha" ("One pound under twenty
stone," Malcolm put in). Silver-tongued
Scott asked the women, "Right who
wants it?" Bertha smiled and walked
his way. "She'd have broken my arm
if I'd refused," he told me. When their
love had been consummated, Bertha
called over to her friend, "Hey, that's
the thirty-seventh this month!" She
showed Scott her little black book to
prove it. Of course, Bertha was about to

be immortalized in "Whole Lotta Rosie."
(In a variant on this yarn, Bertha/Rosie
lived across the road from Freeway
Gardens Motel, AC/DC's last lodgings in
Melbourne.)

Rowdily, the band had charmed
the British summer. But on August 29,
the Reading Festival, an annual binge
of hard rock staged forty miles west of
London, quashed any complacency. It
rained, and AC/DC didn't shine. "They
fucking hated us. We flopped," Evans
told Janssen. "At the end of the first
song, 'Live Wire,' we stopped and there
were 50,000 people just looking at us.
Nothing happened."

Reassurance arrived when Vanda
and Young flew in to produce some
tracks. At Vineyard Studios in South

I've been told we can't say "SHIT." OK, we won't say "shit." They left out "suck," but we won't say that either.

—Bon Scott responding from stage to local Australian authorities during the Giant Dose of Rock 'n' Roll Tour, 1976

London, they recorded versions of "Love at First Feel," "Carry Me Home," "Cold Hearted Man," and "Dirty Eyes" (soon rewritten as "Whole Lotta Rosie").

Although Griffiths had swiftly steered them from £10 a night to £500, Browning transferred them to one of London's biggest agencies, Cowbell, who then delivered twenty-two dates around Europe, headlining clubs or supporting former Deep Purple guitar hero Ritchie Blackmore. In Hamburg, they took in the infamous Reeperbahn strip shows and stayed with Angus and Malcolm's older brother Alex who, since the early '60s, had played bass and sax in Germany (with a short interlude in 1967 when The Beatles signed his band, Grapefruit, to Apple). The following British tour included some half-full venues as they tried to step up a rung, but they knew it was worth impressing 2,000 people even if they were scattered around the 4,000-seat Hammersmith Odeon (as they were on November 10).

That month's European release of *Dirty Deeds Done Dirt Cheap* featured a couple of tracklist changes from the Australian version (which had hit No. 4), dropping "R.I.P. (Rock in Peace)" and "Jailbreak" in favor of the warp-speed rave-up "Rocker" from *T.N.T.* and the recent London recording "Love at First Feel." The album also lacked the Aussie cover art that connected the title to its source, *Beany and Cecil*, a 1960s American TV cartoon Angus loved chiefly for a character called Dishonest John, whose business card read "Dirty Deeds Done Dirt Cheap."

Now, though, frustration did kick in, initially with regard to band members' high American ambitions. Their debut American release, *High Voltage*, had come out on September 28 (with the U.K./European tracklist), and Browning happily told them he had three weeks of gigs fixed for November. Then they were cancelled. Talking to Eliezer from *Juke*, Angus blamed "visa difficulties," but really Atlantic's headquarters in the United States had lost interest in the band. Datelined December 16, *Rolling Stone*'s infamous review of *High Voltage* would refer to the band as "gross-out champions" and the album as an "all-time low" for hard rock.

So, on November 26, they flew to Australia instead, but not for a vacation. They lined up 18 gigs before New Year (notching a 1976 total of around 160). Yet somehow absence had made their homeland fall out of love with them. At least, local authorities had. In a strange Antipodean echo of the simultaneous Sex Pistols tour uproar in the U.K., city fathers suddenly condemned as obscene what they'd previously deemed mischief. Officialdom didn't laugh when Angus dropped his pants on arrival at Sydney airport. Nor when the tour's working title got out: The Little Cunts Have Done It.

The band rechristened the jaunt "A Giant Dose of Rock 'n' Roll," and Radio 2SM in Sydney denounced its double entendres. In response, Angus gave the station a surreal peacemaking interview wherein, live on air, he showed his arse to prove it wouldn't offend listeners. But in Canberra on December 9 and Wollongong the next night, police threatened to cut the power the moment Angus dropped his shorts—which he did, but Scott produced a large "Censored" sign to cover

Hordern Pavilion, Sydney, December 12, 1976. © Bob King/bobking.com.au

Hordern Pavilion, Sydney, December 12, 1976. *Both © Bob King/bobking.com.au*

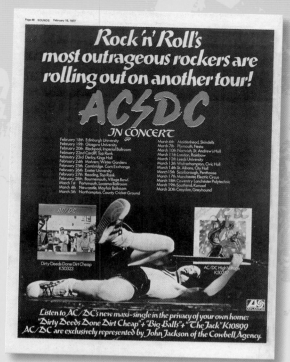

Rock 'n' Roll's most outrageous rockers are rolling out on another tour!

AC/DC
IN CONCERT

February 18th Edinburgh University
February 19th Glasgow University
February 20th Blackpool, Imperial Ballroom
February 22nd Cardiff, Top Rank
February 23rd Derby, Kings Hall
February 24th Malvern, Winter Gardens
February 25th Cambridge, Corn Exchange
February 26th Exeter University
February 27th Reading, Top Rank
February 28th Bournemouth, Village Bowl
March 1st Portsmouth, Locarno Ballroom
March 4th Newcastle, Mayfair Ballroom
March 5th Northampton, County Cricket Ground

March 6th Maidenhead, Skindells
March 7th Plymouth, Fiesta
March 10th Norwich, St. Andrew's Hall
March 11th London, Rainbow
March 12th Leeds University
March 13th Wolverhampton, Civic Hall
March 14th St. Albans, City Hall
March 15th Scarborough, Penthouse
March 17th Manchester, Electric Circus
March 18th Coventry Lanchester Polytechnic
March 19th Southend, Kursaal
March 20th Croydon, Greyhound

Dirty Deeds Done Dirt Cheap
K50323

AC/DC High Voltage
K50257

Listen to AC/DC's new maxi-single in the privacy of your own home:
"Dirty Deeds Done Dirt Cheap" + "Big Balls" + "The Jack" K10899
AC/DC are exclusively represented by John Jackson of the Cowbell Agency.

the offending nether parts. Even so, "outraged" local councils cancelled their gigs at Tamworth Town Hall on December 16 and Warrnambool Palais on January 12, 1977. Throughout the tour, Angus recalled, "The mayor and the councilmen would come along to the show and monitor us. I remember Bon up there saying, 'I've been told we can't say "fuck." OK, we won't say "fuck." I've been told we can't say "shit." OK, we won't say "shit." They left out "suck," but we won't say that either'" (Stenning, unattributed).

Attendances suffered. The 5,500-capacity Sydney Hordern Pavilion remained half empty on December 12, and a sorry sixty attended a gig in Tasmania (probably at Burne Civic Centre, January 9). Over Christmas, Atlantic U.S.A. lobbed in its two cents of trouble by refusing to release *Dirty Deeds Done Dirt Cheap* because *High Voltage* had sold only 7,000 copies and Scott's rude lyrics made executives nervous.

AC/DC reacted with more of the same, only harder and better. After the last "Giant Dose" gig on January 14, they recorded their fourth album at Albert's with Vanda and Young. And, riff by riff, *Let There Be Rock* set new standards of raw grunt with the title track, "Hell Ain't a Bad Place to Be," "Dog Eat Dog," "Overdose," "Whole Lotta Rosie," "Bad Boy Boogie," and, on the Australian version, the down-home comedy blues "Crabsody in Blue" (another tale of STDs at Lansdowne Road). Meanwhile, Scott sang like he looked—leery, lairy, leathery—and came up with some fine earthy verses. That Rosie: "Forty-two, thirty-nine, fifty-six/You could say she's got it all!" Those crabs: "Before you start to scream/That's when you apply the cream/Blues ointment."

After the Giant Dose debacle, AC/DC understandably doubted they had much future in their homeland. When Albert's released *Let There Be Rock* in March 1977, they chose to be half a world away. After a few stray gigs, concluding in Perth on February 15, they flew to London, and, in Australia, *Let There Be Rock* petered out at No. 19. The Youngs rented a flat in boho Ladbroke Grove, Rudd and Evans shared a place nearby, and Scott again moved in with Silver Smith. Ever hustling, three nights after touchdown, they launched a twenty-nine-date tour of major cities, plus oddities such as down-at-heel seaside resort Cleethorpes and country towns Hemel Hempstead and Malvern.

Kursaal Ballroom, Southend-on-Sea, England, March 19, 1977. *Estate of Keith Morris/Getty Images*

On March 11, at the renowned Rainbow in London, they encountered two enthusiastic rockbiz emissaries from America. Quite a surprise. Doug Thaler, an agent from American Talent International, loved "It's a Long Way to the Top" (a flop single in the United States as well as the United Kingdom); heard about the connection with one of his favorite bands, The Easybeats; and brought Aerosmith and Ted Nugent manager David Krebs to see them. Krebs immediately proposed co-managing AC/DC in America. Browning turned him down.

AC/DC hurtled onward into Europe, supporting Black Sabbath. This tour's unforeseen outcome was the departure of bassist Mark Evans. Apparently, at Angus and Malcolm's joint request, Browning did the firing. His final gig was Offenbach, Germany, on April 29

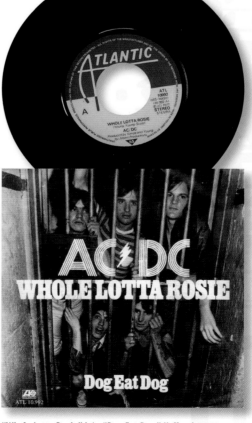

"Grab a Hold of This One" maxi single featuring "Dirty Deeds Done Dirt Cheap," "Big Balls," and "The Jack," U.K., 1977.
Bill Voccia Collection

"Carry Me Home," the B-side to "Dog Eat Dog" that remained unreleased outside of Australia until the recent *Backtracks* boxed set (2009), Australia, 1977. *Bill Voccia Collection*

"Whole Lotta Rosie" b/w "Dog Eat Dog," Holland, 1977.
Bill Voccia Collection

(the night when over-refreshed Sabbath drummer Geezer Butler pulled a knife on Malcolm and Ozzy Osbourne "saved the day," as Malcolm told *Q* in 2003, by ordering Butler off to bed).

In his interview with *Daily Dirt*'s Janssen twenty years later, Evans still struggled to explain his dismissal: "I had a few clashes with Angus, but everyone did because Angus is very intense and very talented . . . ah, there was a general tension in the band. . . . Except for Bon, Bon was just a hippie!" Then he added, "I think basically Angus didn't like me. . . . It actually had become too hard; it was too divisive . . . which was unfortunate because I still loved the band. It was a tough period for me. . . . My health wasn't good at all because I was drinking too much." For his part, in 1979, Angus told French magazine *Best*, that Evans "had nervous depression" and "couldn't stand touring any more." Evans got a $2,000 pay off, handsomely enhanced much later via lawyers.

Cliff Williams, a Browning discovery, replaced Evans on May 27. Born on the outskirts of London, in Romford, Essex, on December 14, 1949, he moved to Liverpool, at age nine, and learned guitar and bass while Merseybeat and The Beatles took over the world. Following the AC/DC blueprint, he left school as soon as he could, worked in a factory, and then gave his soul to rock 'n' roll. Trying his luck in London, he joined short-lived bands and worked in supermarkets and demolition. At his lowest ebb, he slept in a box on the street for a spell. The upturn began when he joined Wishbone Ash guitarist-to-be Laurie Wisefield in a combo called Home that made three albums starting with *Pause for a Hoarse Horse* in 1971 (they supported Led Zeppelin at Wembley Empire Pool that November 20 and 21). When Home split three years later, Williams played with Stars in the United States and Bandit in the United Kingdom until he auditioned for AC/DC in London. A quick thunder through "Live Wire" and "Problem Child," and in June 1977 he found himself on a plane to Australia. ⚡

Adverts for Cliff Williams' early-1970s outfit, Home.

Is It Punk?

By Garth Cartwright

Around 1976 in New York, London, and Australia a handful of like-minded, unrelated rock groups forged a new, raw form of rock 'n' roll. The sound and ethos this gave rise to—especially among the New York and London rockers—would be labeled "punk rock." Australia's new rockers were also branded punks. This included AC/DC.

Thing is, labels have never stuck on AC/DC. Every time a critic or promoter has tried to stick one on the band, the members have shrugged it off, insisting they're simply a rock 'n' roll band. Which is true, as it is for The Ramones, Sex Pistols, and those other New York– and London-based bands that approached playing with a stripped-down, working-class fury comparable to AC/DC. All the aforementioned bands were of a roughly similar age to Malcolm and Angus Young and attempted to play hard-edged, Chuck Berry–flavored rock 'n' roll. If the Ramones sang with mordent, ironic wit, and the Sex Pistols a sneering, politicized nihilism, AC/DC celebrated a bawdy mix of shagging, boozing, brawling, and fleeing. All three bands were led by social misfits (to put it politely) who hoped rock 'n' roll would offer an alternative to menial jobs and petty crime (in the cases of Bon Scott, Dee Dee Ramone, and Steve Jones). And all pursued a personal vision of what a rock 'n' roll band should sound like and ignored prevailing fashions while expressing contempt for a complacent music industry.

By 1975, the Rolling Stones, the Faces, and Mott the Hoople had either split or

were creatively dead. American icons the Allman Brothers, The Band, and Creedence Clearwater Revival had disintegrated or sunk. Glam's crunchy bubblegum rockers—Gary Glitter and David Bowie, Slade and T.Rex, Suzi Quatro and The Sweet—were all finding their time in the spotlight over (OK, Bowie managed to reinvent himself several times over the next decade, but this involved jettisoning his rock 'n' roll stylings for fake soul and German electro angst). Truth be told, by 1975 rock 'n' roll was horribly static, dominated by pompous, ponderous stadium acts—Led Zeppelin and Yes; Emerson, Lake & Palmer and Pink Floyd; Peter Frampton and Foghat—bands that had forgotten it was the joy of the roll, not just the thud of rock, that first inspired and brought them together. These groups were jaded and their music sounded it: pampered, indulged nonsense that only the most privileged and spoilt youths could engage with. Even metal pioneers Black Sabbath and Deep Purple were in severe decline. Iggy Pop was institutionalized. The New York Dolls had collapsed. Only Thin Lizzy and Aerosmith—both on their way up but soon to fall apart—came close to summoning up the spirit of Little Richard's war cry "Awopbopaloobopabopbamboom!" Thing is, rock 'n' roll was by now a primal force in the Western psyche and the kids would not be denied. As Bon Scott proudly proclaimed in 1977, "Let there be rock." As it turned out, lots of other people felt the same way.

Australia, home to Skippy and the Bee

Gees, might seem an odd nation for punk rock to spring from. Not so. Australia excels at selling itself to the world as a land of Nicole Kidmans, Crocodile Dundees, and endless summers, but the reality is it's a nation riddled with fear and loathing (of England, foreigners, homosexuals, Aboriginals, women, bosses—standard prejudices of Irish/Scottish immigrants). Being the most urbanized nation on earth means there are endless suburbs and a huge, white working class. Everywhere, pubs hosted live music, and audiences didn't want fiddly stuff but music to drink, carouse, and fight by. Bands that failed to kick out the jams were likely to find themselves on the receiving end of a rain of beer bottles. Johnny O'Keefe, Australia's first attempt at an Elvis, spelled out the original Oz-rock manifesto with 1958's "Wild One," while The Easybeats' (featuring the teenage Harry Vanda and George Young) 1966 to 1968 hits "Friday on My Mind" and "Good Times" captured the amphetamine buzz of being young and hungry. Having assimilated O'Keefe and The Easybeats, AC/DC set about creating primal rock 'n' roll. AC/DC were not tall, glamorous, or good-looking; no matter, they had a work ethic and a desire to rock hard. The kids heard them and understood.

Not that AC/DC were alone in creating a rock sound that was raw, feral, and distinctly Australian in its "up yours" approach to the world. First there was Skyhooks, a glam rock band best known internationally for "Women in Uniform," a song with which

Nashville Rooms, London, April 6, 1976. *Dick Barnatt/Redferns/Getty*

Iron Maiden scored a U.K. hit. Though Skyhooks were hugely popular in mid-1970s Australia, few today would recall the band as particularly impressive, but their sardonic songs and laddish swagger proved Oz rock could succeed on its own terms. Also forming in 1974 were two Australian bands that would share with AC/DC a desire to shake up rock 'n' roll's complacency. Radio Birdman formed in Sydney, The Saints in Brisbane. AC/DC were based in Melbourne and, as Australia is vast, these bands tended to play mostly for the audiences in their home states. There was then no sense of an Australian "scene" as surrounded CBGB in New York, yet all three bands would go on to make a huge impact both in Australia and internationally. And while AC/DC, Radio Birdman, and The Saints were all masters of their own distinct styles, the world media would briefly label all of them "punk."

The Saints and Radio Birdman drew on similar influences as AC/DC (although both of the former bands shared a love of The Stooges that AC/DC never exhibited). All three wrote short, fast, tough songs and would initially issue recordings in 1976 on their own labels. The Saints' debut single, "I'm Stranded," attracted international acclaim from the likes of Bob Geldof, while Radio Birdman's "Burn My Eye" EP had them hailed as kings of Sydney's underground music scene. Once punk took off and the U.K. music press started praising these uncompromising Aussie bands, The Saints and Birdman got international recording deals. Both bands followed AC/DC to the U.K. but found themselves unhappy with their record companies and frustrated at how the music press expected them to act "punk." The Saints and Radio Birdman would both split by the end of 1979, members retreating

to Australia to lick their wounds, while AC/DC—untroubled by media hype—kept on touring, working harder and harder, building audiences, and slowly conquering the world.

If AC/DC largely avoided being labeled "punk" by the U.K. music press it was more due to good timing: The band arrived in England in summer 1976 and started touring a few crucial months before punk became a media phenomenon. British music fans initially saw AC/DC more as colonial savages, their boozing, brawling, and abrasive music perfectly supporting the widely held English caricature of the Aussie larrikin. In 1976, AC/DC's raw, blues-inflected sound placed them closer to pub rock heroes Dr. Feelgood than any fledgling punk or veteran metal band. Dr. Feelgood, like AC/DC, were a tough, working-class band that eschewed frills and proclaimed a dedication to blues and rock 'n' roll. In Wilko Johnson, they possessed a guitarist almost as manic as Angus. In many ways, the Feelgoods cleared the ground both for British punk to grow upon and for AC/DC to win over hordes of sweaty British rock fans who wanted their music served up hard, fast, and simple.

Yet to the rest of the world—especially the U.S.—AC/DC seemed absolutely "punk," and early reports in *Creem* magazine always described them as "Aussie punks." AC/DC's grimy, hard-as-nails sound and appearance was a world away from the feather-cut, cocaine-fueled, airbrushed bands then sold as "rock." Consider the Australian cover for 1976's *Dirty Deeds Done Dirty Cheap*. The LP features an illustration of the band in a pool hall, Bon flashing tattoos and missing teeth, Angus snarling and giving a two

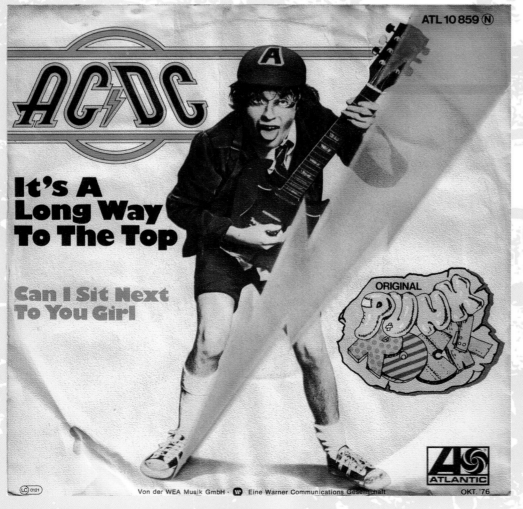

"It's a Long Way to the Top" b/w "Can I Sit Next to You Girl," Germany, 1976. *Bill Voccia Collection*

Some of these idiots wouldn't even know how to tune a guitar.

—Angus Young on contemporary punk rockers, *Juke*, 1978

60

finger salute . . . AC/DC were indeed a lot more punk than many of the poseurs who descended on the scene. Having already played a number of regional dates as an opening act for New York punk heroes The Dictators, AC/DC turned up unannounced at CBGB in August 1977 for an impromptu set, blasting New York hipsters to the wall and attracting rave write-ups in underground U.S. rock magazines (Angus later recalled the legendary club as being "a toilet"). To many Americans this explosion of sweat, snot, and swearing, with their songs about catching VD and getting beat up and broken boned, was the most primal rock 'n' roll experience since The Stooges. AC/DC were a life force, a malevolent energy mass, and alongside punk they were putting pomp, prog, and heavy rock through the shredder. Yet where punks screamed about anarchy, Bon and the lads leered about big, big women.

AC/DC could have played at being punk. Instead, as with their CBGB gig, they chose to doff their collective caps to the movement, acknowledging it had kicked a tired rock scene in the ass while denying they were part of it. While they shared many qualities with The Ramones and Sex Pistols, AC/DC knew that they sounded only like themselves and no one else. Atlantic Records, perhaps aware of the disasters that had befallen The Saints and Radio Birdman when they were marketed as punk, sold AC/DC as a metal band. While the Youngs have always denied any connection with heavy rock, it was the headbanging masses that would prove their first international audience. And if metal ever needed a band to save it from its own ridiculousness it was now, and AC/DC were the music's saviors. Their back-to-basics style—no fuss, no solos, no costumes (beyond Angus' trademark school uniform), no dragons-and-demons lyrics or syrupy ballads—made them contemporaries of Motörhead and helped issue redundancy notices to many a pompous metal band. When AC/DC first post-Bon LP, *Back in Black*, established the band as the biggest rock act going in 1980—Led Zeppelin had split, Black Sabbath were melting down, Alice Cooper was singing ballads, and Rainbow, Ted Nugent, and KISS

were all headed to metal's junkyard. AC/DC reinvented rock 'n' roll by stripping it down to a lean, mean chassis that roared along rock's highway. If the 1980s saw the rise of MTV-sanctioned hair metal, all soft ballads and limp guitars, AC/DC remained a totem for the kids who simply wanted to *rock*. Soon the likes of Metallica and Slayer would rise, all having learned from the Aussie masters, while in New York rap producer Rick Rubin would employ AC/DC's massive, swinging rhythms to reinvent hip-hop. When Guns N' Roses and then Nirvana began laying waste to 1980s hair metal, it was AC/DC who

provided a common spark. Even today, when inept indie bands get too shrill, smug, and clever, it's Angus and Company who kids turn to for a shot of the pure stuff. Rock's scrap heap fills with chancers while the Aussie rockers who swear by Little Richard and Chuck Berry continue to roll.

No waste, no bullshit, take-it-to-the-stage-and-entertain-the-people was as much AC/DC's maxim as it was James Brown's. And like the King of Soul, the Aussies created a sound so simple yet individual, so unique yet engaging, that many imitate but few ever match. ⚡

The LPs
High Voltage

By Sylvie Simmons

International cover art, 1976.

The album considered AC/DC's debut by most non-Aussie fans is actually, of course, their third. The band had already put out two albums with Australia's Albert Productions when the major American label Atlantic stepped up to the plate with an international deal.

Atlantic's plan for the band was to move them to the States and scrub them up a bit before releasing their international debut—and AC/DC was certainly nothing like the polished and manicured AOR artists who in the mid-'70s dominated the U.S. charts (think The Eagles, Peter Frampton, Chicago, Elton John, etc.). As one might imagine, the band was none too enthused at this prospect, so they persuaded Atlantic to let them move instead to London (a longtime dream of Malcolm Young's), where they could play live and build a grassroots buzz.

In April 1976, the night that Bon Scott, Angus and Malcolm Young, Mark Evans, and Phil Rudd took to the stage at a pub in West London for their first U.K. gig, at another West London bar just staggering distance away, The Sex Pistols were playing a show with The Clash. If in America the mainstream rockers ruled, in Britain it was the punks. One month later—May 11, 1976—when AC/DC's U.S. and U.K. debut album appeared in stores, they found themselves between soft rock and a very hard place.

High Voltage features two tracks—"Little Lover" and "She's Got Balls"—from the band's Australian release of the same name (February 1975), with the balance coming from their second album, *T.N.T.* (December

> # With the release of the first U.S. album by these Australian gross-out champions, hard rock has unquestionably hit its all-time low.
>
> —Billy Altman reviewing *High Voltage, Rolling Stone*, 1976

1975), also an Australia-only Albert release. Just to confuse things even more, the *song* "High Voltage" first appeared on *T.N.T.*

The choice of tracks was shrewd move, considering the band was still finding its feet on *High Voltage* Mk. I (an album that still attracts AC/DC completists, if only for "Love Song," their not entirely successful attempt at a rock ballad, complete with keyboards, and their brilliant cover of the Big Joe Williams blues standard "Baby,

Please Don't Go"). The *T.N.T.* material is clearly superior and includes enduring AC/DC classics, such as "The Jack," "Live Wire," and "It's a Long Way to the Top (If You Wanna Rock 'n' Roll)."

At just nine songs in total, none of them epics, the album is short and to the point, even by vinyl standards. But that suited the band and its music just fine. On album as on stage, it's lean and basic, less no frills than stripped to the bone, and as down to

European cover art, 1976.

The 1975 Australia-only release that provided the bulk of the material on the worldwide release of *High Voltage*.

earth and entertaining as the early rock 'n' roll that inspired it—primitive riffs, catchy hooks, and relentless blues-boogie grooves like Chuck Berry in a jean jacket. The band's Atlantic debut presented AC/DC as the ultimate party band—a breath of boozy air sorely needed at a time when bands were arty or angry, pretentious or blanded out.

A number of the songs found here were written when the band lived in Melbourne, sharing a low-rent house. They also shared the girls who came to visit, hence "The Jack," the most popular paean to sexually transmitted disease ever written. Along with "She's Got Balls" (Bon's love song to his wife, really) and "It's a Long Way . . . ," these three numbers encapsulated all the trademark elements of every AC/DC song to follow: good-natured sleaze, sexual double entendres that are part Chuck Berry and part Benny Hill, and a commitment to rock 'n' roll as an end in itself.

As befits a party band, the songs also offer an in-built inclusiveness—it wasn't about *them*; it was about *us*, a communal experience. The choruses are all instant sing-alongs, and the unfussy music leaves space for listeners to punch their fists or bang their heads. The resulting overall attitude and sense of fun make it music to crack a beer to. (It was no accident that when AC/DC released their *Bonfire* box set twenty years later, it came with a free bottle-opener.)

The production by the team of Harry Vanda and Malcolm and Angus' older brother (and mentor), George, perfectly captures the energy, spontaneity, and party spirit. With its ferocious riffing, the album sounds like it could have been recorded in that Melbourne house on any sweaty Saturday night. There's a raw horniness to "Can I Sit Next to You Girl" and "Little Lover," an infectiousness (no pun intended) to "The

Jack," a greasy bluesiness to Scott's piercing vocals on "Live Wire" and "It's a Long Way . . ." (the latter also featuring Bon playing the bagpipe, as proud of his Scottish heritage as Rod Stewart ever was).

It's quite amazing, really, looking back at this album more than thirty years on, how arena-ready the band sounded on its international debut, even if it took the public a little longer to catch up and the rock press longer still. *Rolling Stone*'s review, calling it an "all-time low" in rock, summed up the attitude of most music critics at the time, particularly in the United States. In the United Kingdom, the band's credibility was helped along when it was embraced by mega-popular radio DJ John Peel, who called AC/DC an "Antipodean punk band."

Although *High Voltage* failed to chart on either side of the ocean, over time it would sell three million copies. ⚡

The LPs
Dirty Deeds Done Dirt Cheap

By Anthony Bozza

Australian cover art, 1976.

Recorded as the follow-up to 1975's *T.N.T*, *Dirty Deeds Done Dirt Cheap* is a true gem in the AC/DC canon. The original Australian version of the album was released in 1976, but it did not see the light of day in the United States until 1981, following the success of *Highway to Hell* and the death of Bon Scott. The U.S./international version substituted the song "Rocker" for the song "R.I.P. (Rock in Peace)" and contained an edited version of one of Scott's finest lyrical outings, "Ain't No Fun (Waiting Round to Be a Millionaire)." Malcolm and Angus Young intended the album to be an homage to noir, their version of a Mickey Spillane dime-store thriller by way of a biker gang. It is their succinct, muscular take on a concept album, which, being AC/DC, is worlds away from a concept album. They're no Styx circa *Kilroy Was Here*, that's for sure.

Dirty Deeds features, in the title track alone, proof positive of Scott's prowess as a vocalist and performer. A classified ad for a gun for hire—a fix-it man who will avenge all wrongs for a price—the song sets the tone for what's to follow. The title was taken from the cartoon *Beany and Cecil*, which Angus Young enjoyed as a child. Specifically, it pays homage to the character Dishonest John, who carried business cards that read "Dirty Deeds Done Dirt Cheap. Holidays, Sundays, and Special Rates." The Youngs' appropriately sinister riffs on the track lay the groundwork for Scott's lyrical and vocal exploration of a ne'er-do-well private investigator–cum–hit man. Scott was capable of emoting through several distinct voices: a growl, a taut whisper, a shrill midrange, and a crystal-shattering wail. He used all of them in this song, and the result is quite a showcase of his range.

Unlike his successor, Brian Johnson, Scott brought a theatrical edge to his vocal performances that's evident on every track on *Dirty Deeds*. More so than in his work with any of his earlier bands, Scott convincingly embodied the narrators in AC/DC's songs, likely because his lyrics were recounted tales from his life. But even when they weren't, Bon sold a song like no other. The tangible menace of the song "Dirty Deeds" is inherent in the music, but the deathblow is Bon's delivery.

Among the most overlooked and misunderstood elements of AC/DC are their sense of humor and carefree self-mockery. Nowhere is that quality more apparent than in Scott's lyrics, and they're in full effect here on "Big Balls," which, for all the nudge-nudge-wink-wink entendre, is a deft use of metaphor, a hilarious statement on social class, and a subtle self-castigation.

International cover art, 1976.

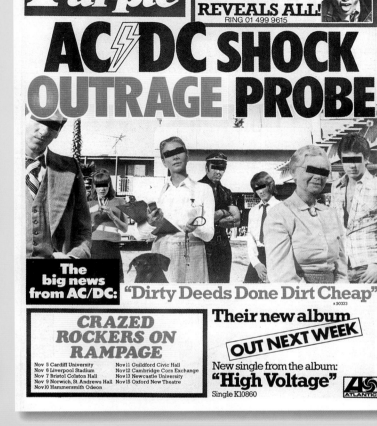

Sounds, November 6, 1976.

The song is ostensibly about high-society ballroom events, but when Scott sings that he's "itching to tell you about" all of the "seafood cocktail, crabs, and crayfish," available in his big balls, the infamous lothario is poetically over-sharing. Scott was a master of layered meaning who built his imagery from the gutter up.

From the first track on, the album is as taut as AC/DC's best outings. It never lets up, and, more than *T.N.T.*, it feels and sounds like a band bent on world domination. There is no denying the musicianship or the attitude of this album: It's a collection of songs celebrating outlaw behavior by a band reveling in the low life. It's not a romanticized view of the other side, either. This is the warts-and-all honesty that only Bon Scott could have delivered. From the lonely rebel soliloquy of "Ride On" to the ode to the roots of rock 'n' roll in "R.I.P.," the album is 100 percent authentic.

Because the Australian and international versions of the album contain some material that was recorded at different times, it's hard to see *Dirty Deeds Done Dirt Cheap* as a moment in time in the same way that other albums in the AC/DC canon are. It may be harder to track a musical evolution as a result, but songs such as "Love at First Feel" and "Ride On" shine as examples of the band at the top of its game. It's no surprise that the pinnacle of the Bon Scott era—*Powerage* and *Highway to Hell*—was at hand. Like those outings, *Dirty Deeds* is a true album, a journey from start to finish that leaves you electrified. ⚡

The LPs
Let There Be Rock

By Sylvie Simmons

Australian cover art, 1977.

Any top-fifty list of the best heavy rock albums of all time would be missing something if it didn't include this early AC/DC classic. Though it was recorded, like its predecessors, back in Australia with Harry Vanda and George Young on production duties, the most important contribution to the sound and content of this 1977 album was what the band was up to in the year and a half since the release of its international debut, *High Voltage*—which, in a nutshell, was playing live, pretty much nonstop.

In the U.K. the band performed everywhere they could, from pubs to the Reading Festival. They toured Europe as the opening act for Ritchie Blackmore's Rainbow and then did the same thing with Black Sabbath. In between, they made their live debut in America—more clubs and opening slots—and somehow, before returning for a second shot at the States, found the time to

fly back to Australia and knock out another quick album, *Dirty Deeds Done Dirt Cheap*. That album was released in Australia and the U.K. at the very end of 1976, but it didn't appear in the U.S. until 1981. In fact, *Let There Be Rock* was the first AC/DC record to get near-simultaneous release in the U.K., U.S. and Australia—although, once again, the albums are not entirely identical.

There's a palpable difference between *Dirty Deeds* and *Let There Be Rock*, not so much in the music but in the sound and feel. Where *Dirty Deeds* seems rushed and a touch unfocused, *Let There Be Rock* is road-honed and energized. And heavier—*much* heavier. The trademark AC/DC hooks are still there, as are the metronomic, rock 'n' roll grooves and the memorable, anthemic melodies, but the greasy, old-school blues-boogie has been turned up several notches in the direction of heavy metal. In short, *Let There Be Rock*

is a powerhouse of an album, a blistering, walloping, electrified rabble-rouser. Although it's a studio album, it sounds so live that, listening to it now more than three decades on, I can still feel my feet sticking to the spilled beer on the venue floor.

Which could be why, for the front cover of the U.K. and U.S. versions of the album, the band chose an onstage photo: Angus Young up front in his schoolboy shorts and blazer, wielding his guitar mid-solo. (The Australian version, released on Albert, featured an oddly drab sleeve: a black-and-white close-up of fingers on the neck of a guitar.)

With *High Voltage* and *Dirty Deeds* having failed to do much outside of Australia, *Let There Be Rock* was a crucial juncture for AC/DC. After all the touring, they were anxious to discover if they could ever break in the U.S. and U.K. When Vanda

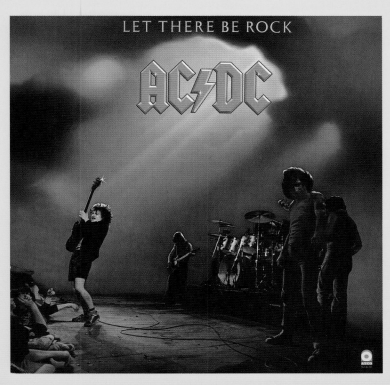

International cover art, 1977.

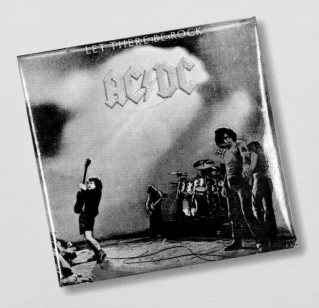

and Young asked them what kind of album they wanted to make, they were so fired up from touring that they told the producers they wanted something more like their live shows. And that's just what the production captures in all its scorching, supercharged glory.

Bon Scott–era AC/DC albums are all bluesy, filthy, and utterly great, and *Let There Be Rock* is no exception. The songs stick faithfully to the already-established AC/DC blueprint, set to insistent, blues-boogie grooves about sex, partying, and an unshakeable belief in the power of rock 'n' roll. The last of these three is at its most devotional on the title track, on which the band borrows and plays with an idea from the Old Testament book: *"Let there be drum/ Let there be guitar/Let there be rock!"* (strike one against the band when it came to their ongoing problems with conservative American Christians).

As to sex, it's all over the album, from "Bad Boy Boogie," where the band gives the blues "Hoochie Coochie Man" template an AC/DC twist, to the blistering, five-minute opening track, "Go Down" (no explanation necessary). All are sung in Bon's best tattooed, testosteroned, alley-cat drawl. But the most memorable and enduring of them all is "Whole Lotta Rosie," the classic AC/DC sing-along inspired, like the equally memorable "The Jack" from *T.N.T.* and *High Voltage* (Atlantic), by one of their female guests at the house they had shared in Melbourne: a 280-pound sex-mad Tasmanian.

As it happens, AC/DC offered another song about a sexually transmitted ailment on *Let There Be Rock*. But although "Crabsody in Blue" appeared on the Albert version Down Under, it was dropped from Atlantic's international release—presumably less an objection to the bad wordplay of

the title than lyrics like "When you start to scream, that's when you apply the cream." Happily, the song that replaced "Crabsody" (which was released on the 2009 box set *Backtracks*) was an abridged version of a track from the Australian version of *Dirty Deeds* and one of the best songs on any hard rock album: the jagged, thrilling, and magnificently played and sung anthem "Problem Child."

Killer songs and performances aside, the album failed to dent the U.S. Top 100, stalling at No. 154 before dropping into temporary oblivion (over time it would go double platinum in the States). It did give the band their first U.K. hit, though, reaching No. 17. *Let There Be Rock* (also notable as the last AC/DC LP to feature bassist Mark Evans) lent its name to the 1980 concert movie (a double live CD of which was released in 1997 as part of the box set *Bonfire*). ⚡

Whisky A Go Go, Los Angeles, August 29, 1977. All © Jenny Lens/Cache Agency

Chapter 4

Ain't No Fun (Waiting Round ...)

Mutt took care of the commercial side while we took care of the riff, and somehow we managed to meet in the middle without feeling as though we compromised ourselves.

—Malcolm Young, *Metal CD*, 1992

Sadly, Australia didn't give Cliff Williams an open-arms welcome. In fact, it deferred his work permit, notionally protecting an Australian bassist's job. So for his first two AC/DC gigs at Bondi Lifesavers in Sydney, he appeared incognito with a band called The Seedies one night, Dirty Deeds the next. However, the shows became what Angus called "a right Babylon." Beer everywhere, fans stripping, Scott's microphone appropriated as a dildo ...

Still uneasy in their homeland,

AC/DC worked on demos with Vanda and Young—"Touch Too Much" and "Up to My Neck in You" among them—then, finally, flew to America for their twenty-nine-date debut tour. Fortunately, new Atlantic president Jerry Greenberg and A&R head John Kalodner did see their potential and agreed an elementary strategy to follow up *Let There Be Rock*'s July 23, 1977, American release: "Work their asses off."

After their U.S. debut on June 27 at the truly wild and western Armadillo

Rebellious, Grungy, Distasteful, Vulgar, Wretched, Putrid, Tasteless, Loud, Raw, Nauseating, Vile, Abominable, Disgusting, Rotten, Repugnant, Crass, Rude, Peculiar, Salacious, Slimy, Perverted, Despicable, Yucky, Raunchy, Repulsive, Revolting, Crude, Gross, Savage, Primitive, Primal, Pornographic, Sleazy, and Wonderful.

AC/DC has the last word.

LET THERE BE ROCK
AC/DC

Watch for upcoming tour in late fall.

AC/DC. "Let There Be Rock." Their latest album from Atco Records and Tapes.

© 1977 Atlantic Recording Corp. ⊕ A Warner Communications Co.

Produced by Vanda and Young for Albert Productions.

Trade ad, 1977. Perhaps the first use of the word *grungy* to describe rock 'n' roll?

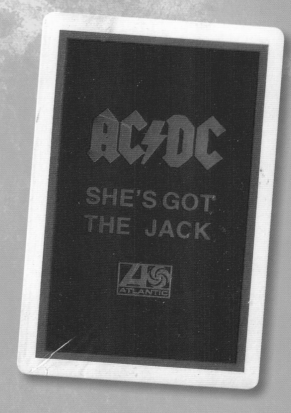
World Headquarters, in Austin, Texas, the tour felt very Australian: an old station wagon with Rudd driving; girlfriends on board at times too, including Malcolm Young's future wife O'Linda Irish; $30 a week each for sustenance; odometer-busting hauls like the nine hundred miles from Dallas (July 30) to Gainesville, Florida (August 4–gig cancelled!).

Yet two days after that fiasco, while supporting REO Speedwagon in Jacksonville, Florida, the band found much of the crowd of 8,000 had arrived early to see them. Promoter Sydney Drashin and local radio had talked them up, creating AC/DC's first American "hot spot." Few and far between at first, every enthusiastic welcome restored their spirits and every crowd got their money's worth and more—especially with Scott interjections, like his introduction of "The Jack" with a parody of *West Side Story*'s "Maria":

"Gonorrhoea, I've just had my first dose of gonorrhoea . . ."

A swathe of their more illustrious peers took a shine to them too. In Jacksonville, Lynyrd Skynyrd befriended them. At the Whisky A Go Go in Los Angeles on August 29 to 31, audiences averaged only eighty, but Iggy Pop, Steven Tyler of Aerosmith, and Gene Simmons came by. The KISS bassist offered support spots that winter. They even encountered Atlantic founder Ahmet Ertegun, though unconventionally. Seeking fresh air after midnight in an alleyway behind New York punk club CBGB (early on August 25), the mogul found himself next to a man urinating into an empty jar—namely, Bon Scott.

A crucial, technical development occurred that night. At the early-evening Palladium show, Angus abandoned his hundred-foot guitar lead and introduced his wireless device invented by New Yorker Kenny Schaffer and pioneered by

On August 24, 1977, Robert Francos went to CBGB in New York City's Bowery to see one of his favorite power-pop bands, the Marbles. As their set ended, Francos noticed a crowd begin moving toward the stage, surrounding a cluster of people. That's when the next band—an unscheduled act—was announced over the PA. AC/DC had played at the Palladium earlier in the evening and wanted to check out the legendary punk club. They proceeded to play an impromptu set, and Francos recalls that, at one point, Angus made his way through the crowd, utilizing the new wireless device that rendered his 100-foot guitar cord moot. Outside on the sidewalk, he talked to the transient gents who were milling outside CBGB—all the while playing his riffs and solos.

Luckily, Francos caught the gig on film, though he didn't have a flash with him. "At first I was disappointed by the blur," he writes, "but after some time I found that the effect was almost like echo from the guitar, giving a true feel to the motion of the moment."

Soon after, Francos bought a copy of *High Voltage* for a buck out of a cut-out bin.
All © Robert Barry Francos/FFanzeen

Legendary L.A.-based music photographer Jenny Lens is most renowned for her work documenting the punk pioneers who paved the way, including the Ramones, the Clash, the Sex Pistols, the Dead Boys, the Dictators, the Runaways, Television, Patti Smith, and more. She was on the scene at the Sunset Strip's Whisky A Go Go on August 29, 1977, to witness and capture on film not-so-punk (but no doubt loud) AC/DC less than a week after their impromptu appearance at CBGB in New York City. Among the curious rockers who turned up for the gig were Aerosmith's Steven Tyler, Gene Simmons of KISS, and Iggy Pop (opposite).
All © Jenny Lens/jennylens.com/Cache Agency

KISS earlier that year. Well worth the $3,300 he paid for it, Angus told French magazine *Best* in 1979: "I'd had enough of continually finding myself with an unplugged guitar. And as I sweat hugely, I don't want to electrocute myself." Not that the technology negated every rock 'n' roll hazard. That September Scott told Howie Klein of *New York Rocker*, the crowd walkabout with Angus on his shoulders could reduce the axe hero to squeals of "Put me down, me balls, me balls!"

The Young genitalia weren't the only part of AC/DC's anatomy under pressure that year. In September and early October, sixteen European dates saw some disappointing turnouts and concluded amid a riot at Thierbrau Sportshall, Kontich, as described in "Bedlam in Belgium" from 1983's *Flick of the Switch* ("There was a cop with a gun/Who was running around insane"). But after *Let There Be Rock* became their first British chart album (No. 17), most of their U.K. shows in October and November sold out. This writer saw them in dazzling form at the Mayfair, Newcastle, again with Scott ever the charming rogue and buccaneer. I wrote, "Give him a wooden leg, a parrot on his shoulder, and he'd be the image of Long John Silver."

However, Scott's girlfriend Silver Smith was worried about his drinking. She gave biographer Clinton Walker (*Highway to Hell: The Life and Death of AC/DC Legend Bon Scott*), her take on the nonstop AC/DC party: "It was a lot of people in a lot of pain, trying to rage on regardless." Impossible to say whether this was insight or over-interpretive hindsight.

Light relief ensued in November when Scott and Smith took a break in Paris, socializing with her friend Ron Wood, in town to work on The Rolling Stones' *Some Girls*. AC/DC reconvened, flying back to America and spending another month in the station wagon, beginning November 16, supporting KISS, Rush, Styx, Aerosmith, and their new best touring mates, Cheap Trick.

An elegant row of even ivories that wouldn't look out of place in the mouth of Donny Osmond.

—The author writing on Angus' new teeth, *Sounds*, 1978

After around 125 gigs in 1977, they went home for Christmas.

The Youngs spent time with their family, while Scott and Smith rented an apartment at Coogee Beach in Sydney. Williams holidayed in England, which caused problems as soon as AC/DC started recording at Albert's again in January 1978. Having overstayed the previous summer, he couldn't get his visa renewed. The band waited, cancelling planned Australian and British dates. Angus fumed to Australian music magazine *RAM*, "We used to think of ourselves as an Australian band. But we're beginning to doubt that now. The fuckers won't even let us play here."

Once Williams won his argument with the London embassy in February, recording *Powerage* proved a happy experience. Malcolm told American website *KNAC.com* in 2000, "George was at the top of his form. . . . We rocked all the way through" (except when they were fishing in Sydney harbor, a sure sign of how relaxed they felt and why *Powerage* remained Malcolm's favorite studio memory). The riffs could be warm and smiley ("Rock 'N' Roll Damnation" and "Riff Raff") or cold and angry ("Down Payment Blues," "Gimme a Bullet," and "Gone Shootin'"), but they were all hard, atavistic, physical to the bone. Scott's crude subtlety with the lyrics emerged in the bleak "Gone Shootin'" (heroin, that is, probably with

Royal Oak Theater,
Royal Oak, Michigan,
September 13, 1978.
© Robert Alford

I love them, man. Angus is such a great guitar player, and the way he plays riffs—man, that kills me. [Lynyrd Skynyrd] played with them in the '70s and it was a lot of fun. And they're just a hard-working band. . . . They're a totally original band.

—Gary Rossington

However, when Atlantic's U.S. offices heard *Powerage*, they worried anew about radio play. Doug Thaler, who'd become AC/DC's agent in America, spoke privately to Vanda and Young in Sydney just before they finished recording. Almost sacrilegiously, he questioned their role, only to find, as he later told Murray Engleheart and Arnaud Durieux in *AC/DC: Maximum Rock & Roll*, "They were indeed interested in giving up the reins. They felt they'd done everything they could do up to that point."

⚡ ⚡ ⚡

When AC/DC flew to London in late April, Scott said an awkward goodbye to Smith, who wanted to end their relationship and emphasized her point by setting off around Asia with a mutual friend, musician Joe Furey.

AC/DC's road-rat year started in May with twenty-five U.K. gigs, extra lighting courtesy of Angus' new front teeth—$2,000 worth apparently, which I described in another review of the

Silver Smith in mind, as she'd been a user for some time) and the lustful, dirty-blues double entendre "Up to My Neck in You." Later in 1978, he surprised interviewer Jay Crawford of BBC Radio Edinburgh by calling the song his "most ardent" song, "written for a woman that I loved very dearly—and I still do." Whether he meant Smith or, more likely, his ex-wife Irene, he clearly deemed serious emotions in no way at odds with raunchy imagery.

Scott fired off scattergun social commentary too. In "Sin City," it was "Diamonds and dust/Poor man last, rich man first," and in "Down Payment Blues" he seemed to tell his own story, from poverty and illusion ("I got myself a Cadillac/But I can't afford the gasoline") to material comfort and inner uncertainty ("Feeling like a paper cup/Floating down a storm drain").

They're an institution, and when the people who don't understand it say all their songs sound alike, you go "HELL YEAH! Who else can be AC/DC?!" We had them on tour with us [in 1977] and they were terrific.

—Paul Stanley

May 5 show at Newcastle Mayfair as "an elegant row of even ivories that wouldn't look out of place in the mouth of Donny Osmond." The tour produced commercial results: Their first U.K. single, "Rock 'N' Roll Damnation," hit No. 24, while *Powerage* charted at No. 26. Malcolm agreed it was the moment for a live album, and on April 30 they recorded their Glasgow Apollo show—chants of "Angus! Angus!" punctuated the staccato opening riffs of "Whole Lotta Rosie."

The band moved on to America, beginning a sixty-four-date marathon in Norfolk, Virginia, on June 24, supporting Alice Cooper. With Angus under orders to keep his shorts up in the Bible Belt, they travelled on, steadily adding to the list of scattered places that loved them—Jacksonville, Cleveland, Columbus, and a big, new thrill when, at Oakland Stadium on July 23 at 10:30 a.m., 65,000 showed up to see them open Day on the Green (Aerosmith, Foreigner, and Van Halen to follow). AC/DC owed it to America's all-time great promoter, Bill Graham, who talked them up until hardly anyone who'd bought a ticket felt it would be sane to miss them.

Angus himself was certainly up for any stunt that might attract attention. At Boston Paradise Theater on August 21—or four days later in New York, depending on which version you believe—he stretched his cordless guitar's reach to the limit (and possibly into the realm of apocrypha) by leaving the building mid-solo, taking a cab to a local radio station, and kerranging all the way up to its fiftieth-floor studio.

Eventually, long before the final gig at Fort Wayne, Indiana, on October

"Whole Lotta Rosie" b/w "Hell Ain't a Bad Place to Be," 7-inch single, Japan, 1978. *Bill Voccia Collection*

3, evidence emerged that these hard-nut Aussies were not emotionally bulletproof. Phil Rudd cracked first. His drum roadie and roommate, Barry Taylor, later an evangelical Christian, wrote in his autobiography, *Singing in the Dark: A Rock 'n' Roll Roadie Comes Clean*, that he often helped Rudd "through situations of extreme stress on the road." Interviewed by Susan Masino, author of *The Story of AC/DC: Let There Be Rock*, Taylor recalled that on August 3 when they supported Aerosmith at Alpine Valley, East Troy, Wisconsin, Rudd suffered a panic attack and "they had to call in a psychiatrist." It happened more than once. Even so, he didn't miss a gig.

Rudd wasn't alone in feeling the strain. On *adelaidenow.com.au* in 2008, Scott's old Valentines band mate Vince Lovegrove wrote about catching up with him in Atlanta, Georgia, on August 11, a few days after Rudd's crisis. Scott said "he was tired of it all . . . that he could

We used to think of ourselves as an Australian band. But we're beginning to doubt that now. The fuckers won't even let us play here.

—Angus Young, *RAM*, 1978

smell the success, but if they didn't make it in the next year or two, he would leave the band. . . . He was certainly lonely. There was unquestionably an undercurrent of resigned sadness behind his impish grin." Back in the late 1970s, writing for *RAM*, Lovegrove further quoted Scott about life in AC/DC: "I love it, you know that. It's only rock 'n' roll and I like it. But I want to have a base. . . . Planes, hotels, groupies, booze, people, towns. They all scrape something from you. . . . Rock 'n' roll, you know that's all there is. But I can't hack the rest of the shit."

When I interviewed Scott and Angus in London for *Sounds* in July 1979, Scott seemed cheerful, but he did say they'd all been "homeless" for the past two years: "I rented a flat here for eight months, but I was only there for six weeks." Angus cut in: "He's always been

of no fixed abode, and I'm in the flat above! I suppose I'll buy a place some time, but . . . I'm quite at home in these hotels. . . . I'll go home to me parents at Christmas, and after a week I'll check into a hotel. I mean I've got brothers who bring their kids round and at six in the mornin'; they'll fuckin' jump on you yellin', 'He's home!'"

Hard to acknowledge inner doubts aboard the AC/DC Express.

After America, AC/DC rushed onward, playing Germany, Switzerland, Holland, France, Belgium, and the U.K. through October and November, promoting their second 1978 album, the live *If You Want Blood You've Got It*. It reached No. 13 in the U.K. and No. 113 in America.

When they flew home for Christmas again, Scott saw his parents in Perth for the first time in three years. But

Royal Oak Theater, Royal Oak, Michigan, September 13, 1978. © Robert Alford

Day on the Green with Aerosmith, Foreigner, Pat Travers, and Van Halen, Oakland Coliseum, Oakland, California, July 23, 1978. © Baron Wolman/Retna (top) and Larry Hulst/Michael Ochs Archives/Getty Images (bottom)

then, says Walker, dissatisfied with his *Powerage* lyrics, he rented a flat near Bondi Beach in Sydney and temporarily disciplined himself to rise every morning at 8:30, swim hard, and then write through the day.

⚡ ⚡ ⚡

It could be the Canning Highway in Fremantle. Or U.S. Highway 666 (since superstitiously renumbered). Back in the 1970s, this latter roadway ran from Douglas, Arizona, to Monticello, Utah. But really, the "Highway to Hell" comprises the tens of thousands of miles of American road AC/DC had traversed in the previous eighteen months.

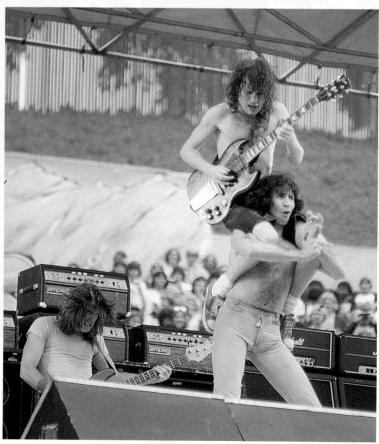

This page and opposite:
Early February 1979, before
departing for Miami and their ill-fated
collaboration with Eddie Kramer, Angus,
Malcolm, and Bon did a surprise show
at the Strata Motor Inn, Sydney, with
George on bass. The drummer is Ray
Arnott of the billed band, the Ferrets.
Philip Morris was the only photographer
to document the appearance.
All © Philip Morris

Recording their seventh album may have begun as early as December 2, 1978. It soon got sticky when Atlantic's Michael Klenfner flew to Australia, his task to secure a sea change in AC/DC's approach to producers. Given Vanda and Young's earlier amenable talk with Thaler—not reported to George's younger brothers—it's not surprising they stepped aside quite readily. The following July, Angus told me for *Sounds*, George agreed they needed "freshness." In 1991, speaking to *Musician*'s Charles M. Young, he elaborated, George "told us, 'Don't let them mess with what you are. Always remember you're a rock 'n' roll band.'"

Even so, Walker and Engleheart/Durieux both suggest Malcolm and Angus initially felt enraged on behalf of their brother. Naturally, the new boy, South African-born Eddie Kramer, bore the initial brunt of their disorientation, even though he had a track record of work with Jimi Hendrix, The Rolling Stones, and Led Zeppelin, and he produced KISS' 1975 breakthrough, *Alive!*.

Angus, Malcolm, and Scott played a see-ya gig for friends at the Strata Motor Inn in Cremorne, Sydney (probably February 5, 1979). But when they flew over to Criteria Recording Studios in Miami, rapport with Kramer eluded them. He liked to start work promptly at midday and expected them to have their songs ready before they arrived at the studio; they'd never worked like that. And Kramer didn't like Scott's drinking. *And* he wanted keyboards!

Malcolm phoned Browning's New York office to convey AC/DC's squirming discontent. Then, as Angus told me, "Someone suggested Robert John, er, Lang . . . Langer . . . Lanj, you know. . . " (*Sounds*). That was Browning on behalf of his temporary New York flatmate, "Mutt" Lange. Born in Northern Rhodesia/Zambia (yet another colonial), he was known only for producing new wavers Graham Parker and Bob Geldof's Boomtown Rats.

Scott later told *RAM*, "Three weeks in Miami and we hadn't written a thing with Kramer. So one day we told him we were going to have the day off, and we [Malcolm, Angus, plus Scott on drums] snuck into the studio put down six songs, sent the tapes to Lange, and said, 'Will you work with us?'"

Heads rolled. Kramer left the album and Klenfner left Atlantic. The band cancelled a March Japanese tour at short notice with their crew already there. Instead, they flew to London and knuckled down to write the album in a cold rehearsal studio before recording at the Roundhouse. Apart from a day off on April 14 when Malcolm married O'Linda at Westminster Registry Office, they surrendered to Lange's insistence on two or three weeks of regular, long working hours.

When I interviewed them for *Sounds* a couple of months later, they'd gotten over any resentments about suffering such strict discipline. Angus told me it had been "good learning for all of us, but in particular [Lange] done a good job on Bon's vocals." As Scott put it, "Bottom line, cobber, he was instrumental in

I love it, you know that. It's only rock 'n' roll and I like it. But I want to have a base. . . . Planes, hotels, groupies, booze, people, towns. They all scrape something from you.

—Bon Scott, *RAM*, 1978

I'm quite at home in these hotels. . . . I'll go home to me parents at Christmas, and after a week I'll check into a hotel. I mean I've got brothers who bring their kids round and at six in the mornin'; they'll fuckin' jump on you yellin', "He's home!"

—Angus Young, *Sounds*, 1979

getting me to project myself . . . in a different area to that in which I'd been projecting myself before." Angus praised Lange to *Musician*'s Young: "Every week he'd be there with the Top Ten of America, listening to the sounds. . . . Bon was very happy with him. Mutt taught Bon to breathe, bring it from your stomach. . . . And I think Mutt was impressed that we knew what a song was, as opposed to just a riff." Observing from the drum stool, Rudd reckoned, "Mutt was fascinated to see how much Angus and Malcolm believed in their music. . . . I think . . . he was savouring our integrity" (*Rock Hard*, 2001).

Still, Lange did effect changes: a degree of refinement for the radio and backing vocals to beef up the choruses ("Highway to Hell" and "Girls Got Rhythm"). Speaking to *RAM*, Malcolm acknowledged Lange's impact: "[Previously] a lot of ideas we wouldn't finish because you'd wait to see what George might spark for us. [Mutt's] way, we had to have all the ideas written, arranged." He elaborated for *Metal CD* magazine, "Mutt took care of the commercial side while we took care of the riff, and somehow we managed to meet in the middle without feeling as though we compromised ourselves."

Highway to Hell had all the pounding-heart sweat, grit, and grunt AC/DC fans loved: the fierce title track, the striding "Girls Got Rhythm," the swaying "Love Hungry Man," the grinding "Night Prowler" (nailed via Lange after four previous failed attempts). What's more, Scott chiseled out a set of lyrics bristling with honesty, salty humor, and vivid imagery.

With "If You Want Blood (You've Got It)," Scott even managed to tell the world—and his fellow band members—how bad rock 'n' roll life could make him feel: "It's animal/Livin' in a human zoo/Animal/The shit that they toss to you." ⚡

Someone suggested Robert John, er, Lang . . . Langer . . . Lanj, you know . . .

—Angus Young on the decision to bring in Mutt Lange to produce *Highway to Hell*, *Sounds*, 1979

The LPs
Powerage

By Daniel Bukszpan

Released in May 1978, *Powerage* is the most overlooked full-length album in AC/DC's Bon Scott–era discography. It's certainly not for lack of first-rate performances or material, because there are plenty of both to be found here. Every song is delivered with the same fury and conviction as anything on their best albums, and there's material that's stronger than some of their most beloved songs. No less a rock 'n' roll luminary than Keith Richards has cited it as his favorite AC/DC album, an unsurprising revelation when one considers how half of its riffs sound like embryonic versions of "Start Me Up."

Indeed, the lack of widespread acceptance enjoyed by *Powerage* is not a mere mystery—it's a shame. A dirty, lowdown shame.

The album hits the ground running from the first chord and rarely lets up. "Rock 'n' Roll Damnation" is an upbeat stomper that could have appeared on any of the first few KISS albums. After a crashing conclusion, things calm down for the subdued introduction to "Down Payment Blues." The tranquility is short-lived, though, and we're back to full-throated volume and attitude before there's even a chance for the energy to flag. In "Fifty Cent Millionaire," Bon Scott laments that he owns a Cadillac but "can't afford the gasoline," lyrics that no doubt resonated with Americans in the Jimmy Carter era. In fact, the song is likely relevant again thirty years on for SUV owners who have gotten their pink slips.

While it's a matter of opinion whether the compact disc is superior to vinyl, the CD has an advantage over its analog counterpart in at least one respect: It is possible to hear three of the best songs on *Powerage* in quick succession without having to get up and turn the record over. Huzzah! The sequence begins with "Riff Raff," arguably the best song on the album. This ferocious track barrels along courtesy of the airtight rhythm section of drummer Phil Rudd and bassist Cliff Williams, the latter making his AC/DC studio debut. But ultimately the song is really all about the two-note guitar stings that Angus Young throws in whenever an opening appears in Bon Scott's vocal. In music-theory terms, this is known as "badass shit."

Next up is "Sin City," which, like "Riff Raff," was one of the only songs from *Powerage* to get a regular airing in the band's live set. It's taken at a slower tempo than its predecessor, but there is absolutely no loss whatsoever in terms of energy or punch. Not bad for a song that's basically the same four-chord figure repeated over and over again at two different volume levels. It's followed up by "What's Next to the Moon," which, like the two songs before it, moves from strength to strength. From its aggressive cadence, to the "It's your love that I want" section that pretty much makes the song, there is reason after reason why

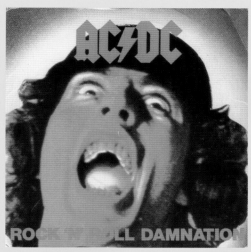

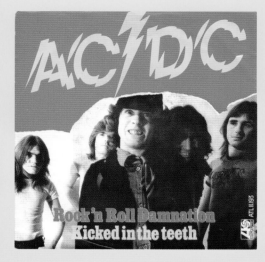

"Rock 'N' Roll Damnation" b/w "Kicked in the Teeth," South Africa, 1978. *Bill Voccia Collection*

"Rock 'N' Roll Damnation" b/w "Sin City," U.K., 1978. *Bill Voccia Collection*

"Rock 'N' Roll Damnation" b/w "Kicked in the Teeth," Holland, 1978. *Bill Voccia Collection*

this track should be an AC/DC classic. That it isn't held in that regard is criminal.

As far as weak spots are concerned, there just aren't that many. "Gimme a Bullet" is perhaps not that memorable compared to the material surrounding it, and "Up to My Neck in You" flirts briefly with filler status, but the guitar solo singlehandedly redeems it enough to warrant keeping it on your iPod. "Gone Shootin'" doesn't really hold its own, either, but it's based around a main riff that's enjoyable enough and that wouldn't sound out of place on *Exile on Main St.* The guitar solo even gets a little southern rock on us, as if Angus Young is channeling the spirits of the Lynyrd Skynyrd members who had perished in a plane crash the year before.

Any Achilles' heel that *Powerage* may have is instantly forgotten when "Kicked in the Teeth" comes along to close out the album in unequivocally satisfying fashion. The song is appropriately named, because it's as close as you're going to get to being mugged by a piece of music. The song starts with Scott's alarming shriek of "Two-faced woman with your two-faced lies" against a backdrop of stark silence. Then we're thrown into the deep end with another fast song

that's downright *feral*. Angus, who seems to have an endless supply of top-notch guitar solos on this album, uses the song as a platform from which to strangle the living shit out of his Gibson SG, which squawks and squeals like a clubbed chinchilla. When the crashing finale is reached, it's hard to imagine a better end to the album.

The worst thing anyone could say about *Powerage* is that not every song is as good as "Riff Raff." An uncommonly well-

realized exercise in brutish thuggery, it's anybody's guess why the song has failed to connect with an audience beyond the band's more hard-core fans. But it doesn't really matter at this point. More than thirty years later, the album has more than held up, and when the more casual AC/DC fan finally gets tired of listening to *Back in Black* for the billionth time, there is a hidden gem in the band's catalog waiting to be discovered. ⚡

"Rock 'N' Roll Damnation" stereo/mono promo single, U.S., 1978.

Outside the *Rockpalast* television studios, Köln, West Germany, late August 1979. © *Robert Alford*

Chapter 5

Touch Too Much

Relentlessly, AC/DC hit the highway again in Madison, Wisconsin, on May 8, 1979. En route, the restless Youngs were looking for new management; Michael Browning irritated them by enlisting a co-manager without consulting them ("He tried to sell us like slaves," Angus told Lynda Lacoste for *Le Mag* in 2000. Then agent Doug Thaler brought David Krebs, rebuffed by Browning two years earlier, to their June 14 show in Poughkeepsie, New York.

Krebs told them he could make them a million dollars on tour that summer. Persuaded by Krebs, the band paid Browning off and concluded their new management deal on July 1. Krebs put AC/DC in the care of his employee Peter Mensch, who told this writer, for *Q* magazine in 1997, he'd befriended

the band when he was Aerosmith's tour accountant and that they'd "talked" before his boss Krebs got involved.

That summer, Krebs and Mensch delivered. A Madison Square Garden debut on August 4 was nice (supporting Ted Nugent). But more importantly, for stadium support spots—and sometimes headlining 12,000-seat arenas, like Charlotte, North Carolina (September 29) and Knoxville, Tennessee (October 2)—their earnings jumped from $1,500 to $5,000 per show to $25,000 to $50,000.

Highway to Hell's late-July release rewarded them with No. 8 in the U.K. and a breakthrough No. 17 in America. It even reached No. 13 in Australia, where their previous two LPs had done poorly. Still, as they played about 146 gigs from

You've got to find someone else, you know that. . . . Whatever you do, don't stop.

—Bon Scott's father, Chick, to Malcolm Young after Bon's interment, *Mojo*, 2000

World Series of Rock with Aerosmith, Ted Nugent, Journey, Thin Lizzy, and the Scorpions, Cleveland Municipal Stadium, Cleveland, Ohio, July 28, 1979. *All © Robert Alford*

May to December 1979, with never more than a four-day break between American and European legs, they plowed all the money back into better equipment and transport.

When I interviewed them that year in London for *Sounds*, Angus seemed particularly cheery; he'd always portrayed himself as "the ugly little guy," definitely no babe magnet, but now he was accompanied by his new girlfriend, fashion student Ellen Von Lochem, whom he'd met when playing a festival in Arnhem, Holland, on July 13 during a U.S. tour break.

Scott seemed in good form to me too. But when he met old friends, he often evinced unease. Before Christmas 1979 in Adelaide, he talked with Fraternity bassist Bruce Howe and then Mount Lofty Rangers keyboardist Peter Head about his inability to commit to a long-term relationship. The latter described the conclusion of their evening, telling Bill Voccia, "We went out to a party down the street, and both got blind drunk. We woke up next day in adjoining rooms with strange women in bed, crawled out with a hangover, said goodbye, and wandered off down the street. It was the last time I saw him." When Scott visited his parents in Fremantle, as his father Chick sadly recollected for Clinton Walker in *Highway to Hell: The Life and Death of AC/DC Legend Bon Scott*, "You'd go into any of the rooms in the house and you'd find an empty bottle."

The following weeks were full of "lasts": his last onstage appearance in Australia, at the Family Inn in Sydney, January 1980, jamming with fellow roustabouts John Swan and

"Johnny B. Goode" with Cheap Trick, bootleg single, recorded July 7, 1979, released 2007.

With Rick Nielsen of Cheap Trick, *Rockpalast* television studios, Köln, West Germany, late August 1979. © Robert Alford

Jimmy Barnes (unearthed by Murray Engleheart and Arnaud Durieux, *AC/DC: Maximum Rock & Roll*); his last gig anywhere, with AC/DC at the Gaumont in Southampton, England on January 27 (postponed from December); and his last recording, in London with his friends, French band Trust, doing the *Dirty Deeds Done Dirt Cheap* song "Ride On," probably February 13. However, this is hindsight. Discontented perhaps, yet vibrant as ever, Scott pitched himself wholeheartedly into AC/DC's future, writing lyrics at his rented flat in Ashley Court, Westminster, while the Youngs carved the riffs.

On February 11 Angus took the day off to visit Westminster Registry Office and marry Ellen—a blacksmith's daughter, the certificate revealed. No honeymoon, though. Over the next few days, Angus and Malcolm, with Scott on drums, sequestered themselves in North London rehearsal studio E-Zee Hire and came up with the beginnings of "Have a Drink on Me" and "Let Me Put My Love in You."

On Monday, February 18, Scott went out to the Music Machine in Camden Town, North London, to see a new band called Lonesome No More. He asked

his ex, Silver Smith, to come, but she passed him on to mutual friend Alistair Kinnear, who drove to Ashley Court in his little Renault 5 and picked Scott up. After a twenty-five-year "disappearance" (turned out he was living in Spain), Kinnear finally told his story to Maggie Montalbano for a 2005 *Metal Hammer & Classic Rock* AC/DC special.

At the Music Machine, they drank "far too much" whiskey. When Kinnear drove them back to Ashley Court, Scott passed out. Kinnear couldn't move him from the car, so he went on to his own flat in Overhill Road, East Dulwich, south of the Thames. There Kinnear called Smith and, following her advice, "I put the front passenger seat back so that [Bon] could lie flat, covered him with a blanket." A friend woke Kinnear that morning, February 19. Hungover, Kinnear asked him to check on Scott. The friend took a quick glance at the car and didn't see him. Presuming Scott had gone home, Kinnear went back to sleep. At 7:30 p.m., he decided to go out. Opening the car door, he found "Bon still lying flat in the front seat . . . not breathing."

Kinnear drove to nearby Kings College Hospital, where Scott was pronounced dead. The post mortem later showed he had died of "acute alcoholic poisoning," no ingestion of vomit reported. Verdict: "misadventure."

Kinnear called Smith. Sobbing, she called Angus, who contacted Malcolm and Mensch. By around 3 a.m. on February 20, Mensch and tour manager Ian Jeffery were at the hospital confirming the worst and handling the formalities. Meanwhile, Malcolm took responsibility for ringing Scott's parents in Australia. Angus told Dave Lewis of *Sounds* the following month, "We didn't want them to be just sitting there and suddenly it comes on the TV news."

The band sank into mourning. In 1994, Angus told Michel Rémy of French fanzine *Let There Be Light*, "Nobody knew what to do. We were so battered. It's as if we'd had an arm amputated." Phil Rudd recalled for *Rock Hard* in 2001 how "his death numbed me. Nobody believed something like that could happen to us." Malcolm recollected, "We were so depressed. We were just walking around in silence. Because there was nothing. *Nothing*" (*Classic Rock*, 2005).

On the plane bearing Scott's body, AC/DC flew to Perth for the cremation at Fremantle Cemetery on February 29 and the interment of the ashes the following day.

The first person to address the unspoken question "What now?" was Scott's father, Chick. Leaving the cemetery, he told Malcolm, "You've got to find someone else, you know that. . . . Whatever you do, don't stop" (Sylvie Simmons, *Mojo*, 2000). Angus recalled for *Classic Rock* in 2005 that amid the consoling rituals of tea and subdued reminiscence, Chick "kept repeating his assurances . . . 'You should keep going, you've still got a lot to give.'"

Below and previous spread: Apollo Theatre, Glasgow, October 27, 1979. © Robert Ellis/repfoto.com

In October 1980, Thierry Chatain of France's *Rock & Folk* asked whether they'd considered giving up. Angus said, "Yes, but it was quickly rejected. It would be very hard for me to stop. I'm young, the group too, and we are doing what we love."

Soon after their return to London on March 4, Malcolm rang Angus. They went back to E-Zee Hire studio. Songwriting became "therapy," Angus would say. "After Bon, I felt horribly grown up in a way," he reflected in the liner notes to *Bonfire*. "When you're young, you always think you are immortal, and that time really spun me around."

Even so, speaking to Dave Lewis for *Sounds* that March, Angus said manager Mensch wouldn't let them avoid the "dreadful" question: "Don't you guys want a new singer?"

⚡ ⚡ ⚡

The Johnsons of Dunston, Gateshead, across the Tyne from Newcastle, were not a typical British working-class family. During World War II, Sergeant Major Alan Johnson had fought in North Africa. Then, during the invasion of Mussolini's Italy, he met his future wife, Esther De Luca, daughter of a prosperous family from Rocca di Papa, near Frascati. The first of their four children, Brian, was born in Dunston on October 5, 1947. Talking to James McNair for *Mojo* in 2009, he imagined his mother's view of their surroundings: "She would look across the Tyne and see Vickers steelworks, the gasworks, the ship breaker's yard, and Dunston Staiths where they loaded the coal ships. . . . It wasn't *La Dolce Vita*." To make a little extra, Esther sewed wedding dresses at home. But, remarkably for those times, foundry worker Alan learned Italian and always spoke it to his wife, so Johnson grew up (somewhat) bilingual.

Because of the Italian connection, Brian sometimes got "picked on" at school. But he developed good lungs from singing with the Boy Scouts Gang Show and the church choir. Rock 'n'

roll he discovered via Johnny Duncan & The Blue Grass Boys' "Last Train to San Fernando" and Little Richard's "Tutti-Frutti." Leaving school at fifteen, he became an apprentice fitter at Parsons' turbine factory in Newcastle, joined the reservist territorial army as a paratrooper, and sang in workingmen's club bands: The Gobi Desert Canoe Club, Fresh, The Jasper Hart Band, and USA. No-hopers all, until USA changed their name to Geordie and, in September 1972, found themselves miming on BBC TV's weekly chart show, *Top of the Pops*.

The name "Geordie" means born or brought up in Tyneside and a live review by James Johnson (no relation) in U.K. music weekly *New Musical Express* certainly portrayed them as regional archetypes, looking "like they just walked off a factory floor." Despite four domestic hit singles (the biggest, "All Because of You", No. 6, March 1973), they endured a puzzling lack of cash flow that sometimes saw Johnson go so hungry he'd rush into restaurants and snatch leftovers off the tables.

Before Johnson quit, disillusioned, in 1975, Geordie did sow one seed for his future—that U.K. tour encounter with Bon Scott's band Fraternity in April 1973 (probably in Devon, though some sources say Grimsby, Yorkshire) proved memorable. When AC/DC auditioned singers in March 1980 at Vanilla Studios in Westminster, rumored candidates included Steve Marriott, Heavy Metal Kids' Gary Holton, and Australians John Swan, Jimmy Barnes, and Allen Fryer. But Angus recalled, "Bon had . . . seen this guy perform in Geordie, and he was rolling around the floor screaming his lungs out. Bon said it was the best show he'd ever seen" (Simmons, *Mojo*).

Yet Scott's posthumous recommendation coincided with a crescendo of acclaim for the unknown around that time. A Geordie fan in Chicago sent a tape to Mensch. Mutt Lange recommended Johnson. Finally, according to Johnson's 2009 autobiography, *Rockers and Rollers*, an

Hammersmith Odeon, London, November 1–4, 1979. © Robert Ellis/ *repfoto.com*

Larking about on the set of *Top Pop*, Hilversum, Holland, November 12, 1979. Phil has commandeered Cliff's bass. © Peter Mazel/Sunshine/ Retna

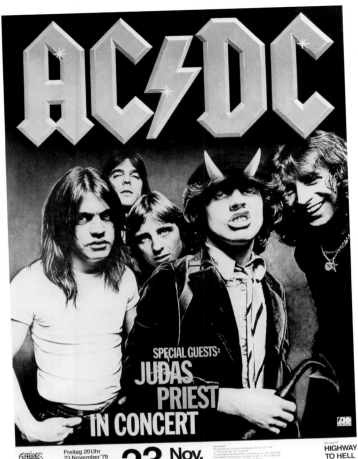

AC/DC gofer nicknamed "Olga from the Volga" phoned him. She said she couldn't reveal the band's name. He said, "How about the initials?" She said, "AC and DC . . . *Scheisse*! I have said too much!"

By then, Johnson and his wife, Carol, had two daughters, but they were temporarily separated and he was staying with his parents. He ran his own business, North-East Vinyls, installing car windscreens and roofs, and sang with Geordie II, a new lineup. But he had heart, soul, and fire in his belly, even though by his own account he "looked like a tramp" (Lacoste, *Le Mag*)—and unsentimental Malcolm saw it the moment he walked into the audition. "[Brian] had tears in his eyes—he was as sad about Bon as we were," he told Simmons in *Mojo*. "We said, 'Do you want to give it a go?' He said, 'I do "Whole Lotta Rosie" with Geordie and off he went. We went, 'Fucking hell . . . Anything else you know?' 'Nutbush City Limits?' He sang that great too. It put a little smile on our faces—for the first time since Bon."

Malcolm added, to *KNAC.com* in 2000, that AC/DC also appreciated Johnson as "working-class, just like us"—school-leavers, ex-apprentices: "He's an open bloke . . . like Bon, a bloke you love."

⚡ ⚡ ⚡

That was probably March 17 or 18. AC/DC asked him back on March 25. The going got tough: AC/DC played new riffs and challenged him to make up words on the spot. Johnson recalled the brief to *Mojo*'s McNair: "It can't be morbid—it has to be for Bon and it has to be a celebration." One of his improvisations became "Give the Dog a Bone." Despite that, from the outset he knew the album would wear its grief on its sleeve: "We got the title before we'd even written a tune. Angus said, 'Why not call it *Back in Black*, make a black album cover, and then it's for Bon'" (Simmons, *Mojo*).

On March 29, Malcolm rang to say he'd gotten the job, with a weekly £170, plus compensation to Geordie II for work lost while they found a new singer. A few days later, a sudden vacancy at Island Records founder Chris Blackwell's Compass Point Studios in Nassau, suddenly took them to the Bahamas. With only candlelight at first in their "breezeblock cells," and trying to settle into a place run by "this big old black lady" who armed them with fishing spears to repel rumored Haitian burglars, as Johnson remarked, "It was a bit of a stretch from Newcastle I can tell you" (Susan Masino, *The Story of AC/DC: Let There Be Rock*, unattributed). However, as he told Chatain in 1980, the band and crew "adopted" him—"It was very important for me."

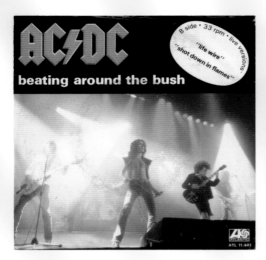

"Beating Around the Bush" b/w "Live Wire" and "Shot Down in Flames," Holland, 1980. *Bill Voccia Collection*

"Highway to Hell" b/w "If You Want Blood (You've Got It)," Japan, 1979. *Bill Voccia Collection*

Bon's last live appearance. Gaumont Theatre, Southampton, England, January 27, 1980. © *Robert Ellis/repfoto.com*

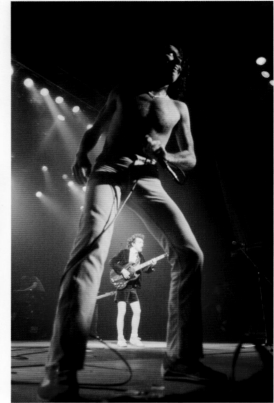

"High Voltage (Live)" b/w "Live Wire," HM-series single, U.K., 1980. *Bill Voccia Collection*

"Highway to Hell" jukebox promo single, France, 1979. *Bill Voccia Collection*

"Girls Got Rhythm" and "If You Want Blood (You've Got It)" b/w "Hell Ain't a Bad Place to Be" and "Rock 'N' Roll Damnation," U.S., 1979.

Nobody knew what to do. We were so battered. It's as if we'd had an arm amputated.

—Phil Rudd recalling the passing of Bon Scott, *Rock Hard*, 2001

Above: Gaumont Theatre, Southampton, England, January 27, 1980. © *Robert Ellis/repfoto.com*

Below: *Top of the Pops*, BBC, London, February 6, 1980. Bon's last appearance—playing "A Touch Too Much." *Both* © *Robert Ellis/repfoto.com*

Geordie, from left: Brian Gibson, Brian Johnson, Vic Malcolm, and Tom Hill. *Chris Walter/WireImage/Getty Images*

Geordie, "Treat Her Like a Lady" promo single, U.S., 1980.

Geordie, "All Because of You" b/w "Ain't It Just Like a Woman," U.K., 1973.

Early inspiration for a young Brian Johnson: Johnny Duncan and the Blue Grass Boys, "Last Train to San Fernando."

Geordie, "House of the Rising Sun" b/w "Electric Lady," Japan, 1973. *Bill Voccia Collection*

Geordie, "All Because of You" b/w "Keep On Rocking," Japan, 1974.

Geordie, "Electric Lady" b/w "Geordie Stomp," France, 1973.

Bon had . . . seen this guy perform in Geordie and he was rolling around the floor screaming his lungs out. Bon said it was the best show he'd ever seen.

—Angus Young, *Mojo*, 2000

Malcolm remembered their new singer worried that he lacked Scott's lyrical "finesse" (*KNAC.com*). But Johnson tackled the vocals with roaring power and improbable top notes—that is, once he'd discovered he couldn't sing in beach gear and switched to work clothes: jeans and cloth cap. While less idiosyncratic than Scott, he wrote lyrics full of fired-up sex, bolshieness, blues double entendres, and cunning rhymes. And they were all his own work, contrary to occasional malicious rumors. Twenty-five years later, speaking to *Classic Rock*, Angus still responded "heatedly" on this topic: "There was nothing from Bon's notebook . . . all his stuff went direct to his mother and family. . . . It wouldn't have been right to hang on to it. It wasn't ours to keep."

Fierce rockin' didn't entirely dominate their six weeks at Compass Point. Malcolm's wife O'Linda gave birth to their first child, Cara, so teetotal Angus glugged some whiskey—shortly before the others had to carry him to bed. Meanwhile, in England the "hell's bell" required to toll for Scott at the start of the album initially

Auditioning singers, Vanilla rehearsal studios, London, March 1980.
© Robert Ellis/repfoto.com

There was nothing from Bon's notebook . . . all his stuff went direct to his mother and family. . . . It wouldn't have been right to hang on to it. It wasn't ours to keep.

—Angus Young, *Classic Rock*, 2005

defied Jeffery's attempts to record it; the original at Loughborough, Leicestershire, war memorial proved impractical, so they had to wait until a nearby foundry finished the smaller replica they planned to use on stage.

Malcolm told Simmons that only when they got the tapes to the mixing room in New York did they realize, "Fucking hell, this is a monster!" In his Bon Scott biography, Walker calls *Back in Black* "the greatest resurrection act in rock history." Statistically, it proved their career peak. Upon its late-July U.K. release, it went straight to No. 1. In America, it reached No. 4 and

remained in the Top 10 for five months. And it went on. Worldwide by 2010, it was estimated to have sold around 50 million copies, second all time to Michael Jackson's *Thriller*.

Even reviewers enthused, although this writer's four-star encomium in *Sounds* provoked anger and threats from the band, I was told, because, among the compliments, it compared Johnson's lyrics unfavorably with Scott's (an unavoidable clash, I think, between a band still in mourning and a critic giving readers an honest opinion). But the heart-stirring, body-shaking oomph of AC/DC turbined through *Back in Black*, whether strutting "Givin' the Dog a Bone," "Rock and Roll Ain't Noise Pollution," and "You Shook Me All Night Long" (their first American Top 40 single) or grinding from their dark R&B soul with Scott-referencing tracks "Hells Bells," "Back in Black," and the paradoxically angry "Have a Drink on Me."

AC/DC vindicated their decision to carry on. They honored Bon Scott. They spent the rest of the year proving it live.

Giving Johnson a chance to acclimate, AC/DC eased into 120 shows in six months with a series of small-venue European gigs. He needed it, as he told *Let There Be Light*'s Rémy; making his debut at the Palais Des Expositions in Namur, Belgium on June 29, when the band played "Shot Down in Flames," he sang the words to "Highway to Hell." Yet he drew strength from the fans' generosity. On tour, he told Robin Smith of U.K. weekly *Record Mirror*: "That poor boy [Scott] was loved by thousands of people worldwide. When we did a warm-up gig in Holland [July 3 or 5] this

Atlantic Records press release announcing Brian Johnson as new AC/DC lead singer, 1980. *Bill Voccia Collection*

PRESS RELEASE ATLANTIC RECORDS PUBLICITY 75 ROCKEFELLER PLAZA, NY 10019 (212) 484-8200

FOR IMMEDIATE RELEASE
FROM: BOB KAUS
APRIL 15, 1980

AC/DC NAMES BRIAN JOHNSON AS NEW LEAD SINGER

Atlantic recording group AC/DC has announced that Brian Johnson has joined the group as their new lead singer. The news comes after the considerable speculation which followed the tragic and untimely death in February of original AC/DC lead singer/lyricist Bon Scott.

27 year-old Brian, who was born just outside Newcastle (England), was previously with the British group Geordie. They enjoyed two Top 20 hits in the U.K. in 1973, "All Because of You" and "Can You Do It." Most recently, Brian had been singing with a re-formed line-up of Geordie, when he was invited to audition for AC/DC last month. Brian was recommended to the group by their producer, Robert John Lange.

Brian has now joined the other members of AC/DC - Angus Young, Malcolm Young, Phil Rudd & Cliff Williams - in rehearsals for the group's next Atlantic album. Current plans call for the band to enter the studio in early May to commence the recording of the new LP.

AC/DC's last album, "HIGHWAY TO HELL," was recently certified platinum by the RIAA. The group most recently toured the U.S. in the Fall of 1979, with a cross-country headlining itinerary.

Rehearsals for *Back in Black* tour, New Victoria Theatre, London, June 1980. © Robert Ellis/repfoto.com

kid came up to me with a tattoo of Bon on his arm and said, 'This bloke was my hero, but now he's gone I wish you all the luck in the world.' I just stood there shakin'. What can you say when people are willing to put their faith in you like that?"

But where Johnson thrived, vulnerable Rudd began to flounder. Engleheart and Durieux report that, deep into their four-month American tour, around September 10 in Lincoln, Nebraska, Rudd called Jeffery at 4 a.m., asking him to help clear a load of people out of his room. When Jeffery got there, he found only a tearful and hallucinating drummer pleading, "Don't tell Malcolm." But on October 8, at Uniondale, New York, Rudd arrived late for a gold-disc presentation prior to a show and then fell off his drum stool during the set. Malcolm walked up to him in the dressing room and punched him.

Nonetheless, Angus resolutely accentuated the positive. Speaking to Chatain for *Rock & Folk*, he said, "People have been very kind to us. I think . . . people like us more because we didn't let ourselves be beaten down by destiny and that we practically started again from zero. . . . In a sense Bon's accident has tightened the bonds inside the group." ⚡

AC/DC — I'VE GOT BIG BALLS

ROCK AND ROLL AIN'T NOISE POLLUTION — AC/DC

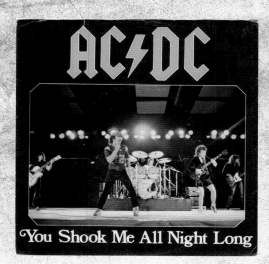

"You Shook Me All Night Long" b/w "Have a Drink on Me,"
Italy, 1980. *Bill Voccia Collection*

"You Shook Me All Night Long" b/w "Back in Black,"
Japan, 1980. *Bill Voccia Collection*

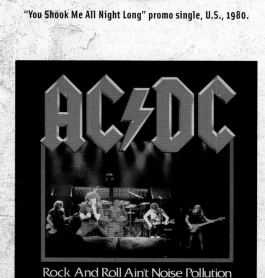

"You Shook Me All Night Long" promo single, U.S., 1980.

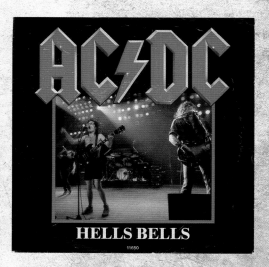

"You Shook Me All Night Long" b/w "What Do You Do for
Money Honey," Australia, 1980.

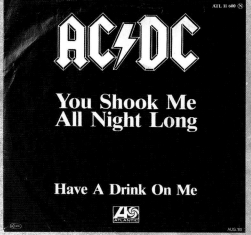

"You Shook Me All Night Long" b/w "Have a Drink on Me,"
Germany, 1980.

"Rock and Roll Ain't Noise Pollution" b/w "Hells Bells,"
Australia, 1980 (first Australian picture-sleeve single).
Bill Voccia Collection

"Hells Bells" b/w "What Do You Do for Money Honey," Belgium, 1980 (left), and France, 1980 (right). *Both Bill Voccia Collection*

I think ... people like us more because we didn't let ourselves be beaten down by destiny and that we practically started again from zero.... In a sense, Bon's accident has tightened the bonds inside the group.

—Angus Young, *Rock & Folk*, 1980

U.K. tour, Fall 1980.
© *Michael Putland/Retna*

Back in Black North American tour, 1980.

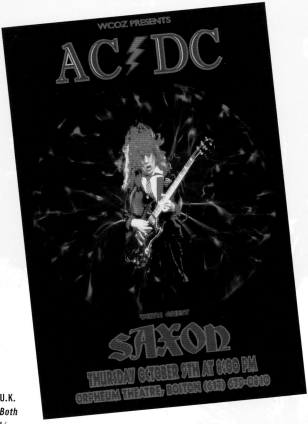

Left and below: U.K. tour, Fall 1980. *Both Michael Putland/ Hulton Archive/ Getty Images*

This page and opposite:
Toledo Motor Speedway
Jam II, Toledo, Ohio,
August 17, 1980—the last
time AC/DC raised the
curtain on another act until
opening for the Rolling
Stones in June 2003.
All © Robert Alford

TOLEDO SPEEDWAY   TOLEDO OHIO JAM 2
TOLEDO SPEEDWAY JAM TWO   81710G.A.
Z Z TOP   GATES
11:30A SUN AUG 17 1980   OPEN
NO CANS/BOTTLES/FIREWKS 9:00AM   GEN
0909/13   08/16
NO REFUNDS/RAIN OR SHINE $12.50 ADM

The LPs
Highway to Hell

By Joe Bonomo

Australian cover art, 1979.

In many ways, the End was the Beginning. When AC/DC gathered at London's Roundhouse Studio in February 1979 to begin recording their sixth album, there was anxiety in the air. The band's shows were growing in size and clamor, their albums were selling in Australia and the U.K., and Angus, Malcolm, and Bon had new, strong material, but there was pressure from Atlantic Records to produce a hit in America. AC/DC had yet to break in the U.S., the vast hometown of blues and rock 'n' roll, the mythic source of their stomping sound. There was a lot was riding on these sessions.

In the late '70s, the name Eddie Kramer had a capital ring to it, and Atlantic wanted the former Jimi Hendrix engineer and the producer of KISS' career-making albums to helm the follow-up to *Powerage*. A notably tight-knit outfit, AC/DC bristled at the ousting of George Young and Harry

Vanda, not only because Angus and Malcolm would be forced to cut loose their older brother, but because the producers had over a half-decade forged a productive bunker mentality. The Young brothers eventually gave in to the bottom line, but the Kramer sessions sputtered. "We did attempt some demos in Australia, and I don't think they were that good," Kramer said. After a few frustrating weeks, he was let go.

The band's manager, Michael Browning, then suggested Robert John Lange, a thirty-year-old producer with a modest industry reputation. He'd helmed the boards for Graham Parker and The Rumour, XTC, Motors, and The Boomtown Rats, among others, but there's little indication in those records of the mammoth, tuneful clamor that "Mutt" Lange would come to create with AC/DC. In the band's new songs, Lange heard anthemic choruses, the timeless appeal of adolescent

uncouthness, and the giddy propulsion of eighth-notes. Lange and studio engineers Mark Dearnley and Tony Platt collectively harnessed the band's energy and buffed their sound to a radio-friendly sheen that had been lacking on earlier records without sacrificing any of the band's muscular wallop. Says Platt now: "It's absolutely, definitively the fact that Mutt pulled together the attractiveness of AC/DC, the commercial edge that it needed."

One of the riffs that the band and Kramer had knocked around in the studio became "Highway to Hell," not only an AC/DC classic and in many ways their signature song, but about as perfect as a rock 'n' roll song gets. In three and a half minutes, AC/DC translates across languages and culture Dionysian excess, the lure of naughty behavior, and the promises made by twin-guitar riffing. The peak fever of the band's combustible sum, "Highway to Hell" has become a touchstone for besotted fans, worried evangelicals, dyed-in-the-wool hard rockers, and indie hipsters who can grin and ironically headbang their way through the song's fun inanity. For their part, the guys have long claimed that the lyrics came from Angus having said that riding around for years in a tour bus with the singer's reeking feet in your face is nothing short of a highway to hell. My favorite origin story is this: Near where Bon Scott was living in Fremantle, Australia, was his favorite pub, The Raffles. To get there, he had to take the Canning Highway that dips into an infamously steep decline as the pub approaches. Allegedly, scores of people died at the intersection near the bottom of the hill, and its descent into mayhem became luridly known as "the Highway to Hell." Bon loved the story and the joint.

The bulk of *Highway to Hell* fires on all cylinders. An unhinged yet committed vocal from Scott gives "Girls Got Rhythm" its ballsy swagger, propelled excitedly by the Youngs' riffing. The song is tactile in its mid-range, compact and focused. Lyrically, with a meaningful grin, Scott was mining his favorite source of inspiration in an epic sweep through the triumvirate of straight men's needs: girls, rock 'n' roll, drink. Though Scott's lyrics lacked the emotional complexity of some of his hard rock contemporaries'—Thin Lizzy's melodramatic sincerity, say, or Van Halen's "Jamie's Crying"— AC/DC created their own kind of drama on *Highway to Hell* in song arrangements, particularly on "Touch Too Much." Though the opening four bars march in assertively, they don't much sound like old AC/DC, and Bon actually sings a semblance of a melody in this song, a new trick allegedly tutored to him by Lange, who convinced Bon that breathing exercises would help him as a singer in the long run.

"Beating around the Bush," fast and riff-driven, is an exercise in sweaty delivery and fret dexterity as much it is as another sexual lamentation. A tried-and-true Chuck Berry model refitted for '70s Camaro culture, "Get It Hot" serves its purpose well. Bon describes a classic, comical scenario: he's riding in a car, a girl by his side, and—most crucially—no one's playing Barry Manilow on the tape deck. Virtually transposed from the band's collective chromosomes, the tune keeps up the party's momentum. "Shot Down in Flames," the funniest song on the album, goes a long way toward self-satirizing the band's macho posturing. The song grooves and rocks with Phil Rudd's punch-line snare shots and a solo made insane by Angus' runs in mocking imitation of Bon's romantic nosedives and his growing frustrations. ("That's nice!" approves Bon during the solo.)

International cover art, 1979.

Relative to the earlier albums, Bon's lyrics on *Highway to Hell* are more universal, if no less personal; the telling narrative details of earlier songs are sacrificed for a broader celebration of hedonistic ethos. Bon would occasionally visit social issues beyond STDs, however. In "If You Want Blood (You've Got It)," his howling about a "human zoo," dealing with "the shit that they toss to you," is disgorged on top of one of Malcolm and Angus' most stirring riffs and backed with an exhilarating performance.

The haunting, haunted, six-and-a-half-minute closer "Night Prowler" is a slow blues with a controlled, vivid band performance. A decade earlier to the month, the Rolling Stones had recorded "Midnight Rambler," an influential slow grinder similar in tone and tempo; both songs begin and end in the source material of the blues, always Malcolm and Angus' first influence and love. "Anyone can play a blues tune," Angus noted to Vic Garbarini, "but you have to be able to play it well to make it come alive. And the secret to that is the intensity and the feeling you put into it." Bon's howling delivery sends genuine tremors throughout the song.

Notorious serial killer Richard Ramirez admitted in the mid-1980s to loving "Night Prowler" to the point of heinous identification, in part prompting L.A. media to dub him the "Night Stalker." When AC/DC learned of Ramirez' sick admiration, they recoiled, claiming that Ramirez wildly misunderstood the tune: It's really just about a horny guy sneaking into his girlfriend's bedroom at night. Yet Bon's more treacherous imagery pushes the song into regrettably mean places.

Highway to Hell was released worldwide in July 1979. Its place in the AC/DC pantheon was hardly immediate. The album debuted on *Billboard*'s "Top LP & Tape" chart at 107, a lowly position from which the band could barely make out the top spot occupied by The Knack. On November 10, *Highway to Hell* peaked at No. 17, destined forever to stare up the backsides of, among others, Michael Jackson's *Off the Wall*, Kenny Rogers' *Kenny*, and—in what must've galled Bon—Barry Manilow's *One Voice*. After four weeks, the title track stalled briefly on the Hot 100 singles chart at No. 69, likely giving the guys a dirty chuckle.

Bon would never see the band's international ascension: He'd be dead within half a year. ⚡

The LPs
Back in Black

By James McNair

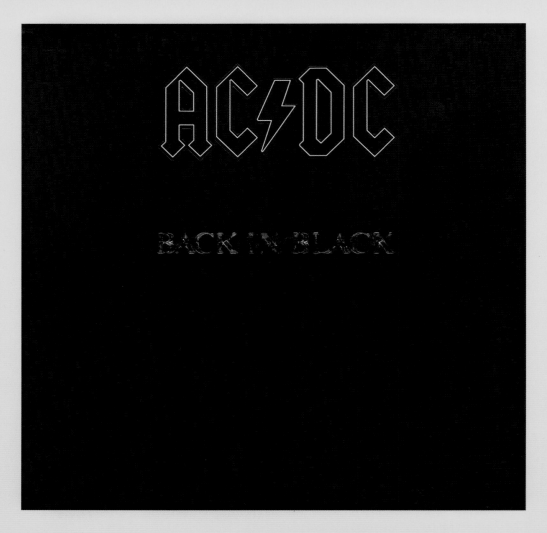

"**We were heartbroken**," recalled Angus Young in 2003. "I was numb for weeks." The death of Bon Scott in February 1980 had come just as AC/DC was preparing to follow up their first million-selling U.S. album, *Highway to Hell*, but for a time it was to Hades with that.

At the funeral, though, Scott's father, Chick, encouraged Angus and Malcolm to carry on. They were still young men, it was what Bon would have wanted, and they shouldn't "sit on their arses." The Youngs took this advice on board, and by March their shock had mutated into a kind of stoical anger. Using music to galvanize themselves, Angus and Malcolm battened down the hatches and began writing and rehearsing at a secret London location.

Soon it was decided that the next AC/DC album would be a heartfelt tribute to Bon, but the band had never penned a ballad and weren't about to start now. Instead, *Back in Black* would be the mother of all wakes—a raucous and visceral celebration of Bon's life. There was just one problem: Who would sing?

Former Geordie frontman Brian Johnson was back working as a windscreen fitter on an assembly line at U.K. car manufacturer British Leyland when he got the call. He sang Ike and Tina Turner's "Nutbush City Limits" and "Whole Lotta Rosie" at the auditions, his taut, gravel-and-broken-glass vocals securing him the job. That Bon Scott had liked and admired Johnson was a bonus, as was Brian's complete lack of pretension. "He was comfortable in his own skin, and before he'd

even sang a note, we warmed to that," said Angus.

That April, the new-look AC/DC jetted out to Nassau, Bahamas, to begin work on their magnum opus at Compass Point Studios. Though the surrounds were beautiful, the accommodations were basic: "We had these rooms like breezeblock cells," Brian Johnson told this writer in July 2009. "Nae television, nae computers, and I forgot to buy a book. One time we could hear this strange clacking noise in the speakers. A crab had got into the drum booth. It was walking across the floor snapping its claws like castanets!"

Like *Highway to Hell*, *Back in Black* was overseen by Mutt Lange, who was by then already well on his way to becoming one of hard rock's most sought-after producers. With fine-tuning lessons learned on *Highway*, Lange made the band sound more expensive and commercial without sacrificing a single volt of their raw power.

Ominous as the lone bell that tolls at the start of "Hells Bells" is, *Back in Black* quickly becomes the no-holes-barred party for Bon his band mates envisaged. The stoked guitars in "Shoot toThrill" jab like a prizefighter, while "What Do You Do for Money Honey" lambastes a gold-digging practitioner of the world's oldest profession. Elsewhere, the double entendres of "Givin' the Dog a Bone" and "Let Me Put My Love into You" recall the work of Tufnel & St. Hubbins, but the honesty of intent and joyous, gobsmacking power of delivery is such that only po-faced killjoys could find fault.

Further in, *Back in Black*'s title track raises the bar higher still. Built upon a

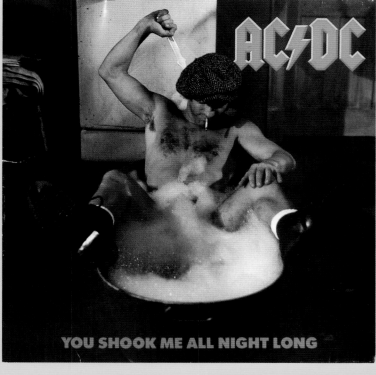

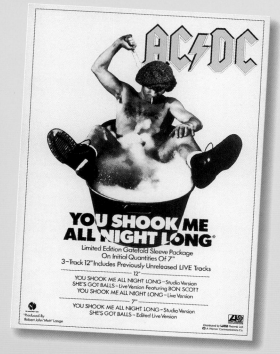

"You Shook Me All Night Long" b/w "She's Got Balls (Live)," U.K., 1986.

wonderfully spacious riff that invites the committed listener to strut, it almost slipped through the net. "We were on tour in America," recalled Angus. "Malcolm came into my bedroom with a little cassette player, and said, 'Listen, I've got this idea that's been bugging me—what do you think?' He was gonna erase it, but I knew it was a keeper."

Johnson, meanwhile, has vivid memories of working on the title track's lyric: "The boys told me, 'It can't be morbid, and it can't be about mourning—it has to be for Bon and it has to be a celebration.' I thought, 'Okay—nae pressure there, then!' I just wrote whatever came into my head, and at the time it seemed like mumbo-jumbo: *I got nine lives/Cats eyes/Abusin' every one of them and running wild.* The boys got it, though. They saw Bon's life in that lyric."

Lange, AC/DC, and the album's

engineer, Tony Platt, spent six weeks at Compass Point. Nothing—not even rumors of a machete-wielding killer frequenting the local beaches—stemmed their flow. With its catchy, sing-along chorus, "You Shook Me All Night Long" was earmarked as a single. It duly did the business, going Top 40 on both sides of the Atlantic.

Given the circumstances of Scott's death, some deemed bluesy, straight-ahead rocker "Have a Drink on Me" insensitive, perhaps even irresponsible. Angus later countered that the song had been written while Bon was still alive. Indeed, the former tub-thumper turned vocalist had even played drums on the demo.

Back in Black closes with the propulsive, Led Zeppelin–meets–Chuck Berry "Shake a Leg" and the truly fabulous "Rock and Roll Ain't Noise Pollution," a slow and sticky standout that goes a way toward

explaining why Mutt Lange later described AC/DC as masters of the "half-time groove."

Had Johnson and AC/DC done a phoenix from the flames? The answer was a resounding yes. *Back in Black* reached No. 1 in the U.K. and No. 4 in the U.S., where it stayed in the charts for 131 weeks. Amazingly, this was only the beginning. As of 2009, the record had sold nearly 50 million units worldwide, making it the second biggest album ever. Only *Thriller* by the late Michael Jackson has sold more.

"*Back in Black* was happy and sad," Johnson told me in July 2009. And for all the plaudits and gongs, his reassurance that AC/DC had done the right thing came in Maur, Belgium, when he played his first gig with the band: "There was a sea of banners saying 'Bon R.I.P.,' but there was one in the middle that saved me. It said, 'The King Is Dead/Long Live The King/Good Luck, Brian.'" ⚡

113

Rosemont Horizon, Chicago, November 20, 1981. *Paul Natkin/WireImage/Getty Images*

Chapter 6

Rock Has Got the Right of Way

What was that one we had in Detroit just now? 'The Bible says the word of the devil is evil and so is rock 'n' roll' . . . I don't remember the Bible *mentioning* rock 'n' roll!

—Brian Johnson, *Creem*, 1982

One solid sign of the way AC/DC turned Brian Johnson's world upside down was the arrival of his first royalty check for *Back in Black*: £30,000. For years, one building society employee had harassed him about late mortgage payments, so Johnson dropped by, dumped an armful of cash on the malevolent clerk's desk, payment in full, and snarled, "Never phone me again, you piece of shit" (VH1, 2003).

But he knew that, suddenly cash rich at thirty-three, he mustn't forget his roots. For instance, the workingman's cap he wore on stage did much more than soak up sweat: "It's not a gimmick to give me an image," he told Thierry Chatain of *Rock & Folk* in 1980. "My father always wore a cap. Everyone did in the North-East of England until 20 years ago." Angus interjected that his father was the same—"Never set foot outside the door with a bare head!"—and Johnson added, "It's a significant detail for me, preserving something of the place where I was born."

THE ONLY MOVIE POWERED BY

AC/DC

LET THERE BE ROCK

Starring BON SCOTT · ANGUS YOUNG
MALCOLM YOUNG · PHIL RUDD · CLIFF WILLIAMS

Let There Be Rock movie
ticket stubs, U.S., 1981.
Bill Voccia Collection

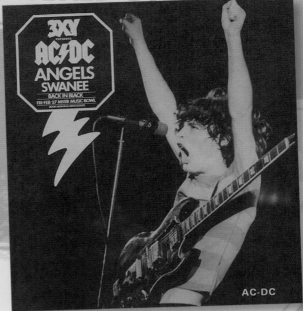

Weekly survey, Melbourne radio station 3XY,
February 20, 1981.

While *Back in Black* triumphed globally, AC/DC's conspicuous problems seemed merely practical—like having to knock a hole in the occasional venue roof to get the hell's bell in. They toured through Europe in January 1981, Japan in February (a first), and Australia later that month (almost four years after the "Seedies/Dirty Deeds" shows at Bondi Lifesaver). Murray Engleheart and Arnaud Durieux, co-authors of *AC/DC: Maximum Rock & Roll*, discovered how thoughtfully the Youngs supported Johnson in Australia. Scott's old friend John Swan opened for AC/DC and he said that either Angus or Malcolm approached him backstage and said, "Do us a favor, have a talk to Brian . . . he's a bit intimidated, he's in . . . Bon's territory." Kindly, Swan befriended Johnson (years later, the Geordie proved an understanding ally when Swan was striving to beat alcoholism).

Less concerned about establishing the new singer, that March, Atlantic in the United States finally released *Dirty Deeds Done Dirt Cheap*, the album it rejected in 1977. Confirming AC/DC's temporary "phenomenon" status, the old album reached No. 4.

Driven as ever, by May Angus and Malcolm were writing *For Those About to Rock (We Salute You)*. In July, the band flew to Paris and developed the new songs at a former factory turned rehearsal space on the city's outskirts. But when AC/DC moved to EMI Pathé-Marconi in the city to record, nothing worked. Two weeks wasted away until Mutt Lange urged them to quit. The sound in the studio just didn't suit them, although a delayed effect from the tidal onslaught of mourning Scott and then becoming fabulously successful may have dampened their fire too. They returned to the former factory and hired a mobile recording studio.

Fortunately, the move coincided with a break to headline the second Castle Donington Monsters of Rock festival in Derbyshire, England, on August 22. Facing a 65,000 crowd after six months without a gig, Johnson told Sylvie Simmons in *Creem*, "We were shitting ourselves" (1982). Then when they climbed the steps to the stage, a security guard told Malcolm, "Get off, you haven't got a pass!" They bulldozed through. But the bass end of the sound system blew and the gig disappointed AC/DC, even though it thrilled faithful tour manager Ian Jeffery, who told Mark Putterford, author of *AC/DC: Shock to the System*, he shed tears of joyful vindication: "That was such an emotional day because I'd gone from pulling kids off the street in London and dragging them into a pub to see the band."

Back in Paris, they tore along, finishing the album by the end of September. Angus supplied the title when he found a hook line for the opening track, telling Simmons, "There's this book about Roman gladiators called *For Those About to Die We Salute You* [maybe given to him by Bon Scott]. We thought, 'For those about to *rock*.'"

Promoting the album, Johnson pronounced the band "dead chuffed with it," but in 1992 Malcolm told Mark Blake of *Metal CD*, "Christ! It took forever for us to make that record, and it sounds like it. It's full of bits and pieces and it doesn't flow properly like an AC/DC album should. . . . By the time we'd completed it I don't think anyone . . . could tell whether it sounded right or wrong."

Listening again in 2010, the album seems rather cold, short on their characteristic self-mockery. Hard-line AC/DC grunts through the title track, "Evil Walks," "Breaking the

> **Christ! It took forever for us to make [*For Those About To Rock*] and it sounds like it. It's full of bits and pieces, and it doesn't flow properly like an AC/DC album should.**
>
> —Malcolm Young, *Metal CD* magazine, 1992

Rules," and the slow, weighty "Spellbound" (this last sports an adventurous Johnson lyric with its car crash metaphor and desperate sense of life out of control). However, sometimes the mighty AC/DC swing just feels dead as lead (e.g., "Snowballed" and "C.O.D.") or evaporates into '80s radio rock ("Put the Finger on You"), while "Inject the Venom" verbally succumbs to uncharacteristic, humorless nastiness.

"Breaking the Rules" is an interesting song because it expresses Johnson's distinctive take on life and political lyrics. As he told Simmons for *Creem*, it says break the rules, but "don't start any fooking revolutions. . . . One of the things that annoys me is these bands in fooking England who play Concerts for Jobs, Concerts Against Nazism. . . . Those people want fooking blowing up." The lyric's are all in favor of being a "black sheep and a renegade" and satirize the rule-enforcing class, yet the protagonist is a rugged individualist who doesn't want to change the system: "No rebellion, not today/I get my kicks in my own way."

Is everyone having a good time? Fans at Monsters of Rock festival, Donington, England, August 22, 1981. *Kevin Cummins/Getty Images*

MONSTERS OF ROCK

AC/DC

Whitesnake

Blackfoot   SLADE

MORE

OFFICIAL PROGRAMME

CIC CONVENIENT TICKET COMPANY

C090C090114
114   EVENT CODE   BRASS RING
CA05 $.00   PRESENTS
10/15   AC/DC
18:49   CA/01   10/15   COBO ARENA
0059   NOVEMBER 14, 1981
59   SATURDAY AT 8:00PM
G   FULLPR
009.   ADMISSION   TIER B-21   FULLPR
$.00   11.00321 G   009   SEAT 45301 $11.00
11.00   PRICE   SEC/BOX   ROW   SEAT

ADMISSION INCLUDES CITY SURCH

Cobo Arena, Detroit, Michigan, November 14, 1981. *Both © Robert Alford*

One of the things that annoys me is these bands in fooking England who play Concerts for Jobs, Concerts Against Nazism. . . . Those people want fooking blowing up.

—Brian Johnson, *Creem*, 1982

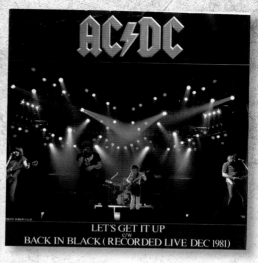

"Let's Get It Up" b/w "Snowballed," Portugal, 1981.
Bill Voccia Collection

"Let's Get It Up" b/w "Back in Black," Japan, 1982.

"Let's Get It Up" b/w "Back in Black (Live)," U.K., 1981.

The band's veiled unease became apparent when, toward the end of recording, for reasons unannounced, they sacked manager Peter Mensch. He told this writer for *Q* in 1997: "I started getting weird vibes after Donington. [AC/DC's] lawyer phoned David Krebs, and he called me and said I was fired. They never told me why. I was stunned. Till then my shit didn't smell." The band stayed with David Krebs' company *pro tem* while Mensch left to set up Q-Prime, who handled Def Leppard, Courtney Love, and Smashing Pumpkins, among others.

Released in late November, in chart terms, *For Those About to Rock (We Salute You)* did well, given the improbability of emulating *Back in Black*: U.S. No. 1 (the band's first, a million sold in the first week), U.K. and Australia No. 3, and Canada No. 4. Meanwhile, fall-to-winter tours of the U.K. and, especially, America showed burgeoning ticket sales: For instance, a 17,000 sellout at Indianapolis Market Square Arena on November 28 compared to 4,000 in that city in 1980, and three nights instead of one

For Those About to Rock dressing-room door sign, U.K., 1982. Bill Voccia Collection

My father wouldn't let us go to church when we were little. You've got that Catholic/Protestant thing in Northern Ireland, and it spilled over into Glasgow. There used to be a lot of gang fights, and he thought it was all bullshit.

—Angus Young, *Musician*, 1991

at Chicago's Rosemont Horizon, from November 19 to 21.

In their evermore spectacular show, cannons joined the bell as an AC/DC signature—twenty-one of them at first (they got the idea from the Di and Charles' royal wedding on TV on July 29, 1981). The cannons brought trouble: At Hartford Civic Center in Connecticut, on December 3, enforcing a bylaw against onstage cannon fire, police handcuffed Jeffery and his crew onstage, so the band had to drop "For Those About to Rock (We Salute You)" for the night.

Touring America, AC/DC's traditional foes, the police, were now reinforced by Christian pickets distributing tracts that claimed "AC/DC means Anti-Christ/Devil Children or After Christ/Devil Comes" and fantasized "hidden messages" revealed if you played vinyl records backward. They took titles like "Highway to Hell" and "Evil Walks" literally. They didn't get jokes like Angus donning red plastic horns (even when they accidentally slipped down over his eyes onstage as they were wont to do). Talking to Simmons for *Creem*, during that Moral Majority-beleaguered tour, Johnson growled, "What was that one we had in Detroit just now [November 14 to 16, 1981]? 'The Bible says the word of the devil is evil and so is rock 'n' roll' . . . I don't remember the Bible *mentioning* rock 'n' roll!" Talking to Youri Lenquette, of French magazine *Best* in November 1983, Johnson looked back on the protesters as "religious maniacs," admitting they "scared" him, and speaking to Tom Doyle for *Q* in 2008, he said, "I don't believe in God or heaven or hell. I'm a complete and total atheist."

AC/DC had no common ground with religious campaigners. In the band's 1991 interview with *Musician*'s Charles M. Young, Angus stood by principles he learned from his father: "I think people need to think there's an afterlife 'cause it would throw them if everything just went black at the end. My father wouldn't let us go to church when we were little. You've got that Catholic/

Protestant thing in Northern Ireland and it spilled over into Glasgow. There used to be a lot of gang fights, and he thought it was all bullshit."

With morality suddenly center stage in AC/DC interviews, *Creem*'s Simmons pressed them on an earthier aspect: Given they'd started to attract girl fans in America, what did they do with groupies? "You shake hands and that's it," Johnson insisted. "Me, I'm married with two kids." Also wedded, Angus confirmed, "You wouldn't catch me in [the backstage groupie room]. None of us actually. We're not that way inclined."

Despite the "morality" brouhaha, on the surface, 1982 looked good. The band picked up armfuls of awards, including Band of the Year, Best Live Gig, Best Single, Top Guitarist, and Top Bassist from British rock magazine *Kerrang!*. They toured, more big-time, more leisurely, in America, Japan, the U.K., and Europe. Except for native Aussie Phil Rudd, they set up first or second homes around the globe: Angus in Holland, Malcolm in London, Cliff Williams (with his wife, Georgann) in Hawaii, and Johnson in Florida (he'd tried to stay in Newcastle, but too many people treated him as "the rich rock star" rather than the plain man they knew).

Still restlessness gnawed at them. In June, they left Krebs' management company and replaced it by promoting longtime tour manager Ian Jeffery. Then, without explanation, they cancelled their July and August European festival dates.

And all the while, as secretly witnessed by Jeffery two years earlier, Rudd was cracking up—driving his Ferrari at crazy speeds, suffering anxiety attacks, hallucinating, drinking, drugging.

⚡⚡⚡

During January and February 1983, in Sydney, the Youngs worked on riffs and chord structures for the next album. Then the five got together to finish songs and rehearse on the Isle of Man (between Ireland and England).

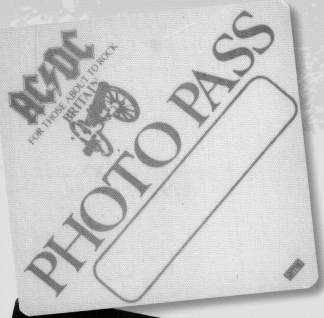

AC/DC
FOR THOSE ABOUT TO ROCK
BRITAIN

PHOTO PASS

AC/DC
FOR THOSE ABOUT TO ROCK

WE SALUTE YOU
TOKYO – BUDOKAN
6/10/82

通行許可証

Working Personnel

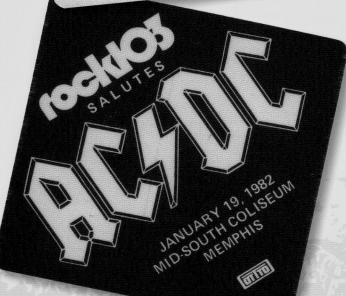

rock103 SALUTES
AC/DC

JANUARY 19, 1982
MID-SOUTH COLISEUM
MEMPHIS

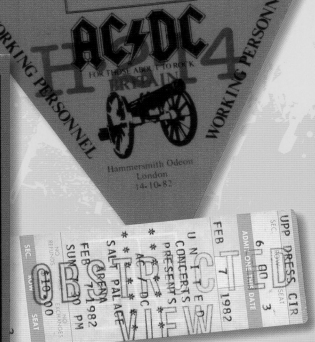

AC/DC
FOR THOSE ABOUT TO ROCK
BRITAIN

WORKING PERSONNEL
WORKING PERSONNEL
WORKING PERSONNEL

Hammersmith Odeon
London
14.10.82

AC/DC
FOR THOSE ABOUT TO ROCK
AMERICA

WORKING
PERSONNEL

LAKELAND, FLORIDA
JANUARY 28, 1982

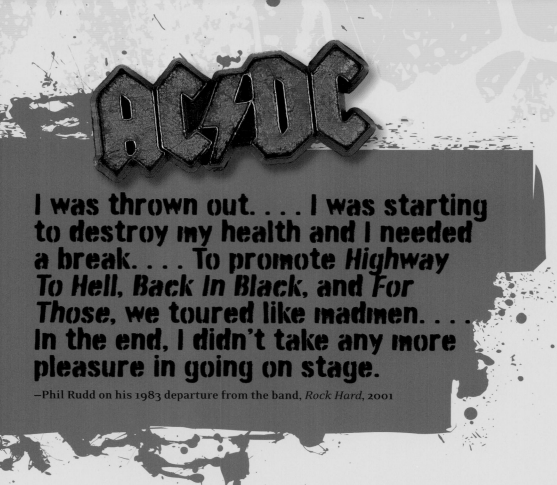

AC/DC

I was thrown out. . . . I was starting to destroy my health and I needed a break. . . . To promote *Highway To Hell*, *Back In Black*, and *For Those*, we toured like madmen. . . . In the end, I didn't take any more pleasure in going on stage.

—Phil Rudd on his 1983 departure from the band, *Rock Hard*, 2001

To record, in April they returned to Compass Point Studios in the Bahamas, crucially without Mutt Lange, although they did hire *Back in Black* engineer Tony Platt. Malcolm had decided he and Angus should take control, even though the credits for *Flick of the Switch* eventually read "Produced by AC/DC."

In February 1984, Angus told Jan Olbrecht of *Guitar Player* he favored "rawness": less reverb, fewer effects, no more "gigantic echo" on the drums. Much later, talking to Brad Tolinski for the *Flick of the Switch* reissue liner notes, he reflected on how much he valued Malcolm's opinion—de facto "production"—regardless of who was nominally in charge: "When I play something in the studio and the producer says, 'Oh, that's great,' I always look around and say, 'Yeah, but what does Malcolm think?' Because Malcolm knows me, and he says 'Yay' or 'Nay.'"

Malcolm often said he aspired to the spirit of Muddy Waters' 1977 album *Hard Again*, produced by Edgar Winter—harsh, shouty, and live-in-the-studio. He clearly didn't feel AC/DC hit the spot at Compass Point because, mixing in New York, he called for help from the "Dutch Damager" and the "Gorgeous Glaswegian"—Vanda and Young. When French fanzine *Let There Be Light* interviewed George Young in 1993 he acknowledged, "Yes, we helped a number of times. . . . But that didn't interfere with them producing themselves."

However, before that, their underlying discontent had exploded into the departure of Phil Rudd. The official version, related by Johnson to Lenquette in *Best*, went, "We were just finishing the album when Phil told us it was over for him. . . . There's nothing traumatic in this story."

However, years later in *Mojo*, Malcolm told Sylvie Simmons that he and Rudd had "an out-and-out go at each other." Different accounts have

Rudd flying out of Nassau "two hours later" or "the next day." As to what provoked the fisticuffs, in 2000 (long after Rudd rejoined the band) Malcolm told American site *KNAC.com*, "It wasn't really alcohol, but he abused drugs and he started to piss around—sooner than I did. . . . We had a dispute about nothing important." Band biographer and *Kerrang!* journalist Putterford wrote that insiders told him Rudd "smoked so much pot he began to hallucinate."

The drummer gave his recollections in two interviews with French fanzine *Hard Rock* in 1996: "I was thrown out. . . . I was starting to destroy my health and I needed a break . . . a certain stability. The incessant tours started to weigh heavily on me. I needed to breathe." In 2001, he told *Rock Hard*, "To promote *Highway to Hell*, *Back in Black* and *For Those*, we toured like madmen and this giantism literally consumed me, emptied me of all substance. My interest withered. . . . In the end I didn't take any more pleasure in going on stage."

Former AC/DC bassist and Rudd tour roommate Mark Evans told Volker Janssen for German fanzine *Daily Dirt* in 1998 that Rudd had always been "a little eccentric . . . nice guy, a real angel, a very good heart, but very withdrawn." Evans concluded that Rudd had "a real struggle" with the aftermath of Scott's death: "I think losing Bon gave him that . . . extra push and he got a little too far out there." And that was no place to be at a time when Malcolm's years of relentless drinking had begun to erode his stability and strategic clarity.

⚡ ⚡ ⚡

Rudd had completed the drum tracks for *Flick of the Switch*, but an American tour had to be cancelled while AC/DC advertised (anonymously) for a replacement. A reported, though improbable, seven hundred auditions over three months in America and the U.K. apparently saw Free and Bad Company's Simon Kirke, Roxy Music's Paul Thompson, and other notables rejected. Finally, they announced

Simon Wright and Brian Johnson. *Chris Walter/WireImage/Getty Images*

twenty-year-old unknown Simon Wright's appointment on August 5. A former bricklayer from Manchester, he'd played with obscure combos Tora Tora Tora, AIIZ, and Tytan. He owned a few AC/DC albums, and he'd seen them live once, at Manchester Apollo in October 1979.

Wright acclimated readily, telling Bill Voccia, "I was shittin' myself. But they were truly great down-to-earth people, a pleasure to work with." However, his arrival coincided with an unforeseen AC/DC career slide. Released on August 19, *Flick of the Switch* reached only No. 15 in America and dropped quickly. In the U.K. it peaked at No. 4, but lasted only nine weeks in the Top 75. The same story prevailed worldwide.

Nobody loved it. AC/DC even debuted in an unwelcome section of the *Kerrang!* readers' poll: Disappointment of the Year (No. 8). In 1984, Malcolm defended the album to French magazine

I was shittin' myself. But they were truly great down-to-earth people, a pleasure to work with.

—Simon Wright on joining AC/DC, quoted by Bill Voccia

Simon Wright. *Bob King/Getty Images*

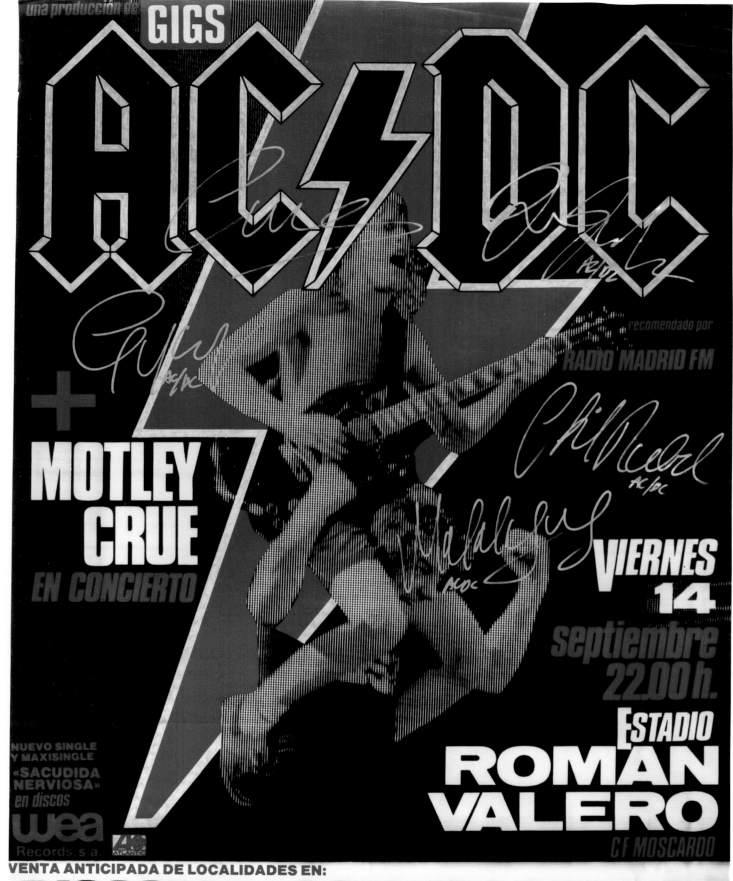

una producción de: **GIGS**

AC/DC

+ **MOTLEY CRUE**
EN CONCIERTO

recomendado por
RADIO MADRID FM

VIERNES 14
septiembre 22.00 h.

ESTADIO ROMAN VALERO
C.F. MOSCARDO

NUEVO SINGLE
Y MAXISINGLE
«SACUDIDA NERVIOSA»
en discos

wea Records, s.a.
ATLANTIC

VENTA ANTICIPADA DE LOCALIDADES EN:
DISCOPLAY, SOTANOS GRAN VIA

La Organización no garantiza la autenticidad de las entradas que no hayan sido adquiridas en los puntos oficiales de venta.

DENVER
COLORADO

AC/DC

AFTER SHOW ONLY

AFTER SHOW ONLY

FLICK OF THE SWITCH

OCTOBER 25, 1983

CLUB PROMOTIONS Presents

AC/DC
CAROLINA COLISEUM

COLUMBIA, SC
SUNDAY
8:00 P.M.
TAX INCLUDED

$13.50

NO EXCHANGE
NO REFUND
NO RESALE

LEFT
FLOOR

DEC. 1.1

Detroit, Michigan,
November 17, 1983.
© Robert Alford

127

Metal Attack: "We could have made a more commercial album . . . but it wouldn't have sounded true." Later, his first-flush enthusiasm waned.

Reconsidering *Flick of the Switch* brings to mind shifty phrases like "you can see what they were trying to do." For instance, from the first track, "Rising Power," the guitars flare much brighter and sharper than on the previous album, a great sound in itself and a credit to producers Angus and Malcolm. "Landslide" delivers a tear-along, body-shaking riff and Johnson ripping into the money-grubbing evangelists he detested. But generally the band just didn't find its intangible, microsecond-timed, rocket-launching oomph.

Eventually, AC/DC toured again, more than thirty-five gigs in North America in October and December. They made one rather old new fan in Johnson's father, Alan, the World War II "Desert Rat." Flown over to see them, he joked to *People* magazine, "I was at Monte Cassino when the Americans flattened the place and I was at El Alamein when we knocked Rommel back, but I've never heard anything as loud as this in my life."

However, even their live pulling power suddenly collapsed, playing one night in venues where the year before they'd done two and finding some venues half-full (8,000 in the 16,000-capacity Nassau Coliseum in New York on December 8). Malcolm took it out on the manager, regardless of old friendship. Jeffery told Engleheart and Durieux, "He turned on me, like, 'You're supposed to be on our side you fucking cunt!' I said, 'I am! Where there isn't two shows, there isn't two shows.'" When they reached Hartford, Connecticut, in early December, Malcolm came to his hotel room and told him his services were no longer needed "I was gobsmacked," Jeffery recalled.

Crispin Dye, who had worked for Albert's in Europe, replaced Jeffery for a short, desultory term of office.

Inconceivably, in 1984, AC/DC played only ten gigs and recorded

This page and opposite: Joe Louis Arena, Detroit, Michigan, November 17–18, 1983. *Both © Robert Alford*

nothing until October. The Youngs went to ground, "writing songs" as ever. Hanging out in Florida and Hawaii, Johnson wondered about going home, maybe hinting that all was not well: "I never see my family [thoughtful silence]. Perhaps one day I'll go back," he told Lenquette. Cliff Williams pitched into a side project with his former Home band mate, lately of Wishbone Ash, Laurie Wisefield. Atlantic rejected them.

In a brief summer outburst of live work, AC/DC headlined a Monsters of Rock package tour around Europe with Van Halen second on the bill. Even so, when they played one of their own gigs in Paris, only 6,000 showed up at the 18,000-seat Palais Omnisports on September 15. Incomprehensible. Bleak.

Their agent Doug Thaler later told Engleheart and Durieux that when he joined them at the Monsters festival in

Italy, "Malcolm had clearly had too much to drink." During "Bad Boy Boogie," Angus' solo and spoof striptease showcase, Malcolm only had to keep a steady rhythm but "He couldn't even do that. And he fell into the drum kit."

In Malcolm's holy order of rock 'n' roll that constituted sacrilege. But he wasn't ready to admit it yet. ⚡

I was at Monte Cassino when the Americans flattened the place and I was at El Alamein when we knocked Rommel back, but I've never heard anything as loud as this in my life.

—Brian Johnson's father, Alan, on seeing (and hearing) his first AC/DC concert, *People*, 1984

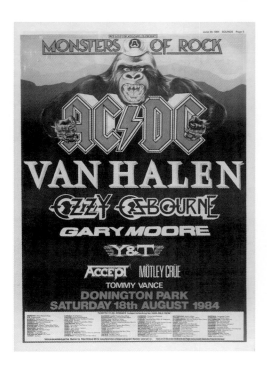

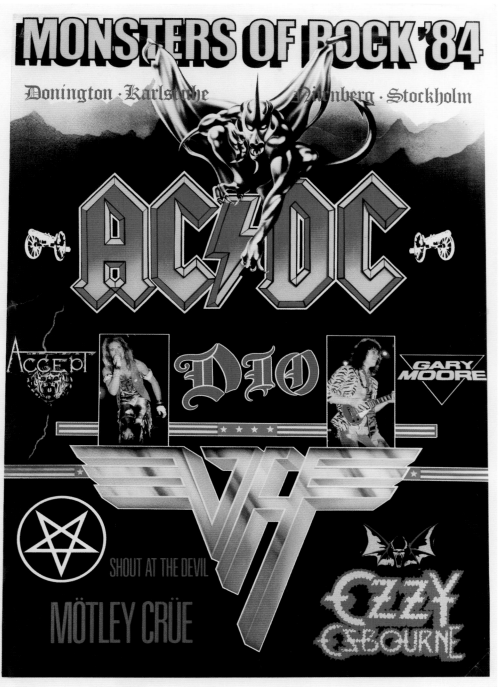

Monsters of Rock poster, England, Sweden, Switzerland, Germany, and Italy, August–September 1984.

For Those About to Rock (We Salute You)

By Bill Voccia

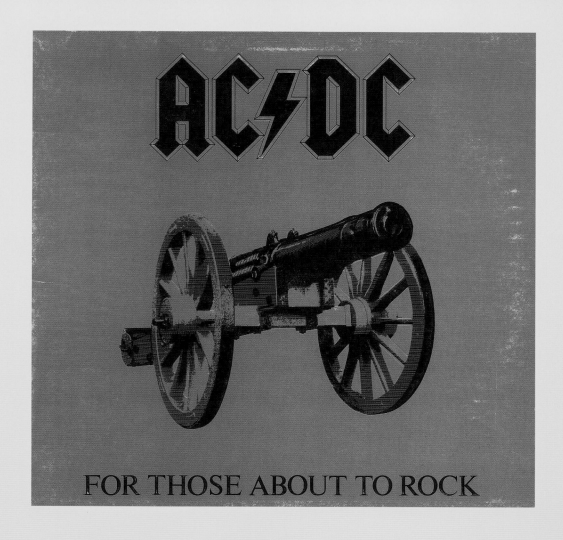

FOR THOSE ABOUT TO ROCK

AC/DC had done the impossible. Not only did they replace their irreplaceable frontman Bon Scott after his untimely death in 1980 with new singer Brian Johnson, but also they released an album that catapulted them to superstardom, giving the band new success and putting them on top of the music world. *Back in Black* quickly went multiplatinum, and the band was welcomed with the addition of Johnson, with his vocal style similar to, but raspier than, Scott's. After the massive success of *Back in Black*, could AC/DC deliver once again?

Paris, 1981, the band enters the studio with producer Robert John "Mutt" Lange, who worked on both of AC/DC's previous efforts, *Highway to Hell* and *Back in Black*, to begin recording their next album.

Angus, always a big fan of history, was inspired by a book about Roman gladiators titled *For Those About to Die We Salute You*, and the title track was born. Gracing the simple album cover sleeve was a single Civil War–style cannon on a golden background, crowned by AC/DC's type logo in black. Angus' ominous opening guitar riff sets the mood. Malcolm lays almost gloomy-sounding chords over Angus' pace, the tone evoking soldiers slowly marching onto a battlefield. The buildup is strong, and like cannon blasts, Phil Rudd's powerful snare-drum hits launch us into the album's title track, "For Those About to Rock (We Salute You)." Johnson's screeching vocals command the song, as a five-star general would command his troops, stating such epic lines as "'cos rock has got the right of way" and resulting in possibly one of rock's great all-time anthems. What better way to finish off than with a twenty-one-gun salute, complete with real cannon blasts (which have been a staple at every AC/DC concert

since the song's introduction to their set). If nothing else, the title track is simply one of AC/DC's greatest compositions. On the tail of the buzz generated by the *Back in Black* album and tour, *For Those About to Rock* quickly shot to No. 1 on the Billboard charts, resulting in AC/DC's (and hard rock's) first ever No. 1 album in the United States, and allowing AC/DC to remain the most popular band in the world in the year to follow.

The second track—the catchy "Put the Finger on You," with its clever Bon Scott–esque tongue-in-cheek lyrics and upbeat rhythm—picks up the pace, a simple foot-stomping, hand-clapping rock song. The guitar chords hit the listener like a battering ram, with an electric charge of high-energy that defines the band. This track could have made a great choice for the album's first single. Instead, the next track, "Let's Get It Up," was the first single release, another good choice with its powerful chorus and one of Angus' more tasteful solos. Phil Rudd and bassist Cliff Williams lay the foundation behind the rhythm of Malcolm's guitar, simple, yet full of dynamics. Williams' bass playing throughout the album is quite possibly some of his most creative to date.

"Inject the Venom" features Angus blistering his fretboard and Johnson barking out the spelling for the listener ("V . . . E . . . N . . . O . . . M!") just in case you might have misunderstood. The fiercely pounding rhythm section demonstrates more than just the laid-back attitude listeners may have come to expect from the pair. This is a heavy track, and overall a heavier-sounding album than anything else AC/DC had done before. Despite the "heavy metal" tag often mistakenly attached to the band, this is a rock 'n' roll album no matter which way it's twisted or categorized.

"Snowballed" was destined to be the Brian Johnson–era "Riff Raff," a boogie-and-blues-drenched track that grabs listeners by the throat. Again, the magic of the Young brothers' guitar work combines with Johnson wailing at the top of his lungs' capacity. The song drives like an Indy 500 race car speeding down the track at full force before slamming into a guardrail shattering the vehicle to pieces.

Throughout, the crisp tone of Malcolm's Gretsch, coupled with the intense attack of Angus' Gibson, assaults the listener's ears with an unmistakable sound that can only be AC/DC. "Evil Walks" is another finely constructed piece, which builds to a more upbeat flow as the Youngs' guitars interplay like two prize fighters in a championship boxing match. Johnson's vocals are well presented here (and throughout the entire album), showing off an incredible range that often goes unnoticed behind the singer's signature rasp.

"C.O.D."—an acronym for "Care of the Devil"—rings in with power chords and powerful gunshot drum hits. Here, Johnson's vocals ooze with soul you would expect from an aging blues crooner, commanding your attention. "Call of the doctor, cash on demand/If you give them a finger, they'll take off your hand" he sings before Malcolm and Williams join him for the chorus. This track was the first radio promo, given to radio stations for airplay before the album was released.

"Breaking the Rules" is AC/DC's answer to authority. Authority makes the rules, and rules are made to be broken—simple enough. The song features an incredible guitar arrangement, and Williams' bass lines keep things flowing along, pulling everything together and driving up to the huge-sounding chorus. In fact, Lange's imprint is exhibited throughout the album in the prominent and melodic backing vocals.

Angus takes listeners on another history lesson in "Night of the Long Knives," the title inspired by Nazi Germany's Operation Hummingbird, which involved at least eighty-five political executions. Notably, the song marks the first time AC/DC took a turn from their standard sex, booze, and rock 'n' roll good-time-oriented lyrics, though it wouldn't be the last.

In "Spellbound," the album's closing track, Johnson uses a traffic accident as a metaphor for his narrator's travails. The rest of the band sets a tense atmosphere behind Johnson during the song's bridge before exploding back into the verse.

Throughout the album, production on every instrument is crisp and clear, and the result is probably one of AC/DC's more musically intricate recordings. So, following on the heels of their breakthrough and featuring the same producer as its predecessor, was *For Those About to Rock* another *Back in Black*? No. As a matter of fact, it was quite different in many ways. Regardless, what we have are ten solid hard rock tracks that remain one of AC/DC's most solid and powerful albums to date. The title track remains AC/DC's final encore at every concert to this day, the real cannon blasts from their artillery of custom cannons designed for each world tour, certain to finish off the night with an ear-ringing 120-plus decibel boom. ⚡

The LPs
Flick of the Switch

By Andrew Earles

Enigmatic and spitting in the face of logic on so many levels, the AC/DC of today is a complex equation of conflicting elements that somehow equals the biggest hard rock band in the world. But rewind a quarter-century and AC/DC were enduring a common denominator linking 99 percent of all wildly successful rock bands throughout history: their first commercial flop.

With *Flick of the Switch*, released in August 1983, AC/DC had unwittingly created their own version of the "critic's album" found in many mainstream pop and rock discographies. But unlike most examples of the form, *Flick* is not a stylistic curveball in the context of the band's previous output. AC/DC probably held critics who would criticize the band's stock and trade in the same regard it held the fathers of sixteen-year-old groupies and negligent concert promoters. Fans bought records, and AC/DC had plenty of those. Young, Young, and Johnson had no sales worries in mind as they invaded the studio in early 1983, free of "Mutt" Lange as producer and gifted with the temporarily energizing idea that the organic intimacy and immediacy of earlier recordings would eventually identify the self-produced *Flick of the Switch* from start to finish.

Flick is an AC/DC album through and through, its greatness originating from a handful of subtle changes and a few creative decisions that clashed with the musical climate the album was released into. Importantly, two other forces clashed several weeks into the recording process: drummer Phil Rudd ran afoul of one of the band's three anchors, Malcolm Young, and the former was served walking papers shortly after laying down his drum tracks. New Wave of British Heavy Metal session workhorse Simon Wright replaced Rudd in time for the album's support tour and remained in the position for the next three albums before leaving in early 1989.

Measured by its blunt-force heaviness, *Flick of the Switch* joins its successor, *Fly on the Wall* (1985), in a stretch of content that is matched (not surpassed) only by the Rick Rubin–produced *Ballbreaker* (1995) and various moments from that album's follow-ups, *Stiff Upper Lip* (2000) and *Black Ice* (2008). It's important to remember that the recent albums cited here are technically, and perhaps synthetically, as "heavy" as the two earlier examples due to natural progressions made in recording technology. *Flick of the Switch* is heavy because a consummately heavy band was operating in its heaviest, and perhaps bleakest, incarnation. *Flick* is a decidedly more abrasive record than anything the band had recorded up to that point, especially compared to the Mutt Lange unit-movers of '79 through '81. Excepting some of *Highway to Hell*, Lange spread a smooth safety coating over Angus' riffs that allowed them to retain their basic heaviness minus any jagged or discordant bits that might trigger a sudden and widespread "AC/DC allergy" among radio programmers and mainstream music consumers. So as Lange helmed the ultraslick *Pyromania* by Def Leppard in 1983, AC/DC took matters into their own hands to record the anti-*Pyromania*.

Problem was that the world didn't want an anti-*Pyromania*. Metal became mainstream, and metalheads were exploring waters heavier and more progressive than what AC/DC was capable of (or interested in), notably Iron Maiden and Ozzy Osborne's magnificent comeback. Thus, *Flick of the Switch* failed to perform like *For Those About to Rock* or *Back in Black*, though it still deserves a mention within AC/DC's canon of classic albums. *Flick of the Switch* is the last great album by a band still vulnerable to outside trends, its lack of a memorable radio staple or two notwithstanding. After all, AC/DC would slowly transform into a band that didn't need radio staples to short-circuit SoundScan with album sales, and this is the beginning of that transformation. ⚡

Brendan Byrne Arena,
East Rutherford, New
Jersey, May 20, 1988.
*Michael Uhll/Redferns/
Getty Images*

Chapter 7

Shaking Foundation

In apparent good working order, AC/DC entered the band Queen's Mountain Studios in Montreux, Switzerland, in October 1984 to start recording *Fly on the Wall*—title and sleeve Angus' ideas from an Australian TV fly-spray ad. Certainly their preparation, having developed songs and arrangements over the previous nine months, impressed previously underemployed drummer Simon Wright. "Malcolm and Angus had all the songs ready to go and Brian had the lyrics," he told Bill Voccia. In 1992, Malcolm told Mark Blake for *Metal CD* that, as producers, the brothers had intended to put "more time and thought into what we were doing instead of just *taping* ourselves."

They broke off from recording only for Christmas and the colossal Rock in Rio festival, where, as one of five acts headlining two nights each, they played to a (very) estimated 50,000 on January 15 and 250,000 on the January 19, the latter with Whitesnake and Ozzy Osbourne.

Returning to Switzerland, they finished the album in February 1985. Despite their fervent efforts, *Fly on the Wall*, released worldwide in June 1985, has commonly been deemed weaker, less consistent, than the unsatisfactory *Flick of the Switch*. In this writer's opinion, a Young and Young production signature did emerge again in the bright, hard guitar sounds found on tracks like "Shake Your Foundations" and "Back In Business," and in the bare R&B and '50s rock 'n' roll inspirations exemplified by Brian Johnson's lowdown

Fortunately, the Young brothers continue to come up with enough inspired riffs to make the tunnel vision justifiable.

—Jim Farber reviewing *Blow Up Your Video*, *Rolling Stone*, 1988

gravelly vocal on "Danger." But too many riffs grind when they should spark fires (e.g., "First Blood," "Sink the Pink," "Send for the Man"). Yet the title track motorvates, as Chuck Berry would say, while "Shake Your Foundations" has that Muddy Waters holler from the groin Malcolm loved so much and "Back in Business" does their deadly, tight ZZ Top speedster thing. What's more, Johnson adds the tang of real adult (rather than fantasy) sex to his lyrics in "Shake Your Foundations" ("Lickin' off the sweat, her favourite trick"), and for "Back in Business" he extends his scope by going into character as a vicious psycho pimp ("I'll do you a favor/Put your soul for sale").

Fly on the Wall continued AC/DC's chart decline, reaching only No. 32 in America and No. 7 in the U.K. But somehow it stuck around longer than *Flick of the Switch* and, by the time AC/DC embarked on a fall American tour, their faltering career had actually begun to revive. However, a hideous imbroglio coincided with this upturn.

"Fly on the Wall" video shoot, World's End, Lower East Side, New York City, June 1985. © *Bob Leafe/Retna*

On August 31, three days before the tour started, a group of Hispanic Los Angelenos citizen-arrested Richard Ramirez, the "Night Stalker" later convicted of thirteen murders committed between June 1984 and August 1985 (come early 2010, he remained on death row at San Quentin). A Satanist and an AC/DC fan, he claimed that the *Highway to Hell* track "Night Prowler" induced him to break into people's homes and shoot or stab them. Coincidentally, September also saw the opening of a televised U.S. Senate committee inquiry

The *'74 Jailbreak* EP featuring tracks previously available only in Australia was released in October 1984.

Sydney, circa 1985. *Bob King/ Redferns/Getty Images*

ＡＣ/ＤＣ

シェイク・エア・ファンデーションズ
Shake Your Foundations
センド・フォー・ザ・マン
Send For The Man

"Shake Your Foundations" b/w
"Send for the Man," Japan,
1985. *Bill Voccia Collection*

[We had to] lie
on the floor
of the bus
and change
the front
so it read,
"Singers for
Christ."

—Brian Johnson recalling the
1985 U.S. tour under threat of
violence, allegedly from the
Christian Right, *Q*, 2008

into rock's alleged malign influence on young people. The hearings were initiated by the Parents' Music Resource Center, the "Washington wives" organization fronted by then Senator Al Gore's wife, Tipper.

Encouraged by this uproar, AC/DC's Christian Right foes regrouped and campaigned to ban their concerts. When cancellation threatened their October 3 show in Springfield, Illinois—after a local pastor called them "immoral, suggestive, satanic, destructive, lustful, lewd"—AC/DC's lawyers argued the Constitution's protection of free speech and won (even so, Johnson told Tom Doyle for *Q*, 2008, threats of "sharp-shooters" waiting to ambush them on the way

into town meant they had to "lie on the floor of the bus and change the afront so it read, 'Singers For Christ'"). Similar onslaughts against the Dallas and Houston dates (October 12 and 13) failed too, but AC/DC did cancel Costa Mesa, California, October 21, after another (probably copycat) killing was committed by a man wearing an AC/DC cap.

This must have been quite testing for all concerned—including their latest manager Stewart Young (unrelated) of U.K. company Part Rock, who also handled Gary Moore and Emerson, Lake & Palmer. That November, when the tour reached Washington, D.C., Malcolm raged about the alleged Ramirez/"Night Prowler" connection to Mark Putterford,

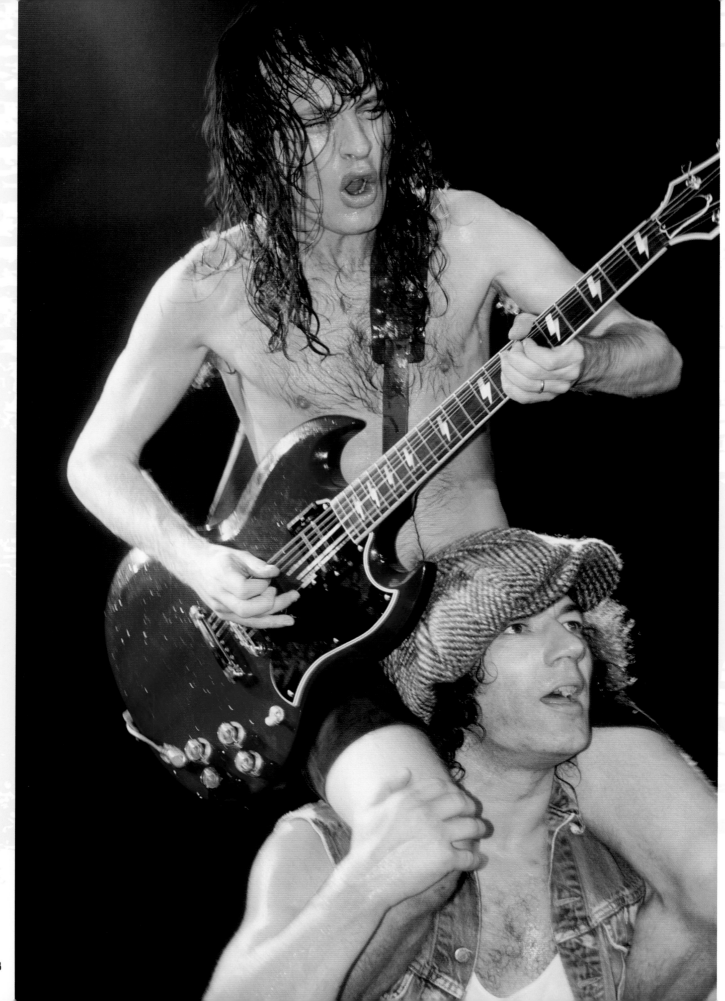

Civic Center, Providence, Rhode Island, November 22, 1985. *Ebet Roberts/Getty Images*

author of *AC/DC: Shock to the System*: "Some loopy loves your band and wears your T-shirt while he's bumping people off. We're not telling the guy to do it!" But Malcolm—who, for reasons soon apparent, may not have been in the best shape to deal with such terrible events and absurd accusations—then either forgot what Bon Scott's lyrics said or resorted to untypical disingenuousness when he added the oft-quoted, "What they can't see is 'Night Prowler' is just about creeping around at night on a couple of old girlfriends and doing the business." It isn't—not by any stretch of metaphorical imagination, when one considers lines such as, "And you don't feel the steel/Till it's hanging out your back." It's a strong, in-character lyric from inside the mind of someone fantasizing murder—by all means an appropriate (and by no means an unprecedented) subject for a song, but it could have used a different defense than the one proposed by Malcolm at the time.

However, the controversy produced unexpected results: AC/DC sold more and more tickets, booked more and more venues. Reports vary, but the original plan may have been for twenty-eight gigs, whereas when the tour ended at Cumberland County Civic Center in Portland, Maine, on November 24, they'd played about sixty.

⚡ ⚡ ⚡

To date, Brian Johnson's experience of AC/DC hadn't included recording with Harry Vanda and George Young. December 1985 fixed that. Oddly enough, this came about via blockbusting horror novelist Stephen King. A renowned fan, he asked them to soundtrack a movie he'd directed, *Maximum Overdrive*, with some old songs plus new material.

AC/DC took the opportunity for a studio reunion with big brother and old friend Vanda. Angus told Dante Bonuto of *Kerrang!*, "I always thought we did the great rock tunes with George . . . Mutt Lange was very conscious of what was

What I love to watch sometimes is Mal or Ang will look at George and just go "ummm." And George will go "hmmm." And they've just had a conversation . . . through the mind without words getting in the way.

—Brian Johnson, quoted by Paul Stenning

popular in America, but with [George] . . . if it was a rock 'n' roll song, he made sure it rocked." Talking to Putterford in 1987, he added, "Also George and Harry are honest enough to tell us if something is crap." Johnson simply delighted in observing the fraternal telepathy. In *AC/DC: Two Sides to Every Glory*, Paul Stenning quotes Johnson: "What I love to watch sometimes is Mal or Ang will look at George and just go 'ummm.' And George will go 'hmmm.' And they've just had a conversation . . . through the mind without words getting in the way."

In two weeks at Compass Point Studios in the Bahamas, they recorded "all the horror noises" (Angus to Sylvie Simmons, *Metal Creem*, 1987) by improvising to clips shown on a video screen. Guitar-driven instrumentals dubbed "D.T." and "Chase the Ace" made it to the soundtrack album. So did one new song, title track "Who Made Who." It opened with a hint of Michael Jackson's "Billie Jean" and then chimed out straight, clean rock while complaining about how video had taken over '80s music—amid ruminations of sci-fi machines controlling people ("The video game she play me/ . . . Who made who?").

Perversely, the video for this anti-video satire turned out to be the first one they'd ever liked. On February 27 and 28, 1986, at Brixton Academy in London, they shot "Who Made Who" with scores of fans toting spoof Angus outfits and cardboard guitars. The self-mocking comedy worked, so director David Mallet—whose C.V. boasted David

Bowie's "Ashes to Ashes" and Queen's "Radio Ga Ga"—became an AC/DC regular right through to 2010. Malcolm told Simmons (interview transcript, 1995): "We hate videos, we always have. . . . Then David came in with [ideas] not far off from the band's, very tongue-in-cheek. Now he's indispensable. He's like the sixth member of the band, when it comes to videos."

Rising from the serial-killer and religious-fanatic mire, AC/DC kept on selling out U.K. and European tours (January to February) and then North America (July to September). Magazines started giving them awards again—and not for Greatest Disappointment as in 1983. Now it was Album of the Year from mass-circulation American magazine *People* (a real surprise) and Comeback of the Year from U.S. rock monthly *Circus*. Although Stephen King's movie proved a midsummer turkey, AC/DC's strangely hybrid *Who Made Who* album, released May 20 around the world, suggested they were developing a new can-do-no-wrong status. The mix of Johnson period highlights ("Hells Bells," "You Shook Me All Night Long"), a moody Scott favorite ("Ride On" from *Dirty Deeds*

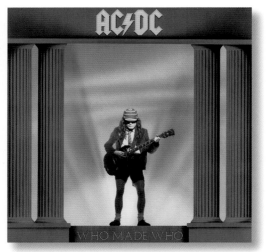

Who Made Who, released in 1986 as the soundtrack to the Stephen King film *Maximum Overdrive*. The new instrumentals "D.T." and "Chase the Ace," as well as the title song, were accompanied by backlist tracks.

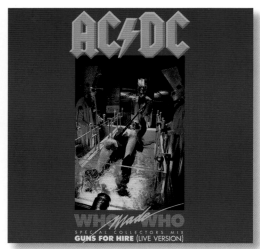

"Who Made Who (Special Collectors Mix)" b/w "Guns for Hire (Live)," 12-inch single, 1986.

Make-your-own-Gibson poster (see photo below) included with vinyl editions of *Who Made Who*.

Done Dirt Cheap), and new tracks continued the band's revival, especially in America where it reached No. 33 but remained in the chart for forty-two weeks and sold a million before Christmas.

Yet AC/DC let their renewed momentum slide so comprehensively it might never have returned. Drained beyond the demands of strategy, it seemed, they took four months off.

Much the oldest member at nearly forty, Johnson grasped the opportunity. He started going to the gym and cutting down on alcohol and cigarettes. He pursued his interest in history, traveling to the World War I battlefields of Northern France around Arras (the experience provoked his lyric for "This Means War" on the next album).

Unprecedentedly, AC/DC gigographies for 1987 read "No known tour dates." But inertia wasn't their style. Angus and Malcolm couldn't stop themselves from playing. That February, Johnson joined them in Sydney, and they began to build tunes and lyrics onto chords and riffs. They talked with Vanda and Young, and all agreed it was time

Angus with doppelgangers.
Nassau Coliseum,
Uniondale, New York,
September 20, 1986.
Ebet Roberts/Getty Images

How many spotted Malcolm Young leaning disconsolately against an amp at one point in the evening and looking positively bored during Angus's striptease routine?

—Mark Putterford writing on the last show of the European *Blow Up Your Video* tour

Mixing *Blow Up Your Video*, 1987.
Bob King/Redferns/Getty Images

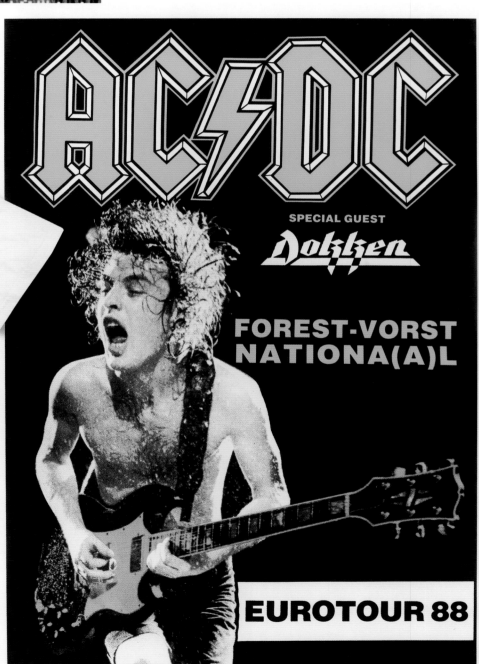

Blow Up Your Video
European tour.

the duo produced a full album again.

Johnson emphasized the combative approach behind the new songs, fulminating to French fanzine *Hard Rock* in February 1988 that hearing "shit on the radio" like the "identical" Bon Jovi, Mötley Crüe, and Whitesnake had moved them to declare, "OK, we're going to show them who's the boss here!" Malcolm's explanation, for once, admitted his insecurities, despite that comeback award: "We'd lost our footing by that time, and we needed to get the old feeling back again," he's quoted as saying in Susan Masino's *The Story of AC/DC: Let There Be Rock.* "So we stuck with Vanda and Young . . . and went back to our roots."

Moving more deliberately than ever before, the band rehearsed in Sydney from April to July 1987. Then in London they did two more warm-up weeks at Nomis Studios before settling into Miraval, a twelfth-century chateau studio near Le Val in the south of France (Pink Floyd recorded *The Wall* there). For six weeks beginning August 10, AC/DC toiled from 11:30 a.m. to 1 a.m., inspired by the in-house cooking, though sometimes alarmed by the exigencies of sharing the stone building

with bats, spiders, and scorpions— especially when they had to bed down on simple mattresses on the floor.

In mid-October, they took tapes of nineteen songs to New York for mixing. "Always the most delicate part of making an album," Johnson told Arnaud Durieux for French magazine *Hard Force* that December. "You have to concentrate to the maximum all day. That's why we took two weeks off after recording, to rest our ears a little." They polished ten tracks, eliminated nine, and *Blow Up Your Video* was ready—a call, Angus told Putterford for *Kerrang!* that December, to "Get off your backsides and go see a rock 'n' roll show live!"

But also buy the album, of course. Jim Farber of *Rolling Stone* recommended doing so in his review, arguing that it "posits loyalty to one's own style as the ultimate virtue. Fortunately, the Young brothers continue to come up with enough inspired riffs to make the tunnel vision justifiable." This writer feels it recaptured a good deal of that late-'70s raw power, not so much in the hit single "Heatseeker," but definitely with the variously funky, juddering, and meaty riffs of "Meanstreak," "Nick of Time," and "Some Sin for Nuthin'." Those tracks inspired some of Johnson's strongest writing, word and thought driven by rhythm (e.g., "Nick of Time": "Wrong track, wrong line/ . . . Bad blood, bad news/ . . . Mad bull seeing red").

Blow Up Your Video and 1988's lengthy tours showed the years of unease and incomprehension, because *For Those About*

to Rock (We Salute You) had not, after all, pushed AC/DC past the point of no return, musically or commercially. In January and February 1988, propelled by the single "Heatseeker," the album went to No. 2 in the U.K., while in America it leapt to No. 11.

Australia ran riot over the band's first homeland tour in seven years (this lineup was entirely U.K.-born): Dozens were arrested when tickets went on sale in Perth; jailhouses crammed in Melbourne and Adelaide after the gigs got a little rowdy.

In February, AC/DC played sixteen dates in Australia's biggest venues, plus one in New Zealand, and then twenty-seven more in the U.K. and eight other European countries. But when band biographer and *Kerrang!*

Where's Malcolm? Thomas & Mack Center, Las Vegas, July 24, 1988. © David Plastik/Retna

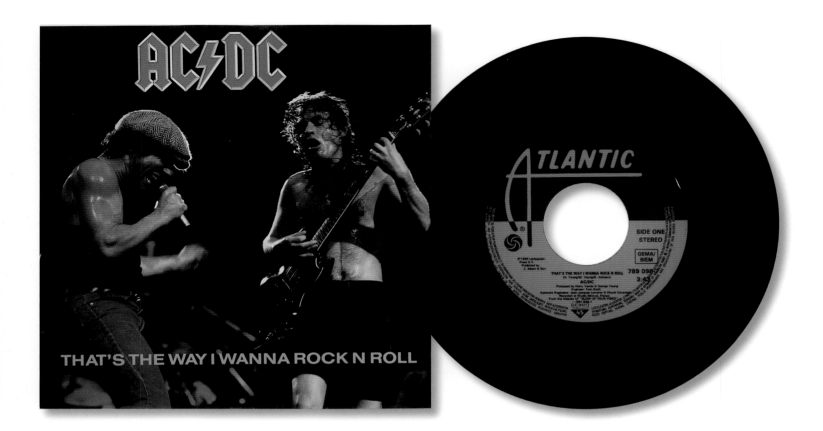

writer Mark Putterford attended the last of those shows, at Wembley Arena in London, something disturbed him: "How many spotted Malcolm Young leaning disconsolately against an amp at one point in the evening and looking positively bored during Angus' striptease routine?"

⚡ ⚡ ⚡

"I can't do this, I just can't do this," Malcolm said when he came offstage one night toward the end of that tour (Simon Wright to Murray Engleheart and Arnaud Durieux in *AC/DC: Maximum Rock & Roll*). The band was due to open in America on May 3, but on April 21 Atlantic announced that Malcolm would miss the tour because of "nervous exhaustion." His place would be taken by his nephew, Stevie, son and namesake of the oldest Young brother (then aged thirty and based in Birmingham, England, having spent much of his childhood in Sydney, Stevie Young was in a band called Starfighters, unknown except for their support spot on AC/DC's 1980 U.K. tour).

Few believed the familiar "nervous exhaustion" euphemism, and, despite their dedication to privacy, within a couple of years AC/DC felt able to give the honest explanation. "I was . . . getting ripped all the time," Malcolm said in a 1990 interview (Howard Johnson, *Get Your Jumbo Jet Out of My Airport: Random Notes for AC/DC Obsessives*, unattributed). "It was always the same story, and I couldn't leave it alone. I was a real Jekyll and Hyde character. I'd lost my self-control. I was still playing the songs OK. . . . Things would get really bad after the gig though. I was the first one to start drinking and the last one to leave any club. I always had to be dragged out." Angus told Putterford in 1990, "He had to stop it, it had just gone too far. From the age of 17, I don't think there was a day when he was sober. . . . I never knew how he could function like that."

Malcolm has elaborated on the feelings that dragged him down: "I was losing my enthusiasm for everything, the group, life in general," he told David Sinclair, writing for *Q* in 1990. "I was

The funny thing was I never drunk heaps; I just drank consistently and it caught right up on me and I lost the plot. Angus was going, "I'm your brother; I don't want to see you dead here. Remember Bon?"

—Malcolm Young, *Mojo*, 2000

into and I couldn't do it alone. We didn't have Phil in the band at the time, we had Simon and I wasn't at ease with that. I was worn out, because we were non-stop drinkers. When you start to get weakened like that . . . ," he told *KNAC. com* in 2000. His brother George added, to French fanzine *Let There Be Light* in 1993, that alcohol "wasn't the only reason. He was very tired and he had big family problems."

Malcolm came to understand exactly what kind of a drinker he'd been. "The funny thing was I never drunk heaps, I just drank *consistently*, and it caught right up on me and I lost the plot," he told Sylvie Simmons for *Mojo* in 2000. "Angus was going, 'I'm your brother; I don't want to see you dead here. Remember Bon?'"

After all his years of leadership and independence, Malcolm realized he needed help. He joined Alcoholics Anonymous. Back home in Sydney, he spent time with O'Linda and their young children, Cara and Ross. He still played guitar for hours a day. In 1990, on the road again, he remarked, "I've never been on tour without a drink inside me before" and admitted it was still "always difficult to stick with the tea when things get stressful" (Howard Johnson, unattributed).

In May 1988, Angus observed his nephew in action for a couple of days during rehearsals in Boston before placing an excited phone call to his big brother. "Angus said, 'Come quickly and see Stevie. He's got the sound, he's got the look!'" George told *Let There Be Light* in 1993. Malcolm himself is said to have flown over and watched Stevie in Long Beach, California, in June and given his approval. In fact, everyone agreed that for the entire enormous tour—May 3 to November 13, around 120 of the 160 or so shows AC/DC played that year—Malcolm could not have fielded a more worthy substitute (a shame then that Stevie never found another good band and quit professional music in the '90s).

After the tour, Malcolm quietly slipped back into band circles. By December, in Sydney, then at Malcolm's home in London and Angus' in Holland, the brothers started work on new songs. ⚡

The LPs
Fly on the Wall

By Andrew Earles

If the AC/DC songwriting team of Young/Young/Johnson found it troubling that 1983's *Flick of the Switch* failed to add to the band's 1979 to 1981 run of mega-successes, 1985's *Fly on the Wall* was an odd way to show it. Despite "Shake Your Foundations," which teased both the band and fans by reaching No. 7 on the U.K. charts (*Flick of the Switch* failed to yield a chart-invading single), *Fly on the Wall* mixed with the musical climate of 1985 like oil with water, even as heavy metal achieved new heights in mainstream popularity. Whereas *Flick* sounded organic and live compared to the Mutt Lange–produced albums that came before, *Fly* ripped through the speakers like a genuinely abrasive and unfriendly prospect more akin to Mötörhead than to the band responsible for the world-dominating *Highway to Hell*, *Back in Black*, and *For Those About to Rock*

(We Salute You) trilogy. It mattered none that an unending stream of Sunset Strip bubblegum metal dominated the charts and made the general idea of "heavy metal" a household one in 1985—compared to Mötley Crüe or Poison, *Fly on the Wall* was almost as challenging (and thus noncommercial) as punk rock. It's not uncommon to find AC/DC namedropped as an influence by punk and indie rock bands going as far back as the early '90s. With the visceral one-two punch of *Flick of the Switch* and *Fly on the Wall*, this makes sense.

However, *Fly on the Wall*, like its predecessor, did not make much sense given its year of release. The songwriting and production, even on the catchier "Sink the Pink" and the aforementioned "Shake Your Foundations," belonged in a netherworld that simply did not exist in 1985. *Fly on the Wall* is an album unwittingly created for the

heavy metal or hard rock fan who lived in the collective mind of AC/DC and nowhere else. It was too punkish and loose to fit into 1985's notion of heavy metal and too "AC/DC-ish" to be accepted by either punk rockers or the growing legions of speed/thrash-metal fans congregating around bands like Metallica and Anthrax. The weird irony is that AC/DC now sonically resembled a sloppier version of circa-1985 Raven or Saxon, once notable forces in a heavy metal movement AC/DC predated but massively influenced some years before. The stubborn back-to-our-roots integrity, while charming and not without direction on *Flick*, combined with the band's internal strife and overall exhaustion on *Fly* to repel any hope of mainstream acceptance.

Further, in the two years since *Flick of the Switch* revealed itself to be an anti-MTV album, the music video channel had grown

"Danger" b/w "Hell or High Water," New Zealand, 1985. *Bill Voccia Collection*

into an entity with little room for AC/DC's blunt-force barroom metal. There was plenty of hair metal and keyboard-driven new wave to go around, and few bemoaned the absence of a new, flashy music video starring the not-so-easy-on-the-peepers quartet. As if to further alienate the more visually in tune, MTV-savvy masses, *Fly on the Wall* gave an incredibly poor first impression even before Angus' opening riffs assaulted any ears.

Barring their shocking-for-the-time foray into staged gore on the cover of *If You Want Blood You've Got It* (Angus' execution by guitar) in 1978 and the subtly disturbing *Dirty Deeds* cartoon art from the 1976 Aussie version of that LP, AC/DC cover art had existed as consistently serviceable afterthoughts. As a visual manifestation of the efficient yet powerful hard rock/heavy metal simplicity contained within, the art didn't need to be complex or fantasy-driven. More often than not, the (quite) literal nature of AC/DC cover art worked perfectly. But *Fly on the Wall* crossed the line into silliness. Using a certain style of cartoon art usually found on forgotten skate-punk albums of the same era, the album sleeve

displays the band's expected lack of metaphor (e.g., a cartoon fly . . . on a wooden wall), but ends up buried under self-parody in a bid to exploit the band's fun-loving sleaziness. (The entire presentation could have enjoyed a somewhat passable legacy had "O" in "ON" rather than the "Y" in "FLY" been replaced with a knothole through which an eyeball peers—or if that sleazy touch had been omitted altogether.)

Surprisingly, AC/DC also went the Michael Jackson route and released the six-song *Fly on the Wall* concept video. Showcasing over half of the album, the *Fly on the Wall* video has the band playing "Fly on the Wall," "Danger," "Sink the Pink," "Stand Up," and "Shake Your Foundations" in a fictional Brooklyn bar as a practically plot-less scenario plays out ("Playing with Girls" plays during the credits) around them. Featured prominently is an animated version of the sneering fly from the album's cover in a possible bid to establish the promotional pull of a regular band mascot. While the video promptly sunk into the abyss of obscurity, AC/DC would continue releasing these videos with future albums, instead

looking to Angus' high jinks when a mascot was needed.

There's no question that the escalating popularity of MTV combined with the explosion of saccharine pop-metal and flimsy new wave guaranteed 1985 a commercially suicidal moment for AC/DC to unleash (a full two years after the unpolished flop of *Flick of the Switch*) an antagonistically raw set of songs fronted by irredeemable cover art. *Fly on On the Wall* was the second (and final) chapter in AC/DC's flirtation with a relatively DIY mindset, and the ensuing product was a commercial, though not an entirely creative, bust. In fact, it was the first fleeting glimpse of the AC/DC of today: a band that pushed forth regardless of changing times and trends, perfecting how to survive (and later flourish) on the only thing that came naturally. The one million people who purchased *Fly on On the Wall* upon its release would increase exponentially until AC/DC stayed on the charts not by virtue of hit singles, but through a massive following of die-hard fans. ⚡

The LPs
Blow Up Your Video

By Daniel Bukszpan

BLOW UP YOUR VIDEO

AC/DC is expected to be stylistically unwavering. As with Slayer, Mötörhead, or The Ramones, fans buy a newly released AC/DC album with the expectation that it will sound *exactly* like the last one, and the one before it, with no funny stuff thrown in, thank you very much. The failure to summon *Back in Black II: Electric Boogaloo* plagued the band throughout most of the 1980s, and it was in the middle of that decade that it hit its commercial low point. That all turned around when *Blow Up Your Video* was released in 1988. It was the first of the band's albums to receive platinum certification in years, and it indicated that Malcolm, Angus, and Company had finally emerged victorious from their struggle with the law of diminishing returns.

So what accounted for the heroes' welcome that the album received among the record-buying public? Was the ten-song offering an angry, back-to-basics rejoinder to the glam metal movement that was then in vogue? Or was it a polished, contrived sellout that introduced AC/DC 3.0 to the public?

The answer is a resounding "neither." The album is nearly indistinguishable from the ones that preceded it, and if there are dissimilarities to behold, they remain a secret.

It starts off in suitably up-tempo fashion with "Heatseeker" and all the classic AC/DC ingredients on full display. Cliff Williams' bass is as insistent as ever. Brian Johnson's vocals are the living embodiment of permanent larynx mutilation. And Angus Young's guitar is outstanding as always. But something just doesn't add up. This feeling carries over to the follow-up, "That's the Way I Wanna Rock 'n' Roll," and then to the slower-paced "Meanstreak." The latter likely was meant to recall the mid-tempo swing of "Back in Black," but actually sounds a little stiff and void of groove. It's during this song that the light bulb over the listener's head illuminates. What's holding things back are the drums.

And the mix.

And the songwriting.

The drums in question are played by Simon Wright, an accomplished musician who acquits himself well in his current position with Dio. That said, he was completely wrong for AC/DC. What they need, and what they had (and have again) in Phil Rudd, is an artless, ham-handed basher who goes heavy on the crash cymbal and makes the songs stomp. Although Wright doesn't do anything wrong here, his lack of pure caveman violence comes across as rigid, uptight fussiness in the context of AC/DC.

Bill Voccia Collection

If any song is a good example of why the album doesn't work, it's "Kissin' Dynamite," not only the worst song on the album, but one that suffers additional damage when the lead guitar break is buried in the mix. This is a frustrating situation, because more than one mediocre AC/DC song has been saved by an Angus solo. The not-quite-visceral-enough volume of the solo here is an apt metaphor for what's wrong with the whole album—all of the necessary elements are there, but they are all held in check just enough to restrain and neuter their effect. It's not that the album is slick—it's that it's just smooth enough to negate whatever aggressiveness might otherwise have made it to tape.

For the majority of its running time, "Blow Up Your Video" consists of material that can best be described as unremarkable.

There are a few interesting moments, such as "Two's Up," an uncharacteristically plaintive, minor-key affair that's somewhat reminiscent of the melodramatic and melodic chord progression from "Poison Heart" by the Ramones. It absolutely does not sound like an AC/DC song, which is probably why it was stranded near the end of the album, deep in filler land. Maybe if it had appeared near the beginning, it would have cast a completely different mood over the album and revealed the rest of the material in a different light.

The album flops to its conclusion. "Ruff Stuff" is based around a riff that is *waaaaaaaay* too happy and that in less charitable moments is reminiscent of Jackyl. The album mercifully closes with "This Means War," based around a fast riff that's probably supposed to recall "Whole Lotta Rosie." But despite the song's high tempo, there's actually not much speed. Even though Brian Johnson turns in a respectable performance, he can't save the song from its own inertia.

So is "Blow Up Your Video" a subpar AC/DC album? Absolutely. But before writing it off entirely, it's important to recognize one respect in which the album actually went right. It was released in 1988, at the height of the glam-metal craze, and quite a few bands from AC/DC's original era were only too happy to jump on the bandwagon. It certainly would have been the easiest way for the band to try and remain afloat. It's to their credit that they refused, and though the resulting album wasn't exactly a world-beater, their decision to stick to their guns is surely part of the reason why AC/DC still fills arenas more than a decade later. ⚡

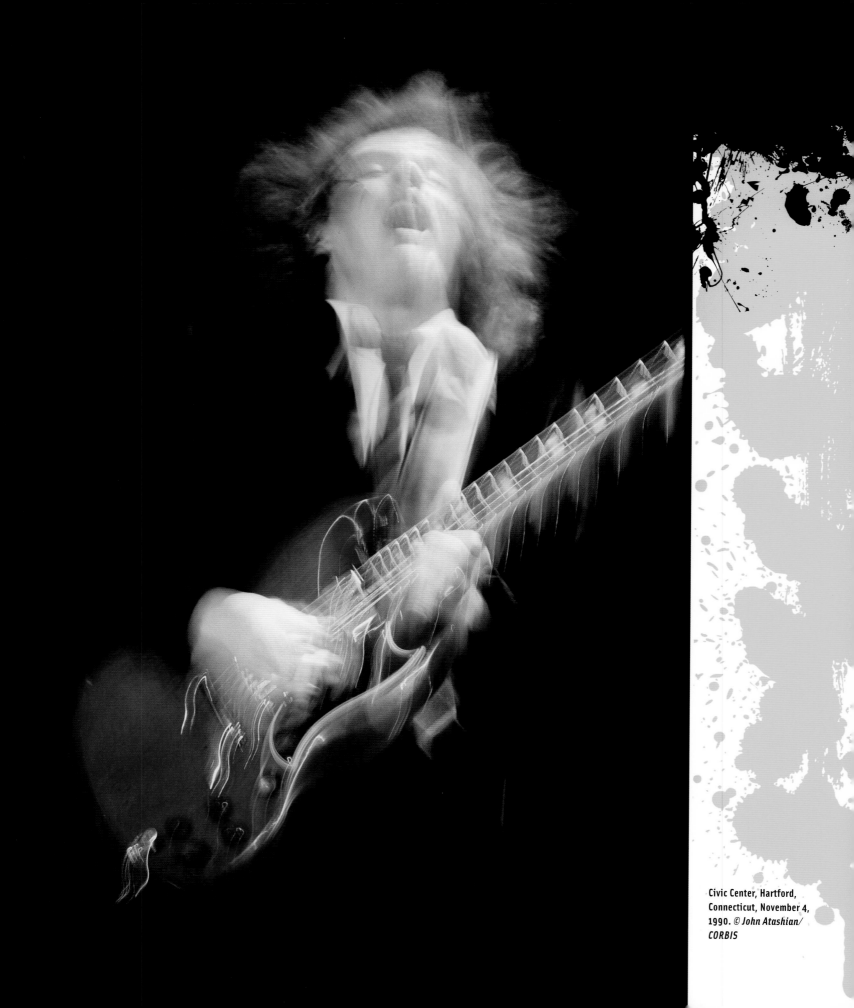

Civic Center, Hartford, Connecticut, November 4, 1990. © *John Atashian/ CORBIS*

Chapter 8

Get Back to the Start

The ultimate confirmation of Malcolm's modest, sober re-emergence had to be musical. Tentatively, he began to write "using some keyboards, just sampling the guitar into it for the sake of trying something different," he recalled for Richard Bienstock at *Guitar World* in 2008.

Restored through relentless willpower, self-discipline, and the quiet support of family, friends, and AA, he soon felt so solid that, with Angus, he took on a fresh responsibility to help a friend. When he realized the seemingly bulletproof Brian Johnson was knocked sideways by his tangled divorce from Carol, his wife of twenty-one years (they had two daughters, Joanne and Kala), Malcolm suggested to his brother that,

for the first time, they should write the lyrics for the new songs, Angus recalled for Howard Johnson in *Kerrang!* (1990).

According to Paul Stenning, writing in *AC/DC: Two Sides to Every Glory*, Johnson expressed only gratitude and relief—for reasons that showed why he never resumed the lyricist role: "I ran out of ideas. I can't think enough. . . . I was having a real tough time thinking of lyrics." Short-term, in absence of official progress reports, word of demos featuring the brothers singing provoked rumors that Johnson had been fired and replaced on vocals by Angus. The story even reached his mother in Dunston: "I said to the guys, 'Me ma says you're kicking me out!' We just laughed. . . . They mustn't have heard Angus sing," he told Sylvie Simmons in *Mojo* (2000).

I want you to sound like AC/DC when you were seventeen.

—Producer Bruce Fairbairn, quoted by Angus Young, *Auckland Star*, 1990

Johnson insisted he suffered no insecurity about it at all, telling Charles M. Young of *Musician* in 1992, "So, I didn't write on this album. It doesn't matter with AC/DC. You're all together and whatever happens, happens." (By then, Young noted, Johnson had married his second wife, Brenda, "a newscaster he fell in love with at first viewing.")

And no worries for the brothers. They'd always been involved in lyrical problem-solving, first with Scott and then with Johnson. "Three of us, sometimes four with George, we'd have this big shoot-around. We'd end up spending two days sitting on one word," Angus told Howard Johnson (*Kerrang!*,

1990). In fact, he added, they found it easier to let the words come while they developed the music, rather than leaving them until they were in the studio. Musing on the new writing process to Martin Aston for the *Auckland Star* in 1990, Angus suggested that, to a degree, it moved them on from "being

riffmakers all the time" and helped them come up with more melodic "full songs." Although the "No Ballads!" rule still vehemently applied, Johnson later joked that *The Razors Edge* made him relearn "what to do with that nonsense— real melodies."

So, I didn't write on *The Razors Edge*. It doesn't matter with AC/DC. You're all together and whatever happens, happens.

—Brian Johnson, *Musician*, 1992

Terry O'Neill/Getty Images

Other changes were on the way. Malcolm's probably unspoken discomfort with Simon Wright seems to have been tacitly reciprocated by the drummer. While the Youngs wrote songs, he went off to record with former Black Sabbath member Ronnie James Dio on an album called *Lock Up the Wolves*. Reasonably enough, as Wright explained to Mark Putterford, "The band was taking some time off and I just wanted to work" (*AC/DC: Shock to the System*, 1992). But AC/DC members had never "guested" with other artists; the Youngs felt it suggested a dilution of commitment. This was pretty much true in the case of Wright, who told Putterford, "I kind of got tired of the straightforward drumming that AC/DC requires." The chatty Youngs also felt uneasy with the drummer's quiet reserve—except when complaining about money, they reckoned. Angus did allow that Wright "always felt he was an outsider because we'd been doing it a bit longer than he had, so maybe that was our fault" (Putterford). But in sum, they decided "we'd better get someone else" and Wright joined Dio full-time.

With the new songs ready, in November 1989 they auditioned-cum-rehearsed in a barn near Brighton, south of London. "Everyone and their uncle" applied for the drumming job, eventual victor Chris Slade told *crabsodyinblue. com*. The others had more or less matched Slade for power, but after three or four songs they flagged, Angus told *Kerrang!*'s Howard Johnson in 1990: "[Slade]'s like Phil, a bit frightening . . . looming over the kit." Thus, AC/DC acquired their first old pro. Born October 30, 1946, in Pontypridd, Wales, Slade started out with Tom Jones in the '60s and played with Manfred Mann's Earth Band, Gary Numan, David Gilmour, Jimmy Page's The Firm, and Gary Moore.

AC/DC had the album's title from the outset. It was political! Angus told Putterford he was "thinking about the moment just before a big storm when you look in the sky and see huge black clouds coming over. . . . People [in

Australia] used to say, 'Here comes the razor's edge.' We thought that fitted in quite well with . . . the ongoing thing between the Russians and the Yanks . . . guess it's just our way of warning about Armageddon. 'Armageddon out of here!'" (Their spelling of *The Razors Edge* also demonstrated their ongoing ecological concern for the world's diminishing stock of apostrophes.)

They moved on to U2's "home," Windmill Lane Studios in Dublin in February 1990, planning to have George Young produce them. But that immediately fell through. He arrived, then pulled out. "He had big personal problems and he had to go home suddenly," Malcolm told French fanzine *Let There Be Light* in October 1992 (the nature of those problems remained private).

While working at Windmill Lane, they asked around about possible replacements. The grapevine responded with one name: Bruce Fairbairn, Canadian producer of two late 1980s phenomena—the reborn Aerosmith (*Permanent Vacation* and *Pump*) and Bon Jovi (*Slippery When Wet* and *New Jersey*). They inquired and Fairbairn was available, but AC/DC expected fashionable American producers to be "high-powered, more business than pleasure." So Malcolm flew over to meet him, and Fairbairn won him over by saying, "I want you to sound like AC/DC when you were 17" (Angus to

Aston, *Auckland Star*). Reassured, in late March 1990, they started work at Fairbairn's renowned Little Mountain studio in Vancouver, British Columbia.

Meanwhile, the band had returned to the news pages, though for more comedic reasons than usual. When General Manuel Noriega, drug dealer, former CIA operative, and dictator of Panama, hid from invading American forces at Panama City's Vatican embassy in December 1989, U.S. "psyops" forces tried to flush him out by playing AC/DC day and night through a massive PA stationed outside the building. Even though the standoff was eventually resolved by diplomacy rather than decibels, as droll Johnson told Ireland's *Hot Press*, 1992, "We were just glad to be of service."

⚡ ⚡ ⚡

After all the disruptions of the previous two years, *The Razors Edge* sessions proceeded with improbable smoothness—the songs all ready to roll, the producer empathetic. When they finished work near the end of May, Malcolm expressed his appreciation of Fairbairn with a meaningful gift: a copy of his beloved Gretsch guitar.

Studio engineer Mike Fraser told Phil Lageat for his website *highwaytoacdc.com* in 2007, "[AC/DC] are pros and good musicians, and they know how to write. And then they are all respectful people. . . . It's easy

I try always to improvise and use the minimum of takes. I base everything on the emotions of the moment. . . . I do have a sort of gift of re-creating on my guitar the melodies that come from my spirit: I often hear my solos before I've played them! But I never prepare my guitar parts in advance.

—Angus Young, *Guitare et Clavier*, 1991

NOW THERE ARE TWO THINGS TO BE AFRAID OF ON APRIL 15TH.

"Are You Ready"

If you're not too busy hiding your assets this April, look for the latest super single from the multiplatinum album THE RAZORS EDGE (91413). It's a blast.

AC/DC

Produced by Bruce Fairbairn.
Management: Stewart Young/Steve Barnett for Part Rock Management, Ltd.

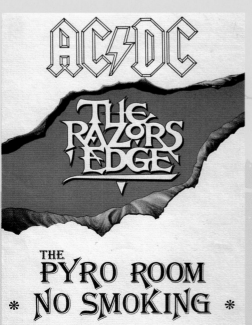

Razors Edge "Pyro Room" dressing-room door sign, U.S., 1990–1991. Bill Voccia Collection

with Angus—he has his soul in what he does." Indirectly acknowledging the compliment, Angus described his approach to recording to French magazine *Guitare et Clavier* in 1991: "I try always to improvise and use the minimum of takes. I base everything on the emotions of the moment. . . . I do have a sort of gift of re-creating on my guitar the melodies that come from my spirit: I often hear my solos before I've played them! But I never prepare my guitar parts in advance."

The brothers felt good about this album from early on. In 2008, Malcolm told Richard Bienstock of *Guitar World*, "When Angus came up with 'Thunderstruck,' I thought, 'Fuck, we've got a great track here.' That set the standard for the album." Sheer terror had inspired him to write the song; on the 1988 European tour, flying from a brief stopover at his wife's parents'

AFTER SHOW
SUMMER 1991

Bill Voccia Collection

vocalizes like a car revving up through all the drumbeats and chorus chants and bagpipey guitar bits. The track swings steadily while remaining quite sparse and unadorned, despite all the action. The brothers launch their lyrical career with a reinvention of Angus's airborne death-terror experience. After the album's arresting start, the riffs come hard in something like the seventeen-year-old way for which Fairbairn and AC/DC longed, hinting at the exhilarating dependability of *Highway to Hell* and *Back in Black*.

When it came to earthy words to match rockin' deeds, Angus and Malcolm couldn't equal Bon Scott, but they hit the spot. Familiarly, "Fire Your Guns" viewed reality from groin level ("She got moves, drips of sweat"). But aside from the sauce, "Mistress for Christmas," "Got You by the Balls," "Moneytalks," and

When Angus came up with "Thunderstruck," I thought, "Fuck, we've got a great track here."

—Malcolm Young, *Guitar World*, 2008

home in Holland to rejoin the band in Berlin, Angus' small plane was struck by lightning, which sounded like a bomb going off (although no harm was done).

As the opening track, "Thunderstruck" evoked a restoration of AC/DC's essential spirit. The opening fancy guitar twiddle, according to Susan Masino in *The Story of AC/DC: Let There Be Rock*, was played "with all the strings taped up, except the B . . . a little studio trick George taught Angus." Johnson

"Goodbye and Good Riddance to Bad Luck" all harked back to what Scott started to chew on with "Down Payment Blues" in 1978: hard-bitten, back-alley stories and ruminations about sex, money, and power. (Johnson had avoided such sociopolitical references on principle, except for "Meanstreak," even though "Down Payment Blues" was his favorite Scott-era AC/DC song.)

156

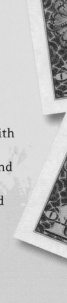

"Goodbye and Good Riddance to Bad Luck" laid it out as flat-broke, sleazy, loveless, and hopeless as it can get: "Gettin' bombed out on booze/Got nothin' to lose/Run outta money/Disposable blues." Then, quite different amid all this squalor, came "The Razors Edge," Angus's metaphor for global politics and zeitgeist anxiety: "Don't look up in the sky/You're gonna die of fright/. . . The razor's edge/You could be cut to shreds."

This album reemphasized that AC/DC, while not an "intellectual" band, are not just about headbanging. It's notable that after Angus found the "razor's edge" metaphor, but before the album's release in September 1990, the first Gulf War began and triggered a yearlong, worldwide recession. In no way pretentious, these political lyrics arose straightforwardly from what the Youngs read and saw. Asked about "Mistress for Christmas" ("He got it, I want it/They got it, I can't have it"),

Angus told Young of *Musician*, "Money's the big divider. . . . So it's just our little piss-taking. It's just our dig at that lifestyle of the rich and faceless."

In this period preceding grunge's eruption with Nirvana's *Nevermind* in October 1991, allowing themselves to grow as writers only accelerated AC/DC's steady comeback.

The Razors Edge reached No. 2 in America and No. 4 in the U.K. (a contract-end label change within WEA from Atlantic to ATCO/Eastwest made no difference).

That October they rehearsed in London and then set off for the first leg of their world tour, beginning in the United States (November 2 to December 16), no expense spared: the bell, the cannons, the giant inflatable Rosie, a new giant inflatable Angus, 100,000 "dollar bills" dropped on the audience every night during "Moneytalks"—souvenirs rather than spendables since Angus' face had replaced George

"Moneytalks" promo-only credit cards, U.S., 1990. *Bill Voccia Collection*

"Angus bucks" rained down on concertgoers during the 1990–1991 Razors Edge tours.

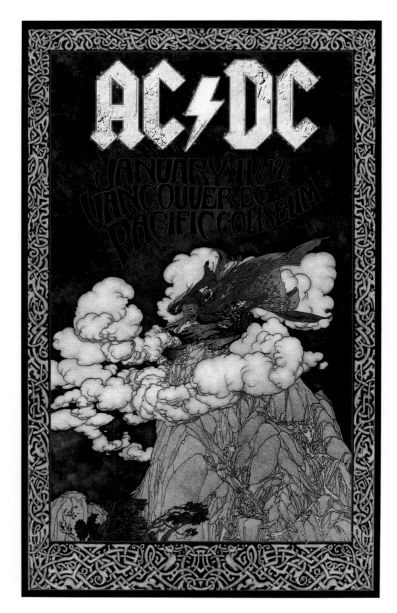

Above: The Razors Edge North American tour, 1990. *Artist: Michael Dole*

Left: The Razors Edge North
American tour, 1991.
Artist: Bob Masse/bmasse.com

Washington's. They got fined £2,000 in London the following year when they illegally replaced the image of the Queen on a snowstorm of facsimile pound notes.

⚡ ⚡ ⚡

After their Christmas break, the tour was overshadowed by a tragic accident at the Salt Palace in Salt Lake City, Utah, on January 18, 1991, which caused the deaths of three teenagers: Elizabeth Glausi, nineteen, and Jimmy Boyd Jr. and Curtis Child, both fourteen. It happened in the general admission standing area in front of the stage (4,400 tickets out of 13,300 for that show). An eyewitness, talking to Cathy Free for *People* magazine, said that, in one spot, for no obvious reason, the usual pushing and shoving "escalated" during the second song and "people four feet from the stage started falling on top of each other." Security men struggled to extricate them, but they couldn't do it quickly enough.

In the aftermath, some blamed AC/DC for carrying on, playing for two or three songs more songs, but from the stage they couldn't see anything going on and their management explained that they did stop "as soon as the gravity of the situation was communicated to them." Then they "stayed onstage [not playing] to minimize the confusion," discussed how to proceed with the city fire marshal (passing on messages to the crowd through Johnson), and, on the marshal's instructions, completed the show "to maintain calm and order."

Within weeks, an investigation completely cleared AC/DC of blame, but the parents of two of the children sued the venue, promoter, security, and the band, who may have contributed to a confidential out-of-court settlement that closed the case in December 1992. After that night, the band insisted on an improved safety zone at their concerts with more barriers to break up crowd surges.

The rest of 1991 passed more normally as they toured Europe (twice), the U.K., North America (twice), and Australasia. *The Razors Edge* benefited from hit singles in many countries for "Thunderstruck," "Moneytalks," and "Are You Ready."

At King's Hall in Belfast, Northern Ireland, on April 27, levity reasserted itself when Angus suffered a revelatory wardrobe malfunction. At the nightly moment when he ripped off one pair of shorts to reveal another beneath, in his stomping, thrashing, duck-walking frenzy, he didn't realize he'd ripped the front out of the second pair too. "I turned around to the audience and they're all sort of stunned," Angus once recalled (Stenning, unattributed). "I look down and there's my wedding tackle hanging out."

In August and September, they headlined a Monsters of Rock European tour that included countries in the former Eastern Bloc: Poland, Hungary, the Czech Republic, and, finally, at short notice, the U.S.S.R. The band heard about

this last event three days in advance, after playing the Estadio Olímpico in Barcelona on September 24. The logistics would have been impossible except that the Russian government de facto promoted the event as Soviet President Mikhail Gorbachev's and Russian President Boris Yeltsin's thank you to the young people of Moscow for their key role in holding off the hard-line Communist military coup attempt of August 19 to 21 (they'd barricaded streets with trolleybuses and, unarmed, mobbed army tanks until their crews gave up and turned around).

Masses of gear, two hundred fifty roadies, and the bands were summarily piled into two huge Antonov military transport planes—"outside toilets, hammer-throwing stewardesses," Johnson drily notes in his 2009 autobiography, *Rockers and Rollers*—and

Monsters of Rock program, Donington Park, England, August 17, 1991.

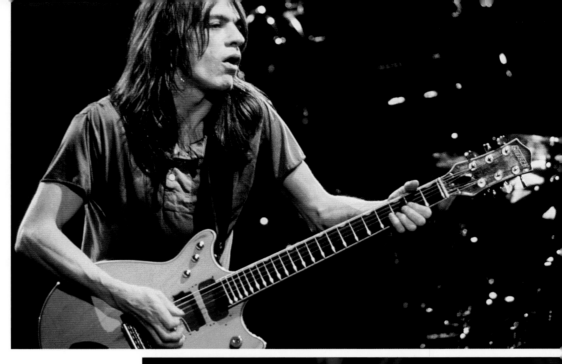

flown to Moscow within hours. Crowd estimates for the free show at Tushino Airfield ranged wildly from 100,000 to 2 million. The hippy vibe faded somewhat when the 20,000 to 50,000 police and soldiers present fell back on old habits and started pounding festival-goers with batons. Still, Johnson optimistically told the crowd this was a whole new kind of cultural exchange: "Opera and ballet did not cut the ice in the cold war years . . . it takes rock 'n' roll to make no more cold war" (Masino, unattributed). Conversely, *Pravda*, just granted independence from its traditional role as mouthpiece of the Party Central Committee, was less hopeful and gloomed that the clashes between fans and security forces "had put an end to short-lived post-coup euphoria" and the illusion that East and West might be "united at last."

After such a year, it must have been a relief for AC/DC to play Down Under again in October and November. The Youngs could see their families—although their father, William, had died of lung cancer in the 1980s. The whole band as usual spent time with Scott's parents in Fremantle. His father, Chick, would only visit them at their hotel but his mother, Isa, always came to the shows.

When they played New Zealand for the first time ever, they invited an old friend backstage in Auckland after the year's final show on November 16.

"It was the first time I'd seen them since I left the group," Phil Rudd told French magazine *Hard Rock* in 1996. "We talked about the good old times and our memories until three in the morning. I met Chris Slade who's an excellent drummer. . . .

He was well in and there was no reason for the situation to change rapidly. I wasn't thinking I had a chance of coming back to the group. But, after a few beers, that didn't stop me saying to Malcolm, 'If you need me, I'm available again.'" Malcolm's response is unrecorded, but Angus at least noted that Rudd "radiated health."

It gave AC/DC something to ponder as, after playing about 158 shows in twelve months, they subsided into another quiet year with avid reader and enthusiastic artist Angus for one starting to feel he had some living to catch up on. "There's a lot I missed, playing in a band," he told Martin Aston for the *Auckland Star*. "Don't get me wrong, I enjoy it, but sometimes you feel a bit hemmed in because you think, 'Jeez, I'd like to nick out and go down the road and spend a couple of hours reading a book, or nicking off down the art gallery. . . .'" ⚡

Don't get me wrong, I enjoy [playing in a band], but sometimes . . . you think, "Jeez, I'd like to nick out and go down the road and spend a couple of hours reading a book, or nicking off down [at] the art gallery or something."

—Angus Young, *Auckland Star*, 1990

This spread: Sydney Entertainment Centre, Sydney, October 14–15, 1991. *All Bob King/ Redferns/Getty Images*

The LPs
The Razors Edge

By Martin Popoff

Hard rockers stomped a crowded arena at the turn of the '90s, the genre having celebrated a full decade of dominance, kicked off by the New Wave of British Heavy Metal and then kicked up through MTV and a prolific and creative splintering into hair metal, thrash death, and finally grunge. Through buzzing eardrums, the old guard soldiered on, some flourishing, some on the wane.

AC/DC, unfortunately, found themselves on a bit of a bring-down. *Back in Black* was the happiest metal celebration of 1980, turning what could have been a wake for Bon Scott and a bomb for the band into—for millions—reason to live and live large through the travails of high school. *For Those About to Rock (We Salute You)* further pressed AC/DC into the patched denim of male teen culture—its sales, at the time and then over time, became a fraction of *Back*

in *Black*'s, but what a fraction. *Flick of the Switch* . . . don't get me started. This writer figures it's the best AC/DC record ever, and more objectively, the band's heaviest. But *Fly on the Wall*? *Blow Up Your Video*? There was a palpable gut feel that AC/DC had been consigned to obsolescence, that the one-note joke had run its course, that there were faster, hungrier crowds of fingers-a-flyin' bands worthy of taking over.

God luv 'em though, 'cos other than a tarting up of Angus' school uniform and an attendant slight poofing of the man's thinning mane, AC/DC resisted the explosion-at-the-paint-factory insanity that attacked acts like KISS and Ozzy and to some extent even Priest and Tony Iommi's revolving-door Black Sabbath. Even if the records reflected a malaise, cheerily, the aforementioned dull duo didn't clog up with power ballads and gang choruses and coke-

spoon productions. AC/DC in '86 and in '88 was still AC/DC, just a tired version thereof.

But it is of no mind, because the story ends happily, just as it did for Aerosmith (*Permanent Vacation*, *Pump*), Mötley Crüe (*Dr. Feelgood*), and yes, even KISS (*Revenge*), who all found a way to focus, work hard with what they had (sometimes not much), and turn out a creditable comeback album or two (true to the core but written smartly and with enthusiasm), and patiently and soberly taking a lot of time with a producer who cared.

This is exactly the AC/DC story at the turn of the dawn of the '90s as well. Dispensing with a few nitpicky negatives, 1990's *The Razors Edge* featured an ironically dull cliché of a title (and grammatically incorrect at that). Keeping up with Foreigner and Def Leppard, it also came wrapped in a crappy sleeve. Finally, there's the oft-debated presence of one Chris Slade on the drum throne. Like Mick Taylor in the Stones, Slade didn't look the part, and many fans attributed the slightly stiff and incredibly more-basic-than-usual performance on *The Razors Edge* to his creative limitations or lack of lubrication. Perhaps a kernel of truth to that, but one has to remember that the job description on the stool for this band is the most restrictive in the biz and that a strong-willed producer like Vancouver golden boy Bruce Fairbairn (gone too young) might have had some say as well, certainly, when it came to the porcelain clatter of the bass drum and high-hat sounds, dialed in, one would think, to make the record sound immediate and sharp.

Then the music begins, and AC/DC makes a remarkable turn, entering the decade as ambassadors of hard rock, a band no longer slightly unwelcome with their smutty jokes set to unsatisfying permutations of the same ol'. Nay, *The Razors Edge* is paced and braced and sequenced with invigorating peaks and valleys of songs and anthems and near-metal moments and all is right in the world again. "Thunderstruck" opens the record with an atmospheric dynamic similar to "For Those About to Rock" and "Who Made Who," the boys in no hurry to get to the rocking as Angus diddles a little, creating tension, building to an epic happy rock climax, good grooves, and football-match holler-alongs added for good cheer. "Thunderstruck" would find its way into

any respecting fan's tight fistful of concert favorites, the crowd perennially exploding for the myriad pregnant pauses that make it a creative triumph.

Elsewhere, *The Razors Edge* takes on a toughness that also made it competitive in a world about to go grunge. "Fire Your Guns" is a quick-hitting hard-charger with an aggressive, intelligent riff. The title track is an uncharacteristically dark plodder, as is the "Hells Bells"-ish "Are You Ready," which nonetheless gets beery and cheery again come chorus time. "Got You By the Balls" stomps a bit more predictably, but Brian Johnson's committed snarl and the geometric zag of the riff turn this one into another argument for calling *The Razors Edge* an agreeably metallic record.

Down a "You Shook Me All Night Long" tack (some call this southern-y, or melodic, or for the ladies), there's a second grammatical gremlin called "Moneytalks," which is this fairly hit-less record's

secondary, second, and last hit. Infectious tune to be sure, and again a concert fave, its simple charm enhanced by Fairbairn's uptight, ripped production. "Shot of Love," "Let's Make It," and the dimly monikered "Rock Your Heart Out" are of similar spirited party rock posture, while "Goodbye and Good Riddance to Bad Luck" rides a recline that recalls the warm sprawl of *For Those About to Rock*.

And the remainder? Well, let's call them amusing eccentricities, diversions, coloring, and shade for an album to give the sequencers something to sequence. "Mistress for Christmas" forever anchors the record seasonal. A combination of bells and balls, the best joke folded into this one is the discovery of how under-written it is. The final eccentricity is album closer "If You Dare," which combines an arch-AC/DC plod with the band's always bubbling-under bluesiness, some dark metal marching, and the tidy, book-ended idea of pregnant pauses, the standout feature of the album's first track eleven songs back.

All told, fans were satisfied, the album sold well, and, as alluded to, there was the happy, palpable shift that AC/DC was now forever, that they had become an essential and irremovable chapter in the book of rock, comfy worn slipper and bathrobe originals that had made a considerably good album, one that would put the band in the good graces of the rock public—hell, the general public!—forever. ⚡

Brisbane Entertainment Centre, Brisbane, February 4, 2001. © Newspix/Steve Pohlner

Chapter 9

Rock on the Richter Scale

In 1992, AC/DC's Great Slowdown began. For the next four years, this formerly peripatetic, hyperkinetic group played no gigs at all. Even so, Malcolm dealt fiercely with any journalistic suggestion they'd taken "a holiday." Through the summer, they put in a heap of work on *Live*. They believed it was the right moment because Brian Johnson had accrued his fair share of material in the set. Again with Bruce Fairbairn producing in Vancouver, they toiled through recordings of thirty shows to assemble two versions: one with twenty-three tracks, the other a recession-challenging cheaper model with fourteen.

Asked how live *Live* remained, Angus told American magazine *Circus* they'd cut out accidental feedback and general squeaking, but "when it comes to a bum note . . . if you were going to fix up that sort of thing, then it becomes a studio album" (Martin Huxley, *AC/DC: The World's Heaviest Rock*, unattributed). Malcolm candidly told Howard Johnson for *Metal Hammer* in 1992, he preferred 1978's *If You Want Blood You've Got It*: "We were young, fresh and vital and kicking ass." But when released worldwide in October and November, *Live* hit No. 15 in America, No. 5 in the U.K., and topped the chart in Australia.

Compiling *Live* wasn't the Youngs' only claim to still being at work. As usual, about three months after the previous world tour ended, Malcolm had called Angus with an invitation to "put our noses down to the grindstone"

[Angus] was running around with bruises all over him, blood pouring out his back, blood all over his elbows and knees.

—Brian Johnson on the then-forty-one-year-old lead guitarist's stage antics, *Sydney Daily Telegraph*, November 1996

(Simmons interview transcript, 1995) and start writing.

The first song emerged in early 1993, just as MTV cartoon slackers *Beavis and Butthead* became generational icons and confirmed AC/DC's standing by wearing their T-shirt. The band wanted to try out producer Rick Rubin, then renowned for his work with rappers Run-DMC and The Beastie Boys, but also with AC/DC emulators The Cult. He said he was a fan and agreed to handle "Big Gun" as a dry run.

They recorded it specifically for the soundtrack of Arnold Schwarzenegger's anticipated summer blockbuster, *Last Action Hero*, hence the lyrical references to "Terminators, Uzi makers/ Shootin' up Hollywood." Quid pro quo, Schwarzenegger appeared in the video. Heroically indeed, in front of hundreds of AC/DC fans, he donned an XXXXXL school uniform, duckwalked in giant step with tiny Angus, and then picked him up on one arm like a pet Chihuahua. The track did OK as a single—the movie lost $25 million.

⚡ ⚡ ⚡

[T]hose who replaced me weren't there except temporarily.

—Phil Rudd, *Hard Rock*, 1996

By July, AC/DC had agreed Rubin "seemed genuine" and agreed he should produce their next album, *Ballbreaker* (Angus to Sylvie Simmons, interview transcript). They started to get serious about developing the songs, sometimes with Chris Slade drumming for them. But the encounter with Phil Rudd in New Zealand at the end of the *Blow Up Your Video* tour had got Malcolm thinking. "He seemed just like the old Phil," Malcolm told Simmons for *Mojo* in 2000. "Me and Angus said, 'Let's bring him down and have a jam and see how it goes.'"

Malcolm rang him. "If I leave aside moments with my family, that phone call from Malcolm is one of the moments that I will never forget," Rudd told Phil Lageat for *Hard Rock* in 1996. "My feet didn't touch the ground, as I was trying to find a pen to write down his number." Come back to the band after ten years? Impossible. And yet, as Rudd told Lageat, he'd "thought about it a lot" and come to feel "that those who replaced me weren't there

"Big Gun" b/w "Back in Black (Live in Moscow)," U.K., 1993. *Bill Voccia Collection*

except temporarily." Maybe his interim life had run its (very active) course.

After his scrap with Malcolm in Nassau, Rudd had intended to go to America, but his mother died and he spent a few weeks with an uncle in New Zealand. He liked it, and, with his wife, he settled in the country between Tauranga and Rotorua: "Down there nobody knew me, it allowed me to start again on a sane basis," he told Lageat. He enjoyed a life involving hobbies and his children. He ran the ten-acre farm they lived on ("a few sheep and kiwis"), raced cars, won pistol-shooting competitions, operated a helicopter charter company (flew them too), and built a studio called Mountain where he produced various bands. After AC/DC sacked him, he didn't play drums for six years until he started a pub band.

Rudd flew to London.

Malcolm told Simmons in 1995 that, musically, he wanted to "get back to where we were on the old records" and felt their former drummer could be "the missing ingredient." When Rudd arrived at the studio, Malcolm simply asked him to sit down behind the drum kit and play. They started with old songs, "Gone Shootin'" and "What's Next to the Moon" (both from *Powerage*, 1978).

It felt astonishing. It felt normal. Rudd told Lageat, "We hadn't played together for a dozen years, [but] it was as if I'd just gone out for a packet of fags." His old rhythm twin Williams enthused to Lageat, "I love to play with Phil . . . with [Wright and Slade] we just tried to remake Phil's game. . . . . [Phil's] got this sixth sense, a natural feeling."

The Youngs agreed. Malcolm offered the drummer his job back. Rudd immediately thought he couldn't refuse, but he had other responsibilities. Back in New Zealand, he told Lageat, "My wife and I discussed it at length. But I am a drummer. That never left me. . . . And I didn't want my children to grow up hearing about what I *had* been. I thought it would be a good thing if they saw me play while I could."

The timeline on these events is unclear. Rudd's return may have been agreed upon as early as August 1993, yet not fully confirmed until the following May (Malcolm to Simmons, interview transcript, 1995). Although Malcolm always sincerely praised Slade as "the perfect drummer" and a good bloke, he perhaps didn't realize how much Slade loved AC/DC and how wounded he felt by the replacement process. Eventually, Slade told Lageat about it, for *Rock Hard* in 2001. Early on, he said, Malcolm warned him what might be afoot, but he asked him to "wait a few days" to

see what happened. "Days turned into months," said Slade. When the axe finally fell, he reacted much as Rudd had in 1983: "I was so disappointed, disgusted, that I didn't touch my drum kit for three years."

⚡ ⚡ ⚡

The cozy feelgoodness about Rudd's restoration soon dissipated when the *Ballbreaker* sessions sputtered. In October 1994, AC/DC came to the Power Station in New York raring to go, but Rubin couldn't get a drum sound that pleased him. Thump-thump. He shifted the mikes. Thump-thump. He had the walls and ceiling carpeted. Thump-thump. He put Rudd and his kit in a tent!

Mike Fraser, the engineer who'd worked on *The Razors Edge* and earned co-producer status on this album, told Lageat for *highwaytoacdc.com* in 2007, they "stayed there for six weeks because

I think that was paid for in advance." They had fifty hours on tape. After the Christmas break, once they moved to Ocean Way in Los Angeles, they dumped the lot.

Ex-Black Flag hardcore-punk icon Henry Rollins dropped by to see them in action. "AC/DC were like five roadies, zero pretension," he told Murray Engleheart and Arnaud Durieux in *AC/DC: Maximum Rock 'N' Roll.* A fitness fanatic, Rollins noted their "horrible posture" and "smoking endless cigarettes" as they "warmed up" by talking and drinking tea. When Rubin said the studio was ready, they went in and hammered out "Caught with Your Pants Down." Two takes. Work done, they vanished. Rubin told Rollins, "They walk in, they hit it, they leave. They don't fuck around." Awestruck by such simplicity, Rollins concluded, "It was watching genius at work."

United Center, Chicago, March 9, 1996.
James Crump/WireImage/Getty Images

However, he'd struck lucky. More often, the Rubin and AC/DC approaches clashed horribly. Sometimes the producer would demand maybe fifty takes, until, Johnson said, "You'd be sitting there going, 'Jesus, I'm sick of this bloody thing!'" (Simmons, *Mojo*). It provoked even Williams to impassioned eloquence: "Playing those tracks again and again," he told Lageat, "I thought we'd lose the sacred fire." Rubin's other eccentricities included sitting on the floor in his sunglasses doing yoga and absenting himself for hours (working on Red Hot Chili Peppers' *One Hot Minute* at the same time, apparently). He rubbed the rugged rockers raw. But Fraser's plain efficiency saw them through. "Mike knew what we wanted and could get it," Malcolm told Simmons. "So we had a kind of intermediary. . . . You've got to hang a medal on Mike."

Band opinion of Rubin never mellowed. In 2008, Malcolm told Richard Bienstock for *Guitar World*, "Rick's not a real rock 'n' roller, that's for sure. We would never go back to him. We thought he was a phony, to be honest!" (Of course, longtime Rubin client Johnny Cash, among others, would have completely disagreed—and, in fact, Rubin always spoke well of AC/DC.)

Nonetheless, the record rocked, from the solid grind of "Hard as a Rock" (another two-take job) through the slower, fruity swing of "Boogie Man" to the hard-driving "Ballbreaker." As intended, *Ballbreaker* harks back to the dynamics of earlier albums: consistent, unadorned, loud-and-quiet, girderous riffs and vocal howls alternating with maybe a tapping cymbal and the barest bass pulse.

Lyrically, in aggregate, *Ballbreaker* may be the crudest AC/DC album. "Cover You in Oil," "The Honey Roll," "Love Bomb," and "Ballbreaker" are in-your-face sex. But the Youngs did have wider interests. Fraser observed that Angus "has an opinion on everything, and he's concerned with everything that happens in the world" (Lageat, *highwaytoacdc. com*); the older they got, the more they

wrote about it. Malcolm's preoccupation with the Youngs' working-class roots as a common ground with their audience came through in his argument that "Hard as a Rock" is more than priapic. As he told Simmons in 1995, "It's also

Rick [Rubin]'s not a real rock 'n' roller, that's for sure. We would never go back to him. We thought he was a phony, to be honest!

—Malcolm Young, *Guitar World*, 2008

about a guy who's had enough . . . he's going to stand up hard as a rock. There's a lot of kids out there who've not got work, there's misery. . . . It's about fucking, but there's also a little message in there—stand up for yourself!"

The same working-class/rugged-individual bolshieness fires up *Ballbreaker*'s three overtly political songs: "The Furor," "Hail Caesar," and "Burnin' Alive." The last even takes a contemporary swing at "PR President" Bill Clinton's failure to avert the Waco tragedy in February 1993 (fifty-four adults and twenty-one children died in Texas when the FBI raided religious fanatic/megalomaniac David Koresh's Branch Davidian settlement).

Released in late September 1995 with Marvel Comics sleeve art illustrating the songs, *Ballbreaker* confirmed the

stability of AC/DC's commercial revival, even after four years' near silence. It hit No. 4 in the U.S., No. 6 in the U.K., No. 1 in Australia, and Top 10 in almost every "major market."

Technical rehearsals in January got the show-opening wrecking-ball-wall-smashing routine right—as well as the usual bell, cannon, and inflatable Rosie stunts. Then they hurled themselves into a tough year's touring, with more than 150 shows, beginning on January 12, 1996, in Greensboro, North Carolina, and ending November 30 in Christchurch, New Zealand. They visited North America twice, Europe, South America, and Australasia. En route, they began to feel their age for the first time; Johnson collapsed onstage in the heat of St. Louis (April 1) and later expressed his own concerns about Angus: "He

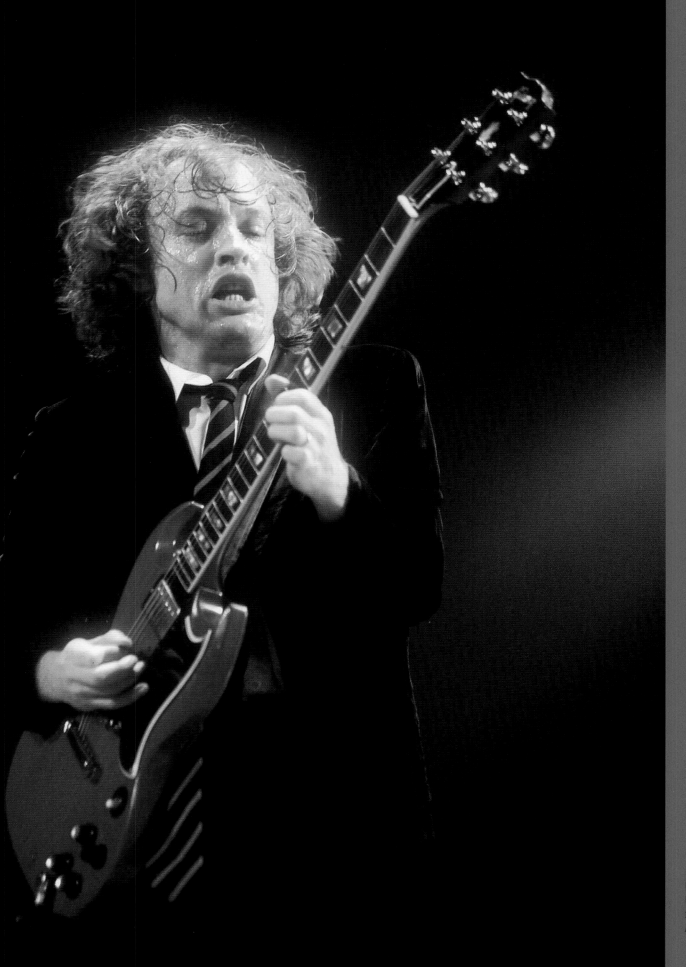

Melbourne Park, Melbourne, November 7, 1996. *Martin Philbey/ Redferns/Getty Images*

was running around with bruises all over him, blood pouring out his back, blood all over his elbows and knees," the singer told Angus Fontayne of the *Sydney Daily Telegraph.*

These huge, well-oiled-machine tours rarely gave rise to colorful anecdotes (although in Phoenix in September 2000, as one video available on the Internet shows, Angus did jump offstage to tweak a beer-chucker's nose), and as a business entity, AC/DC became even more staid when they switched management again. The new incumbent was New York–based Alvin Handwerker of weighty Prager & Young, whose clientele had included Irving Berlin, Bing Crosby, and Frank Sinatra.

Even so, the year closed with Cardinal Joseph Ratzinger (later Pope Benedict, then Prefect for the Congregation for the Doctrine of the Faith—formerly known as the Universal Inquisition) using the occasion of the November 22 Mass for Saint Cecilia, Patron Saint of Music, to describe rock as "an instrument of the Devil." Vatican officials enlarging on the sermon named AC/DC and, inevitably, explained how their initials stood for "Antichrist, Death to Christ" (Richard Owen, *The Times*). Of course.

⚡ ⚡ ⚡

The Youngs, including George, spent the first part of 1997 immersed in a project close to their hearts: a Bon Scott memorial box set. He'd proposed his own title way back, telling Malcolm "When I'm a fucking big shot . . . and they want me to do a solo album, I'll call it *Bonfire*." Combing through old tapes, they assembled two albums of previously unheard tracks, including a nicely raw historic moment: "She's Got Balls" from the night of Williams' incognito "Seedies" debut at Bondi Lifesavers (Scott extemporizing, "She makes my heart race/Every time she sits on my face"). They threw in the *Live from the Atlantic Studios* mini-album (recorded in 1979, only 5,000 promo copies pressed originally), a CD

from the *Let There Be Rock* film (from 1979, live in Paris), and, strangely, an optional extra remastered *Back in Black*. Released that November, *Bonfire* reached No. 21 in Australia and soon sold a million worldwide.

Their devotions concluded, in summer 1997 Angus and Malcolm started writing AC/DC's next at Angus' home in Holland, taking turns on guitars, bass, and drums. Angus quickly hit on the idea for the title track; driving in heavy traffic, thinking about Elvis, he mused on that tough-guy sneer he'd put into his upper lip. They worked on. Slowly. Other band members took their ease, though Johnson showed the unwritten rule on exclusivity had been relaxed by producing Florida band Neurotica's album *Seed* (April 1998) and co-writing a song with Jackyl.

45-cent AC/DC stamps issued in 1998.
Courtesy Australia Post

Coincidentally, 1999's two major AC/DC events happened in Vancouver. That May, Bruce Fairbairn, producer of *The Razors Edge* and *Live*, died suddenly; Angus and Malcolm showed their respect and loyalty by flying over for the funeral.

Promo pole poster, Australia, 2000.

There was this wonderful feeling of light-heartedness, a devil-may-care attitude. The lads went, "Aw fuck, just sing it the way you want to," whereas in the past the producers would always go "Sing high!"

—Brian Johnson on welcoming George Young back to the fold for *Stiff Upper Lip*, *Mojo*, 2000

Stiff Upper Lip album release private party guest pass, 2000. *Bill Voccia Collection*

In July, they returned there to record in Brian Adams' Warehouse Studios with a new-old team at the controls: regular Fairbairn associate and AC/DC favorite Mike Fraser engineering for producer . . . George Young! Hardly ancient at fifty-one, George had remained "semiretired" for five years after an amicable end to his partnership with Harry Vanda. But Angus and Malcolm still habitually sought their big brother's "stamp of approval," they told Simmons for *Mojo*. And George had talismanic status too. He represented their best chance of finding the true path back to their early days—a quest that had become *the* preoccupation of their middle years.

"George wants passion and performance," Malcolm told *KNAC.com* in 2000. "He doesn't give a fuck about technology." In later interviews, they constantly raved about how their brother understood "the swing," the spirit of Little Richard—the things that inspired all the Youngs as children.

AC/DC
NO BULL

Plaza De Toros De Las Ventas, MADRID | FILMED LIVE ON SUPER 16mm FILM

LOS DIAS 10 DE JULIO DE 1996 | EastWest Records America #40192-3

No Bull concert film poster, 1996 (VHS) and 2000 (DVD).

Johnson loved it too. Speaking to Simmons in the pages of *Mojo*, he alluded to another Young childhood hero: "There was this wonderful feeling of light-heartedness, a devil-may-care attitude. The lads went, 'Aw fuck, just sing it the way you want to,' whereas in the past the producers would always go 'Sing high!' But George Young threw a whole different light on it . . . on *Stiff Upper Lip*, I sound like Satchmo!"

After all their preparatory meanderings, the album really didn't take long. By October, Fraser was mixing the twelve tracks that emerged the following February, the other side of the millennium. It didn't do brilliantly—No. 7 in America, No. 3 in Australia, and No. 12 in the U.K.—though it did top the charts in Germany, Austria, Sweden, and elsewhere. But to this writer, *Stiff Upper Lip* is one of AC/DC's very best, fulfilling their instinctive, timeless ambition to simplify.

The track "Stiff Upper Lip" actually opens with a

Above and opposite: Philips Arena, Atlanta, Georgia, August 17, 2000.
© Robb D. Cohen/Retna Ltd.

Stiff Upper Lip North American tour.
Artist: Lindsey Kuhn/swamposters.com

guitar run that could have been conceived by Chuck Berry. But after that the album is all riffs, that big swing of theirs the more powerful because of the open space around it, plus an intangible: warmth. The guitars, in tight unison, in close harmony. Johnson's salty, lower, older voice (admiringly applauded by the band at the end of "Can't Stand Still"). Lyrics that get the joke about almost everything, whether it's sex ("All Screwed Up") or the TV going on the fritz ("Satellite Blues"). Is lighthearted hard-and-heavy possible? AC/DC pull it off, even with their now expected acid drop of politics, sideswiping Mayor Rudy Giuliani's crime-fighting campaign with "Safe in New York City" and bemoaning smoking restrictions in "Damned" ("Don't light no cigarettes/Else you'll wind up in the can").

Off around the world for another year, beginning July 31, 2000, in Grand Rapids, Michigan, and ending July 8, 2001, in Cologne, Germany, the band did about 145 shows in North America, Europe, Australasia, and Japan. They brought along a couple of new friends too: a giant inflatable stripper for

Manchester Evening News Arena, Manchester, England, December 1, 2000. *Jon Super/Redferns/Getty Images*

Guitar Center Rockwalk induction, Hollywood, September 15, 2000. *Robert Knight Archive/ Redferns/Getty Images*

"Whole Lotta Rosie" and a forty-foot "statue" of Angus that turned out to be quite a performer, breathing smoke during "Thunderstruck," growing horns for "Hells Bells," and turning into a firework display at the climax of Angus' "Let There Be Rock" solo.

Veterans that they'd become—from Angus' forty-six to Johnson's fifty-three, the band in its twenty-eighth year—they began to acquire recognition for sheer longevity. *Kerrang!* magazine gave them its Lifetime Achievement award in 1998, and Madrid named a street after them (Malcolm typically expressed satisfaction that it was in

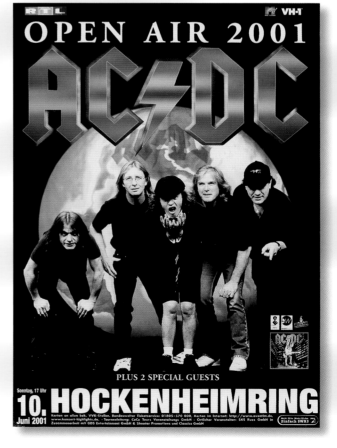

"a working-class area"). Meanwhile, in rural Scotland, on July 9, 2001, little Kirriemuir opened the Gateway to the Glens Museum featuring exhibits dedicated to the town's most famous sons: J. M. Barrie, creator of Peter Pan, and Bon Scott, creator of "Whole Lotta Rosie." ⚡

The LPs
Ballbreaker

By Garth Cartwright

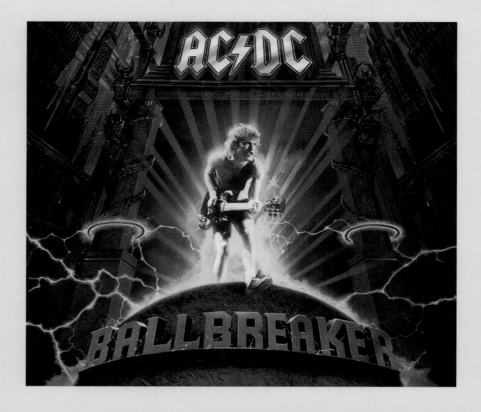

Back in 1995 the news of *Ballbreaker*'s forthcoming release had longtime AC/DC fans cheering. Original drummer Phil Rudd back behind the kit for the first time since 1983! Über-producer Rick Rubin at the controls! Ohmigawd, sounds too good to be true! Was *Ballbreaker* "too good to be true"? Some would say so. Some would say not. Let's consider what happens when you put the Aussie pit bulls in the studio with a New York metal and hip-hop guru.

First things first: Let's give the drummer some! Phil Rudd's indelible contribution to AC/DC was evident to anyone listening to the albums the band made after his departure. The two drummers who occupied the AC/DC drum seat across the next decade—Simon Wright and Chris Slade—may have been consummate professionals, but they lacked Rudd's simplicity, the ability to play in the pocket, to lay down a swaggering, fatback rock 'n' roll beat that galvanized the Youngs' guitar boogie. Fans noticed this. I interviewed Metallica's

Lars Ulrich in 1989, and he commented that since Rudd's departure AC/DC hadn't sounded right, adding how studying Rudd had allowed him to stop being such a fussy, showy drummer and get down to driving the rhythm along. Playing Auckland, New Zealand, in 1991 they invited Rudd (a New Zealand resident) to attend. Over cigarettes and tea, they established Rudd was now sober (Malcolm Young had fired Rudd over his drug/alcohol dependency during the recording of 1983's *Flick of the Switch*—and bygones were bygones. The young AC/DC was known to have sorted out interband disputes with fists rather than words. Now, older and very much richer, they must have seen in Rudd—who appeared to have barely aged during his absence—a reminder of when the band was a gang and every gig was an adventure. When AC/DC regrouped in 1994, Rudd was reoffered the drummer's seat. A decade of easy living (he flew helicopters, raced cars, won target-shooting competitions, and farmed) hadn't rusted his skills.

If resurrecting Rudd suggested a desire to revitalize AC/DC's sound, then hiring the world's most celebrated producer hinted at a willingness to push the musical envelope. New York–born Rick Rubin had loved AC/DC ever since hearing *Powerage* as a teenager. Rubin became rich and famous with his pioneering productions of rappers LL Cool J, The Beastie Boys, and Run-DMC. Having paired the latter with Aerosmith for "Walk This Way" and produced Slayer, Rubin had proved to be the most inventive hard rock producer of his generation. Rubin loudly praised AC/DC (so making many a hipster suddenly decide to check the band out for the first time) and sampled their records (without permission) on early Beastie Boys' singles "Rock Hard" and "She's On It." (Both remain unavailable today, as AC/DC have refused to allow their music to be sampled.)

Rubin often described Mutt Lange's productions of AC/DC as what most influenced his own work (those huge, swinging rhythms, crunching guitars, and raw vocals—no sweetening, no clutter)

and continually suggested in interviews that he believed he could do something fresh with the band. He even produced an imitation AC/DC album with The Cult's 1987 opus, *Electric*. AC/DC, who have never displayed the slightest interest in following fashion or being associated with media favorites, stridently ignored Rubin (he even approached them to produce *The Razors Edge*).

Then the producer got his chance. In 1993, Rubin was put in control of producing the *Last Action Hero* soundtrack and managed to get AC/DC in the studio for one song: "Big Gun." The film flopped, but the recording experience was considered a success by all involved and AC/DC signed Rubin for their next studio album.

Rubin was very hot at the time. He had transformed The Red Hot Chili Peppers from alt-rock also-rans to stadium superstars and reinvented Johnny Cash for a new generation. AC/DC may have been hoping for some of Rubin's magic to rub off on *Ballbreaker*—the half-decade gap between it

and their previous album, *The Razors Edge*, had seen Nirvana reinvent hard rock and left AC/DC looking a little, well, over the hill. In teaming with Rubin, AC/DC looked to reconnect with their elemental rock 'n' roll roots.

The resulting album is streamlined, turbocharged, hungry. As one would expect from Rubin, there is no clutter and the sound is dynamic. But if fans expected something new, or even a re-creation of their Mutt Lange–era greatness, they were to be disappointed. *Ballbreaker* is, ultimately, a journeyman AC/DC album—not their worst but nowhere near their best, either. The hard work is evident in listening to it, but little magic spills from the speakers. Inevitably, perhaps, the band and Rubin

clashed in the studio. The producer worked slowly and expected the band to go away and rework songs. AC/DC refused. Tension had sabotaged relations with Mutt Lange during the *For Those About to Rock (We Salute You)* sessions and *Ballbreaker* involved a similar clash. Rubin (who was simultaneously working on The Red Hot Chili Peppers' *One Hot Minute* album) was unable to make the AC/DC record he wanted and so left things in control of engineer Mike Fraser (who gets a co-production credit). That Fraser also mixed the album suggests Rubin had washed his hands of it before completion. Malcolm Young would later dismiss Rubin as a "waste of time."

Released in September 1995, *Ballbreaker* nevertheless quickly sold a solid million copies in the United States— a success, if a disappointing one compared to the five million U.S. sales for *The Razors Edge*. That the band has kept "Hard as a Rock" and "Hail Caesar" in their live set suggests they like *Ballbreaker*'s songs if not the recording sessions. And, hey, it was nice to hear Phil Rudd's minimalist thud again. Give the drummer some! ⚡

The Boxes
Bonfire

By Gary Graff

By the time 1997 rolled around, AC/DC was at a point where it could do things any way it pleased, no matter how much sense it made—evidence the quizzical release of the *Bonfire* box set.

The lavishly packaged five-CD salute to the late Bon Scott, put together to fulfill a contractual obligation, wasn't timed to the frontman's birth or the anniversary of his death. Nor did it reflect any meaningful mark in the history of *Back in Black*, the blockbuster studio release with new frontman Brian Johnson that's included in the *Bonfire* package because, as Malcolm Young explained, "It was our tribute to him, so it felt right to include it with the rest of the stuff."

Fortunately, that "stuff" amounted to a treasure trove for fans of Scott-era AC/DC and a tutorial for later arrivals aboard the group's rock 'n' roll train. The most notable material appears on the disc subtitled *Volts*, an odds 'n' sods collection of demos and rarities whose ten tracks nicely complement the official catalog. Among the highlights are: early, in-progress versions of "Whole Lotta Rosie" (titled "Dirty Eyes") and "Beating around the Bush" ("Backseat Confidential"); the first recording of "If You Want Blood You Got It"; alternative versions of "Touch Too Much" and "Get It Hot," whose primary differences are lyrical; an eight-minute stomp through "She's Got Balls" from the Bondi Lifesaver concert in 1977; and a performance of "Sin City" from a September 1978 appearance on *The Midnight Special*. Tossing in the cover of Chuck Berry's "School Days" from the Australian *T.N.T.* album was a nice touch as well, nodding to the roots that bound AC/DC together.

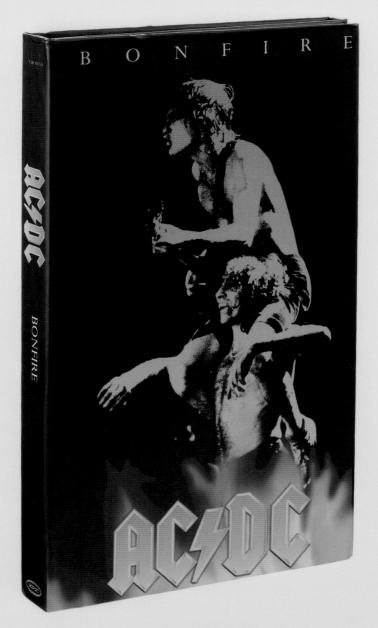

Bonfire also brought to market some other material much sought-after—and frequently bootlegged—by the AC/DC faithful. It marked the first official release of *Live from the Atlantic Studios*, an eight-song in-house performance from December 1977 for the group's then-American record company that was previously available only as a promotional vinyl release. If the group's studio albums at the time sounded like it was still finding its footing, *Live from the Atlantic* was something of a head-turner that gave radio programmers, press, and others lucky enough to be on the promo list a taste of the band's live power. There's a kind of claustrophobic, caged feel to

the set that actually works to its advantage, preserving the raw grit of what you'd have imagined AC/DC's early club performances to be like.

The flip side of that is on the two discs of *Let There Be Rock: The Movie—Live in Paris*, the previously unreleased soundtrack that does the official 1978 live album *If You Want Blood You've Got It* one better by capturing an entire set from December 9, 1979, with "Walk All Over You" restored to its full length after being edited for the film, and "T.N.T.," which had been dropped from the movie altogether. *Live in Paris* is AC/DC in their post–*Highway to Hell* glory, finally tasting a degree of arena-sized mania and making the most of it, with Angus Young letting loose particularly during long workouts on "Bad Boy Boogie," "High Voltage," and "Let There Be Rock," while Scott's flamboyant, bare-chested machismo showmanship is on full display. It's the most definitive concert document of Scott's tenure with the band.

Bonfire also loaded up on the extra treats, including guitar picks, posters, and a booklet that featured some of Scott's handwritten lyrics—and, of course, the iconic cover image of Angus soloing while perched on the singer's shoulders. All told it's an odd set of stuff, and one wonders how Brian Johnson felt about living under the specter of yet *another* salute to his predecessor, but it certainly puts some aural flesh on the myth that grew around Scott after his death. ⚡

The LPs
Stiff Upper Lip

By David Dunlap Jr.

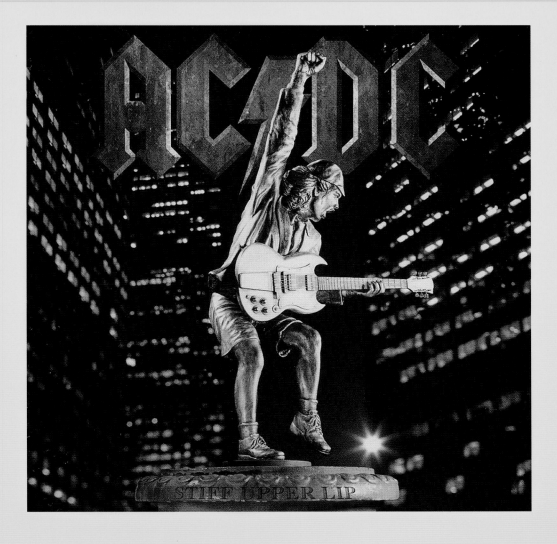

Critics have derided AC/DC for essentially playing the same song over and over for decades. Even die-hard fans would concede that the group rarely strays from its proven hard-rocking formula. Of course, if AC/DC could make a record that is as fun and riff-laden as *Stiff Upper Lip* in 2000, twenty-seven years into their career, fans won't mind a bit if the legendary five-piece stays the course.

Despite the obvious priapic connotation, *Stiff Upper Lip* is a more sophisticated work than *Ballbreaker*, the band's previous release, which came five years earlier. The Anglophilic title evokes P. G. Wodehouse's aristocratic comedy of manners; *Ballbreaker*'s name did little more than allude to testicles. The striking image of Angus Young with fist raised in statuary form, bronzed like a baby's bootie, graces the front of *Stiff Upper Lip*; the cover of *Ballbreaker* features an electrified Angus

duck-walking on top of a sphere and is nondescript by comparison.

However, those differences are merely cosmetic. The biggest upgrade is evident in the album's production. No offense to Rick Rubin, who was credited with helming *Ballbreaker*, but on *Stiff Upper Lip* he is surely outclassed by George Young, ex-Easybeat and older brother to Malcom and Angus. In addition to the fraternal connection, George had minded the boards on the classic, early AC/DC run from *High Voltage* to *Powerage*. Most recently, he had co-produced *Blow Up Your Video* (1988). More than anyone, he knew when to lead and when to get out of the way and let the band make its gritty brand of heavy blues rock. The opening title track is a great example. It's an energetic, but unhurried rocker that sets the proper tone for the rest of the album.

Other standouts include the swaggering

"House of Jazz," the slow-boiling "Can't Stand Still," and the defiant "Can't Stop Rock 'n' Roll." All were great ammunition against those who claimed that Brian Johnson's voice had become too laryngitic and strained to be effective. Johnson sounds like he's having a blast and his pipes are remarkably intact. Although "Stiff Upper Lip" was the first released single and most popular song from the album, Johnson favored "Satellite Blues" and petitioned that the band release it as well. It's a simple, powerful rock song that blends lyrics about a sexy dancer and poor television reception in the seamless way that only AC/DC can.

"Safe in New York City" didn't chart as well as "Stiff Upper Lip" or "Satellite Blues," but it's the strongest track on the album. The staggered arrangement is a great showcase for the other members of the band who sometimes get overlooked behind Johnson and Angus. The younger Young brothers had

Stiff Upper Lip
European tour, Praha,
Czech Republic.

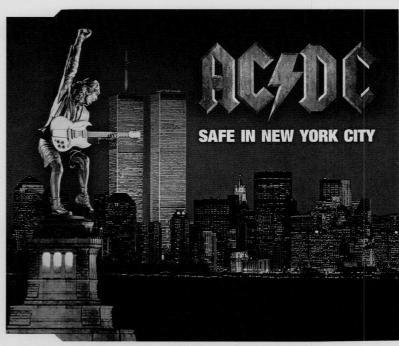

"Safe in New York City" b/w "Cyberspace" and "Back in Black (Live)," CD single, 2000.

originally intended the song to poke fun at the sanitized, post-Giuliani Big Apple, but it's the catchy, fist-pumping, chorus that edges the song from good to great.

In a perfect world, "Safe in New York City" might have been one of the band's most popular songs since 1990's "Thunderstruck," but after September 11, 2001, many no longer felt safe at all in New York City. Since then, the song has essentially been removed from the band's live repertoire. It didn't help matters that the song's single cover featured the bronze Angus statue with the twin towers featured prominently in the background.

AC/DC is known for their elaborate stage sets and the *Stiff Upper Lip* tour was no exception. The star of stage was a thirty-foot recreation of the bronze Angus statue that the band nicknamed Junior. The statue breathed smoke and fire and its horns even glowed red during "Highway to Hell." The intro film for the tour featured the bronze Angus going around the world causing mischief and mayhem to famous monuments. He crushes the Colosseum, clambers up the Eiffel Tower, and carries off the Statue of Liberty like a conquered cavewoman. Unfortunately, a scene in which two fighter jets streak past the World Trade Center and explosive missiles at Junior ensure that the intro film won't be in heavy rotation.

The members of AC/DC dealt with their own more personal tragedy of Bon Scott's untimely death by throwing themselves into their work and making some incredible records along the way. They've held steadfastly to their credo of keeping their music simple and fun. *Stiff Upper Lip* may sound highfalutin', or it may be just another adolescent phallic reference, but it also connotes steely resolve. And it's that quality that gave AC/DC the ability to make such an uncompromising, entertaining record so late in their career. ⚡

Stiff Upper Lip North American tour.
Artist: Mark Arminski/arminski.com

The Live Releases

By Ian Christe

In the beginning, back in 1973, man didn't know 'bout a rock 'n' roll show and all that jive. But very soon after, the brothers Malcolm and Angus Young joined forces with ex-Valentines singer Bon Scott, and rock 'n' roll started careening recklessly toward nonstop headbanging heavy metal. No AC/DC studio album can compete with the live records, where the band is captured naked and raw in its natural environment. I mean, who else makes James Brown's previously untouchable *Live at the Apollo* sound like easy listening?

Basically, AC/DC's live albums are part souvenir program, part instruction manual—especially in the early days. And now for younger listeners, these field recordings reveal what to expect when the time comes (as it does in every rocker's life) to enter the darkened arena. First the spotlight waggles, and then the first resounding chords jangle

out of Angus' Gibson SG. Then all hell breaks loose for a furious couple of hours.

All the clever art direction and posed studio shots of the early albums didn't define AC/DC—this band's image hangs on touchstones of the live show: the curled sneer of Angus Young's loose upper lip, the tight jeans of Bon Scott, and, in later years, the confident index finger of Brian Johnson thrust outward against the screaming throng of thousands.

By late 1978, when their first live release, *If You Want Blood You've Got It*, burst forth, AC/DC had been put through their paces by five years of conquests and hard knocks—including opening slots with Black Sabbath, Rainbow, Alice Cooper, Scorpions, KISS, UFO, Journey, and, yep, REO Speedwagon. Angus' schoolboy getup was just a front—but audiences had not all figured that out yet. He wasn't an icon

yet, he was a gimmick: a trick to lower expectations so that the band could wallop unsuspecting concertgoers over the head and give them a mark to remember.

Historical essays tend to reveal inconvenient truths about live albums—that such and such a classic was released to fulfill a recording contract, to cover up a creative dry spell, or to buy time during a stint in rehab. I prefer to believe that AC/DC shrewdly wanted to burst out of the prim album format and let the sweat and electricity run wild. The AC/DC unleashed displayed everything rock 'n' roll had ever offered in a sexed-up, high-octane slam. Maybe somewhere in some remote blues bayou, the answers came this hard, but AC/DC had ten times the duck of Chuck Berry, five times the speed of The Ramones, twice the chops of Led Zeppelin, and all the grit of Mötörhead.

While punk rock bit the heels of the heavy rock forefathers, AC/DC stood their ground with a kind of street class. On *If You Want Blood* (recorded largely at the Glasgow Apollo during the *Powerage* tour), they were Australian jackals chewing up the punk rats, with the musical weapons to back up their belligerent attitude. "Riff Raff" with its black-and-blue riffs showed what kind of punks they were. Practice made AC/DC nearly perfect. The band had played "High Voltage," "Problem Child," and "Whole Lotta Rosie" only dozens of times before the official recordings. By the time *If You Want Blood* hit, the band had made those songs set staples, polished by hundreds of performances.

Two things that stand out about *If You Want Blood* compared to any live film or video are Malcolm Young and Phil Rudd. Close your eyes and forget about the herky-jerky visual circus of Angus, because on this recording the feet-planted Malcolm, the wizard in his dirty T-shirt, is at the foreground, stomping all kind of ass. He's deadly. And Rudd the metal stamper is equally in your face, no doubt chain-smoking while throbbing and racing like a thoroughbred.

If You Want Blood was Bon Scott's last album before *Highway to Hell*, the record that changed everything. *Highway to Hell* went gold in America in the first week of December 1979, and by February 19, 1980, Bon had become a victim of "death by misadventure." The live album had made a big difference, helping push the hot former opening act over the top. The lyrics and mannerisms anyone could have copped—but the call and response, the greetings, and the impromptu screams were all and only Bon, and they became pure legend.

A great record of Bon performing material from *Highway to Hell* exists in the form of *Let There Be Rock: The Movie*, a concert film recorded in Paris on December 9, 1979. The fourteen-song live soundtrack was released as part of the *Bonfire* box set in 1997. Compared to *If You Want Blood*, which was meticulously constructed from prime 1978 shows, *Let There Be Rock: The Movie* is not the handpicked best of the best, but simply a typically great performance from the last hours of the Bon Scott era. The lengthy solo breaks are probably more interesting with the visuals turned off. But you can tell that AC/DC had triumphed by 1979, that their angry rise had won them the prize.

Another fantastic live document, *Live from the Atlantic Studios* was recorded in 1977 and predates the recordings that made up *If You Want Blood*. The problem was that

for over a decade, nobody officially heard the tapes except the lucky few rock radio programmers, in their satin jackets and ponytails, who scored vinyl promo copies back in 1978.

The eight songs on *Live from the Atlantic Studios* were like the sacred scrolls of AC/DC when uncovered for a CD in 1986, especially once unveiled on a wider scale on the *Bonfire* box set in 1997. Though the band was playing to a small crowd in a controlled environment, they showed that *If You Want Blood* was no fluke—the band was simply always on time. Who else can throw out so much energy without ever derailing the rhythmic momentum?

The pounding pulse of Atlantic Studios is closer to "Rocker" than the pompous heights of "Let There Be Rock" (how the world's most immediate band ever wrote an epic song that mentions Tchaikovsky,

only the 1970s will know, but it made for great stagecraft). And *Live from the Atlantic Studios* is one for the Cliff Williams fans, as the rhythm section is pumped loud for a change, exposing every thump, boom, and wicked change of pace from one of the most underrated and valuable bassists in rock.

Live from the Atlantic Studios was an exclusive affair, though recorded live. *If You Want Blood* was the product of theatres. Following Bon Scott's death, with the success of the *Back in Black* album and the mighty stewardship of Brian Johnson, AC/DC became truly massive—an arena band outselling sports teams on their own turf. So the band traded its sharp edges for the massive-bore firepower needed to level stadiums.

By 1992, the band's energy had downshifted to a more powerful gear, and that year brought *AC/DC Live*, a new nod to tradition that finally gave Johnson his turn

to shoot for posterity with a live album. The majority here are post-1980 anthems, most of them from *Back in Black*—including "Shoot to Thrill" and the band's three most famous songs ever—settling the score somewhat without upsetting the Bon Scott legacy. To his enormous credit, Johnson from the very start knew how to stand *beside* Bon's shadow, never underneath it.

If the album doesn't sound powerful, you aren't doing it right—*AC/DC Live* means to be played loud at serious wattage. Bigger is better in this case. Significantly, the record documents hell's bell clanging and the twenty-one-gun cannon salute of "For Those About to Rock," by now cornerstones of the event. These cues charged up a new generation heading to the concert halls, including AC/DC neophytes of 1992 who were not yet born during Bon Scott's lifetime.

AC/DC concerts have come to seem eternal, reliably outpouring huge amounts of power on a frequent basis for decades. For those of us who already know how the story goes, the ringing tones of that haunting bell, the mass chants of the familiar sing-alongs, and the roar of the dark, primal electric blues on a worldwide stage live in many ways and many formats, including in our memories. After the heads are shaken and earth has quaked, the band's live albums are the best way to say, yes, AC/DC really happened. ⚡

Etihad Stadium, Melbourne, February 11, 2010. © *Newspix /Ian Currie*

Chapter 10

No Wuckin' Furries

Come the new millennium, AC/DC's old exclusivity rule relaxed even more. Less than three months after their world tour ended, Brian Johnson was back in action with Geordie II, the band he'd left to join AC/DC. They played grand Newcastle Opera House on September 28, 2001, and then three workingmen's clubs, concluding on October 8 at Heaton Buffs, which had paid them a handsome £120 on the night when Johnson returned from his first AC/DC audition. Their setlist, the same as twenty years earlier, ranged from "Whole Lotta Rosie" through covers of Led Zeppelin and Tyneside's own The Animals to folk and mining songs ("Geordie's Lost His Liggie"). The old crowd loved it, and Johnson talked to dozens of them in the bar afterward.

That month Phil Lageat of *Rock Hard* asked him about the next AC/DC album. "Malcolm told me last week he was working on new compositions," said Johnson. "We're going to do everything we can to get an album out as quickly as possible."

Mmmmm . . .

⚡ ⚡ ⚡

While fans waited—until 2008—AC/DC's new label Columbia's re-release program from 2003 onward sold more than 20 million albums worldwide, building toward AC/DC's prodigious 2010 career figures of about 200 million albums, 50 million of *Back in Black* alone. So how did they do it?

Looks-wise, their rugged, sweat-soaked charm has certainly appealed to

> **Does it make you want to boil your sneakers and make soup outta your girlfriend's panties? If it doesn't, then it ain't AC/DC.**
>
> —Aerosmith's Steven Tyler inducting AC/DC into the Rock and Roll Hall of Fame, March 10, 2003

some males and attracted some females, though Johnson suspects they're past it in that regard as he confessed to Lynda Lacoste for *Le Mag* in 2000: "This superb girl, 21, big breasts, legs up to here, came up to me and said she'd like to take me home. I said, 'OK, super.' Then she said, 'I want to introduce you to my mother'!"

The one member of the band who really did have sexual charisma was Bon Scott. As Angus told Richard Bienstock for *Guitar World* in 2008, "You could see him coming from a mile away." Once AC/DC lost him, their appeal had to shift back to the collective: the music, the show, the shared knowledge that what they do is honest, believable, and reliable (partly because it's always the same, more or less, and no apologies for that). In his teens, Malcolm determined it should be that way, having studied how The Beatles and The Rolling Stones diversified and then got back to rock 'n' roll: "It's best just to stay where you're at. You're going to come back there anyway," he told David Sinclair of *Q* in 1990. "Why not simply work better and harder at what you've got?"

AC/DC understand their relationship with their audience because it's a matter of principle. Angus always sensed the school uniform helped "the kids" recognize themselves in him. In return then—in good faith—he once said, "You've got to go all the way. I believe you've got nothing to fear. . . . I've never been afraid" (Paul Stenning, *AC/DC: Two Sides to Every Glory*, unattributed). Johnson, who's often seen Angus snort "Fuck it!" and play a gig when doctors told him he mustn't—gashes, infections, illnesses—associates this full-on, no-surrender attitude with the working-class background he recognized when he joined the band: "They had this wonderful air of just being at work with some mates," he told James McNair of *Q* in 2009. "I still call them my workmates to this day. AC/DC are the most industrious bunch of guys I've ever known."

"I look at it this way," Angus told *Rolling Stone*'s David Fricke in 2008. "I didn't have any great prospects for a career, with the education I had. When I started doing this, I thought, 'You gotta give it 200 percent.' Because it was your survival. It was the job, what was going to put food on the table." AC/DC and their music are a living fanfare for the common man—and woman.

Not that they never put a foot wrong, of course, but this almost puritan honesty is embodied even in the small detail of how they make their music. Angus and Malcolm hardly ever use effects pedals. Phil Rudd never uses an electronic click track to keep time ("Man, you can't rock to a click, it just doesn't happen" he told *cyberdrum.com* in 2000). Inevitably, because music isn't easy, the rock 'n' roll Holy Grail integrity they want is sometimes more sought after than achieved. Malcolm expressed the difficulties of finding a true path through old/new, real/artificial, live/recording to Sylvie Simmons for *Mojo* in 2000, reflecting on AC/DC's production problems after *Back in Black*: "It was the *sound* [Mutt Lange] was looking for, whereas we were thinking of the *music*. . . . [In the old days] we used to finish a gig at about two in the morning, then drive down to the studio. George and Harry would have a couple of dozen cans in and a few bottles of Jack Daniel's, and we'd all have a party and rip it up . . . so it was the same loose feeling like we were onstage still. The studio was just like an extension of the gig back then."

The music always is simple, too, because "everything comes from the rhythm," Angus explained to Thierry Chatain for *Rock & Folk* way back in 1980. "It's the base and the feeling of what we play. We want people to physically feel the energy we put out. Every watt." But then there are discombobulating times

> # It's best just to stay where you're at. . . . Why not simply work better and harder at what you've got?
>
> —Malcolm Young, *Q*, 1990

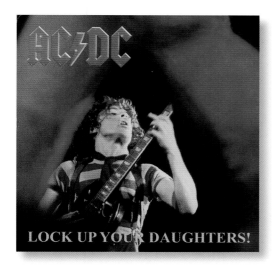
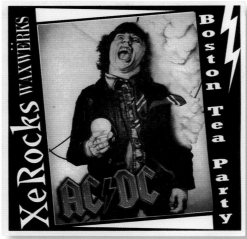

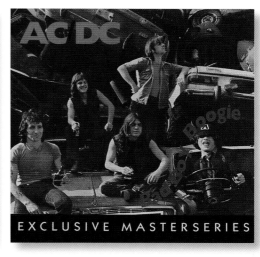

Unofficial releases.

when even Angus can't find that beat. "If I'm bouncing up and down and having fun, then that's music," he told Danny Eccleston of *Q* in 1995. "But if my foot is swimming round in the dark or it's like randomly stomping on cockroaches, I'm a little bit lost." Even the lyrics fit the picture at times: "Bon began as a drummer, so he took care that the words fell *rhythmically*," Angus told Lageat for *Hard Rock*, 1998.

Even Bon Scott may play a posthumous role, although in another aspect of AC/DC's dependability: their well-controlled egos. His memory hangs in the ether around them. These rugged unsentimentalists occasionally talk of seeing him in a dream, of a strange incorporeal force taking a blocked lyricist's hand (Johnson experienced the latter while writing "Hells Bells" in

1980). While he joked to Tom Doyle of *Q* about "keeping the light on all night, man," he didn't feel spooked for long. On the contrary, he told Lacoste, "Bon is always there, and his memory has been a great help to me . . . the lads talk about him as if he were still among us, and that's marvelous. . . . I only have one regret; that I never knew him. I think he'd have been a real mate." It's as if Scott, in absence, is AC/DC's higher power, reminding them that ego must take second place to the group.

But anyway, they really are good at getting over themselves. For instance, AC/DC haven't been immune to addictions, which diminish individual contributions and lead to introversion and self-pity. But they fought their way out: Malcolm, Rudd, and Johnson too. (He admitted to Doyle that soon after

Back in Black, "I tried my first line of cocaine, and I thought, 'Ooh, this is the answer to everything.' I was on it for about six months, and I just went, 'What the fuck am I doing?' I couldn't even talk, never mind sing.")

And when it comes to playing, as a team with a leader, they work to keep their minds on the music, the band, the audience. Mike Fraser watched them in action while engineering or co-producing four AC/DC studio albums. "Malcolm talks most, he's the captain of the ship, but he always consults Angus," he told Phil Lageat for *highwaytoacdc. com* in 2007. "Brian gives his opinion and makes suggestions, as do Phil and Cliff." And that's fine. Cliff Williams is quite clear and content about his support role—sometimes the Youngs tell him what to play, sometimes they ask

> # Malcolm talks most; he's the captain of the ship, but he always consults Angus. Brian gives his opinion and makes suggestions, as do Phil and Cliff.

—Engineer and co-producer Mike Fraser, *Let There Be Light*, 2007

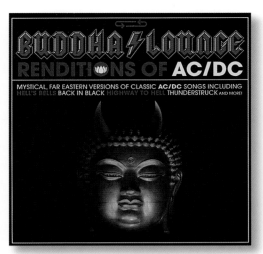

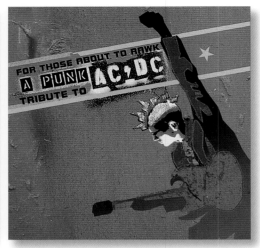

him to create a bass line. Either way, concentrating on the song, forgetting himself, "I give 'em what they want," he told Lageat (*Hard Rock*, 1996). "I don't have any problem doing this because I enjoy playing simply. I never feel angry or like a prisoner."

Sibling rivalry, though—that's a different test. In 2000, *KNAC.com* asked Malcolm whether he'd ever felt a moment of jealousy about younger brother Angus taking center stage in the band he founded? "Angus is a star, no doubt about that," Malcolm replied. "[But] I found my place in the group." Reciprocally, even in middle age, and bar the odd shouting match, Angus still fundamentally defers to his brother's fiery leadership. Speaking to Jan Olbrecht of *Guitar Player* in 1984, he explained, "Malcolm does inspire me. He has very high standards. Like, he'll say, 'I want this to rock like thunder,' and you've got to make it rock. . . . I need my brother, the two of us together. . . . He's the solid thing; he pumps it along. I don't think anyone can do what he does. He's very clean; he's very hard. It's an attack. Anyone [who] sees him or knows about guitars can tell."

It comes down to a love of rock 'n' roll that's like immersion in the faith and a heartfelt understanding of what

the five individuals mean when they stand together. "We know the band's bigger than anything," Malcolm told Murray Engleheart and Arnaud Durieux in *AC/DC: Maximum Rock & Roll.*

⚡⚡⚡

Even so, none of the above made their sixteenth studio album a matter of urgency. Instead, they took their time, with Angus and Malcolm writing away separately. Malcolm lived quietly with his wife O'Linda at their sandstone mansion in Balmain, Sydney, and

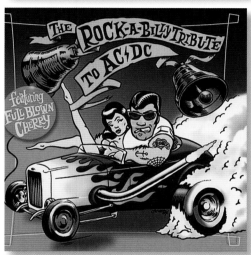

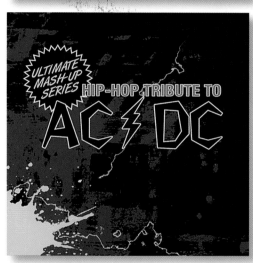

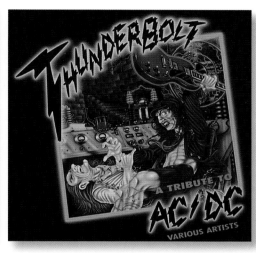

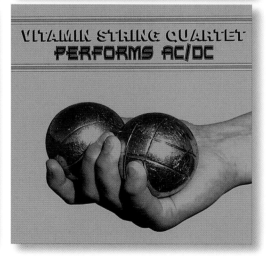

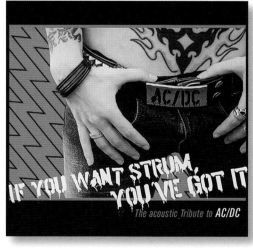

Angus, still drawing caricatures and painting landscapes for fun, lived quietly in Holland, where he and his wife Ellen built a large house in her hometown, Aalten.

The others waited, without obvious impatience. Johnson, in Sarasota with his wife Brenda, raced vintage sports cars, wrote songs with friends, delighted in cooking ("little fancy fanny fucking things"), and tried very hard but (as of 2010) failed to get a musical he'd co-written called *Helen of Troy* off the ground. Williams and wife Georgann, their son and daughter away at university, laid back in Fort Myers, the bass man playing in a bar band, sometimes jamming with Florida "neighbor" Johnson, and, more exotically, in 2002 gigging in Croatia with a band he'd befriended, Emir

Performing with presenter Steven Tyler at 18th Annual Rock and Roll Hall of Fame induction. The Ritz, New York City, March 10, 2003. *Kevin Mazur/WireImage/Getty Images*

Bukovica and Frozen Camel (his serious hand injury from falling on broken glass in the kitchen in 2005 meant eighteen months during which the AC/DC album could not possibly be recorded).

Sequestered in New Zealand, Rudd produced local bands at his own studio. Private as he always wanted to be, he seems to have had children with his wife and two more with a subsequent partner, but that relationship broke up too, and in 2006 he was convicted of assaulting the unnamed woman on a

With boyhood hero, Keef. Molson Canadian Rocks for Toronto, July 30, 2003. *Kevin Mazur/WireImage/Getty Images*

boat at Mount Manganui Marina, where he appeared to spend most of his time. The incident involved grabbing and pushing, not throwing punches, and the judge freed him. Ensuing rumors that various problems would prevent him rejoining the band proved false.

During the hiatus, the group's only public appearances together occurred in 2003. First, they accepted their Rock and Roll Hall of Fame induction on March 10 from Aerosmith's Steven Tyler, whose oration concluded with a flourish: "Does it make you want to boil your sneakers and make soup outta your girlfriend's panties? If it doesn't then it ain't AC/DC." Then they supported The Rolling Stones . . .

It started in February when true fan Keith Richards invited Angus and Malcolm to jam with them at the Enmore Theatre in Sydney. That led to three big European outdoor shows in June—AC/DC acceding to their first support spot since August 17, 1980 (ZZ Top at Toledo Motor Speedway in Ohio), for hero-worshipping reasons plus, apparently, $4 million.

They played four other scattered gigs in 2003. But then they vanished again for five years, bar receiving an array of awards and commemorations ranging from the Recording Industry of America's Double Diamond Award for 20 million U.S. sales of *Back in Black* (2004), to unveiling a Bon Scott statue in Fremantle (2008) and *Maxim* magazine readers voting Angus "Greatest Short Dude of All Time."

⚡ ⚡ ⚡

In March 2008, Angus told Paul Cashmere for *undercover.com*, he walked into a hotel in Vancouver and the first thing he saw was "Brian leaning against the bar, where he was when I left him" in 1999 when they finished recording *Stiff Upper Lip.*

Their songs ready at last, AC/DC went straight to Bryan Adams' Warehouse Studios. After lengthy rumination, they'd decided not to "inflict" production on George Young

again. Instead, with the familiar Mike Fraser engineering, they enlisted Brendan O'Brien. Forty-seven at the time, the Atlanta native was hot from his work with Bruce Springsteen, Pearl Jam, and Rage Against the Machine. In 2008, O'Brien told Robert Levine of the *New York Times* that he liked "'Highway to Hell' and 'Back in Black,' which I view as pop songs done in a very heavy ferocious way" and hoped the new album, *Black Ice*, would make people say, "I've missed AC/DC, and I'm glad they're back."

Instructed by the Youngs to "be brutal," in six brisk weeks O'Brien won AC/DC's respect. Johnson told Jacqui Swift for U.K. tabloid *The Sun* in 2008, "There's a little awkwardness when you first get in the studio with a new guy because he's butting into your little gang. But, by Christ, after five minutes, we could see how wonderful he was." O'Brien even worked around Johnson's enduring tension in the studio—all those machines!—by suggesting he sing in the lobby. "The receptionist had a German shepherd dog, which started howling," he recalled. So he laughed, loosened up, and soon reckoned he discovered both his young voice and a new "soul croon."

This writer hears more of a tough R&B/hard rock holler from Johnson on *Black Ice*, especially "Rock 'N Roll Train," "Money Made," "Rock 'N Roll Dream," and "Black Ice." And then the guitars have that steam-hammer punch throughout, and the gods of riffing smile as they keep it sparse in the old way of Free or 1970s ZZ Top. But they're still AC/DC-hard—very R&Bluesy, too, when Angus wails on "Decibel" or, for once, takes to the slide for "Stormy May Day." After all that preparation, it's odd that *Black Ice*'s lyrics make you go "Huh?" rather than "Yeah!" More than usual, they're down to the occasional strong phrase rather than anything coherent. You've got "Big Jack" ("He said he's the only one who got a full sack") and the winking puns of "Money Made" ("Her swimming pool, is the biggest around"), but overall, an appropriate

middle-aged cooling on the saucy sex front. Regardless, in sound if not word, *Black Ice* really does honor AC/DC's whole musical life—it shakes the ground beneath your feet.

And the world liked it.

It turned out to be AC/DC's time again. When Columbia released *Black Ice* in late October 2008, it hit No. 1 straightaway in America, the U.K., and twenty-seven other countries. It sold 5 million worldwide by New Year's Eve. Phenomenal again. Why? Because of the new fan generation Columbia had drawn in through the back-catalog remasters? Because AC/DC refused to do downloads? Because of the controversial exclusive deal with Wal-Mart in America? Because it had *Black* in the title?

⚡ ⚡ ⚡

No holding back, AC/DC took on the biggest tour of their lives. After seven years, it demanded a lot of effort to get back in the zone.

For Johnson, the struggle was mainly physical. A year into the tour, he told *Mojo*'s James McNair, "The truth is I have a constant fear of somebody going, 'You should have seen him twenty years ago when he was in his prime.'" He hired a personal trainer and flogged himself until "when I came off-stage the first night of this tour, it was like [Russian strongman voice], 'I fear no man! I am strong, like bull.'" So the wine and the working-man's Old Holborn roll-ups would take care of themselves.

Angus saw his own re-entry problem as a matter of identity. "Yeah, I've gotta be this guy again," he told Doyle for *Q* (meaning the one in the shorts and cap). "I told myself, 'Just put them on, don't think.' If you start thinking about it, then you go, 'What *am* I doing?'"

But he knew the onstage "thrill" would come back, those times when, as he told David Fricke of *Rolling Stone*, "I don't know where my fucking brains are. They ain't on this planet, I can tell you."

According to official figures, the band grossed $441 million on a four-continent

continued on page 199

Artist: Jeff La Chance

Artist: Ken Taylor/kentaylor.com.au

SUNDAY, NOVEMBER 23, 2008
XCEL ENERGY CENTER

MONDAY, JANUARY 19, 2009
SAINT PAUL, MINN.

ACDC.COM XCELENERGYCENTER.COM

Artist: Adam Turman/adamturman.com

BANKATLANTIC
DEC 20 CENTER
ST. PETE DEC 21
TIMES FORUM
FLA
2008

LIVENATION.com

Artist: Iron Forge Press/
ironforgepress.com

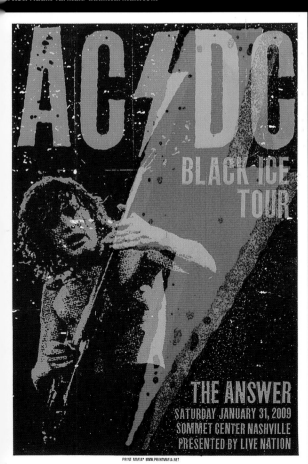

BLACK ICE
TOUR

THE ANSWER
SATURDAY JANUARY 31, 2009
SOMMET CENTER NASHVILLE
PRESENTED BY LIVE NATION

PRINT MAFIA® WWW.PRINTMAFIA.NET

...erican tour. *Artist:*

Hampden Park, Glasgow, June 30, 2009. *Angus Blackburn/ WireImage/Getty Images*

Fans wait in line outside Auckland's Real Groovy Records on July 28, 2009, to buy tickets for AC/DC's February 4, 2010 concert in that city. *Phil Walter/ Getty Images*

Etihad Stadium, Melbourne, February 11, 2010. *All © Graeme Plenter/rockvision.net*

ANZ Stadium, Sydney, February 20, 2010. *Both © Graeme Plenter/rockvision.net*

run of 160 dates beginning October 28, 2008, in Wilkes-Barre, Pennsylvania, and ending June 28, 2010, at Estadio, San Mamés, Bilbao, Spain. They were second only to U2 in concert grosses. Everybody wanted them.

Aptly, the setlist stretched all the way from 1975's "The Jack" to 2008's "Big Jack." The show's new star turn was the Rock 'N Roll Train, towering above the band. Of course, it had its Spinal Tap moments, even if they were all pneumatic Rosie's fault—that first night, when she was supposed to *ride* the train, she just flopped instead. And later in Chicago, she went wobbly again and collapsed over Rudd and his drums.

But Rosie wasn't the only member of the cast to wobble. Fighting fit Johnson missed six American dates in September 2009 because of "my insides . . . ulcers and such." He started to mention that this might be his last tour, and yet there was always that feeling he'd talked about to *Q*'s Tom Doyle: "It gets harder, y'know. But when you . . . look into the crowd and you've driven them into this sweat-soaked, fucked-up state. They're looking at you, going, 'Who's gonna give first?' And it's not gonna be *me*."

With AC/DC it comes down to that—and what Angus said to me back in July 1979 for *Sounds*: "The only image we've ever had is what we really are. . . . We can't just sit on our arses and say the world owes us a livin' because we've paid our dues. Me, I think if I fluff a note I'm robbin' the kids. You're gonna pour it all on until you drop."

"If you want blood — you got it." ⚡

Tributes adorn Bon's memorial in Perth on February 19, 2010, the thirtieth anniversary of his death. *Paul Kane/Getty Images*

Black Ice

By Martin Popoff

With wood-and-strings rock fans and major label bean counters alike starved for a big hard rock record, both Metallica and elusive part-timers AC/DC found themselves obliging (all manner of industry watcher also paying attention) for what was set up as the last gasp for CD sales before another wave of those darned kids forced all the old-timers into an increasingly digital direction. It wasn't like the old days, but *Black Ice* would go platinum, blessed by a confluence of timing and the fact that the boys turned in a rocking, event-filled, brightly recorded album of modest, approachable anthems.

So we had *Ballbreaker* in '95 and *Stiff Upper Lip* in 2000 and then dribs and drabs of tiny rumors for years that the guys were writing and not writing, a record was imminent and then not, and then finally, wee leaks that an album, made in Vancouver with Brendan O'Brien producing, was right 'round the corner.

As with the ramp-up to *The Razors Edge* in 1990, AC/DC had previously made two spotty records. Only this time the predecessors were weird and obscure albums filled with arcane blues melodies, neither record that heavy, curios really, like Status Quo after 1980, an eccentric pop persona of the band's previous self proposing experimental permutations. Also different, *Ballbreaker* and *Stiff Upper Lip* were distant memories, classing *Black Ice* as a comeback or welcome back or please come back into my life and give me something real, something I can recognize (like guitar, bass, and drums), something to believe in, as Bret Michaels is wont to say.

And like the fine *The Razors Edge*, *Black Ice* arrived swaggering, committed to the cause, well-crafted, long and involved, no doubt much credit going to a fresh set of high-priced ears, this time in the form of O'Brien, more of a hard alternative producer, but hey, who didn't drink their first beer to AC/DC? If anything negative can be spread o'er *Black Ice*, one could call it safe, efficient, maybe even surprisingly uniform. But safe means we got what we, as fans, might have drawn up and requested, and efficient means we got a lot of immediate music, and uniform means, well, no ballads but also—was this an oversight?—no fast, riffy, diddly rockers.

I loved the show. The train came through the backdrop and exploded. I sat there watching it going, "This is great!" I went back and said hi to the guys—I didn't realize that I could pick them up with one in each hand. You know, Malcolm can't weigh more than ninety pounds. . . . But they really did rock. They really *played*.

—Alice Cooper

So there's lots to munch on, and it's a satisfying meal. Fifteen songs from this band is a lot (again, some grumbled too many), and inside of each is quite a bit of construction, some serious playing with guitar tones, and vocals out of Brian Johnson that are more expressive and sung (see "Rock 'N Roll Dream" and "Anything Goes") rather than howled.

Highlights are many, beginning with pre-release single "Rock 'N Roll Train," a track that plays up the band's almost subconscious southern-rock attitude (remember, Cliff Williams and Brian now reside in Florida), along with the Young brothers' rolling rock Keith Richards jones. 'Course come solo time, Angus chafes and strafes his meat-and-potatoes note-taking out of his Gibson SG like he's playing it perpendicularly. Like Zakk Wylde, there's a sense of Angus wrenching and wrestling sounds out of his guitar—there aren't many of them, but each one is hard-won.

Speaking of tone, one of the interesting aspects of *Black Ice* is that the songs are written heavier than they come off, due to an astringent, highly electric vibe to some of the riffing, "Big Jack" being an example. Had this one shown up on *Flick of the Switch*, it would've positively roared, and incidentally, everything from this album thrown to the stage on the insanely celebratory *Black Ice* tour juiced the metal quotient ferociously. Tones aside, it's a pretty heavy album, but, weirdly, you can sometimes hear the strings more than the power chords.

But there are various forms of lightness or quietness. "Anything Goes" is a strange pop experiment. "War Machine," built like metal and menacing, is actually a good example of AC/DC in that stealth mode they carry off so well, as is "Decibel." "Smash 'N Grab" is possibly the poppiest thing next to "Anything Goes," and "She Likes Rock 'N Roll" is a little light in the loafers as well. The blues tinge of the band's two previous platters can be heard in "Money Made" and "Stormy May Day," but again loudly, brightly. Nothing's written too intensely, but this time you're getting rocked by lots of splashy cymbals and Brian leaning into it like he can't believe he can still belt it out at sixty-one.

And man, along the ol' substantial meal line, I'd argue with anybody who doesn't think *Black Ice* doesn't end on a headbanging, pool cue–swinging beer buzz. "Rocking All the Way" opens with a classic dirty-blues mumble and then gets going, headed for trouble, before giving way to the intense title track, the album's heaviest, most note-dense riff rocker, the band working through a sharp, staccato, violent arrangement that approaches a form of funk.

Which wraps up a bulging fifty-six-minute spread of invitingly compromised AC/DC, each track—again uniformly—building a case, with the quite lofty and abstract concept being sumthin' along the lines of deceptively simple blues- and melody- tinged hard rock songs put through enough of an electric grinder that the sum total sounds like the first record since *The Razors Edge* that fully dares to participate in a volume war, air guitar unleashed, AC/DC once again as screeching upsetters of the polite pop equilibrium. ⚡

Chapter 11

The Rocky Road to Rock or Bust

Until you drop . . . if you want blood . . . When this writer signed off on the first edition of this book in 2010, nobody knew just how much such rock 'n' roll lines rung true in AC/DC's real life. Before 2014, no one outside the band knew that Malcolm Young had begun to suffer a form of dementia—from the very start of *Black Ice*, perhaps as early as 2003, onwards.

"With hindsight I could tell something wasn't right with him," Angus told Keith Cameron for *Q*.

"Mainly memory things. I said, 'Maybe you should see someone?' He just said, 'Och, it's nothing.'"

At first, they got by, with Angus picking up the dropped stitches if, say, Malcolm wrote and recorded a guitar part then lost track of it. "Before, Malcolm was always very organized, date, time . . . all neat and tidy. So I had to sharpen up *my* processes."

By the time they started recording *Black Ice* in March/April 2008, Malcolm had accepted the nature of what was

> "Malcolm said to me one day a long time ago to play perfectly above all things. The rest is bonus."
>
> —Angus Young

happening to him. Angus faced it with him. He said, "Are you sure you want to do this? I have to know that you really want to do it." Malcolm replied, "Yes! We've really got to do it" and "I'll keep going till I can't do it" (to Michael Hann for the *Guardian*).

In the early American stages of the tour, he went to a doctor for the first official diagnosis: certain medicines might help, but there was no cure, no stopping it.

To fight it, Malcolm spent time every day rehearsing/relearning his parts for songs he'd known like his own heartbeat. Then after the show, he'd ask Angus, "What didn't I get?" Nothing anyone would notice, said his little brother—and it was true: "Some days he was really good, he was Malcolm again. Other days he was lost" (Cameron).

The band, despite the roughneck image, expressed their care in quiet ways that protected Malcolm's privacy, even in front of 20,000 people. And they enabled him to ask for help when needed. Johnson told Cameron, "Once, about halfway through the tour, he'd started to go forward to do vocals on choruses where there weren't any.... After the gig he said, 'Hey Johnna, if you see me doing that again just put your hand out would you?' 'Nae problem, mate.'"

He got through the tour—only to be assailed by lung cancer and heart trouble. Surgery and a pacemaker beat them back. At every turn, by all accounts, Malcolm deployed more stoicism than should be demanded of anybody.

Determined to catch the last of the light, the brothers started songwriting again a few weeks after the *Black Ice* tour ended—Malcolm's final gig with the band, June 28, 2010, a 37,000 sellout at Estadio San Mamés, Bilbao, Spain.

Both had ideas and archived fragments to work from. Inevitably, though, Malcolm's contribution "kind of faded" (as Angus told David Fricke of *Rolling Stone*). Sole responsibility for finishing the songs—and writing all the lyrics—fell to Angus. Again, he wondered whether they should keep going. "I talked with my brother George and he said, 'You know Mal better than anyone. Mal always liked to go forward....' I thought, 'OK, I'll give it a shot. I'll try'" (Cameron).

"It was very difficult, above all, emotionally," Angus told François Barras of *www.24heures.ch*. More so, when Malcolm finally realized he had to withdraw from the group: "It was hard to take because he was aware of what was happening to him.... We couldn't do anything except observe his

Malcolm Young of AC/DC performs at Datch forum on March 19, 2009, in Milan, Italy. *Morena Brengola/Redferns/Getty Images*

deterioration.... AC/DC was his baby." To David Fricke, he added, "When I worked on things on my own I'd always think how Mal would hear it."

Now alone, but ever faithful, Angus got on with it.

As Johnson ruminated to Fricke,

Guitarist Angus Young performs on stage at Cartuja Olympic Stadium in Sevilla, Southern Spain, in June 2010 as part of the band's Black Ice Tour. *Jose Manuel Vidal/ EFE/Sipa Press*

"You can imagine Angus going into his studio without this person—not just his brother but his mentor, his workmate from the age of 15 when he left school … always this man he could turn to."

Of course, a wider AC/DC inter-album life did go on—fun, hobbyist private enterprises and the occasional bit of big-time brand development.

⚡ ⚡ ⚡

Johnson bounced around, as is his natural wont: racing his vintage cars, publishing an autobiography, *Rockers and Rollers: A Full-Throttle Memoir* (2011)—no ghostwriter job, either. It stirred controversy by cheerily declaring his atheism, which provoked various American clerics to an excited state of fulmination.

Down in New Zealand, that September Phil Rudd opened a fancy waterside restaurant called Phil's Place near his home in Tauranga—then closed it for many months the following year after a bust-up with the staff, which eventually saw him pay New Zealand $72,000 in compensation.

Meanwhile, a month earlier, corporate AC/DC—with the band's OK, if not their full-blooded participation—launched AC/DC Monopoly ("allowing fans to build their own AC/DC empire" while bounding round the board as the "For Those About To Rock" cannon or Angus's schoolboy cap, among other pieces).

A range of four wines, Australian of course, also debuted (Highway to Hell Cabernet Sauvignon, You Shook Me All Night Long Moscato). Connoisseur Cliff Williams, in an interview about his own extensive wine collection, chuckled a confession of unfamiliarity with the entire range, although he did have a bottle of each in the rack … saved for a rainy day, perhaps.

Four bottles of Warburn Estate wine bearing the AC/DC name are displayed for the national release of 'AC/DC The Wine' in Melbourne on August 16, 2011. *WILLIAM WEST/AFP/Getty Images*

Still, the feeling remained that this period would prove a hiatus rather than a middle-aged band's wanderings down the leafy lane to retirement. In May 2012, they returned momentarily to their real business when Columbia released *Live at River Plate* (from Buenos Aires, December 2009) as a DVD/Blu-ray. Nothing outstanding, but solid, said the reviewer consensus—and devout fans welcomed it, of course.

Rumors of serious action on a new album started there as well. In *River Plate* promotion interviews, Johnson spoke optimistically, if vaguely, about something afoot for 2013, the band's 40th anniversary. In the month of the DVD's release, Eric Mackinnon—photographer, writer, and rock fan—at the *Stornoway Gazette* in the Outer Hebrides islands, north of Scotland, had the remarkable good luck to spot Malcolm Young along with his wife and son Ross on a holiday visiting the land of their ancestors, and some remote family members, too (Malcolm's in Glasgow, O'Linda's in the outer isles).

Finding Malcolm in fine and friendly form, the well-informed Mackinnon asked about the Johnson-initiated rumors and Malcolm said: "You know what Brian's like. He just says things and then walks away. It'll be a little while—a year or two anyway. I've been doing some jamming on some song ideas, but I do that all the time, as do the rest of the band. We're still working, [but] I think we need a couple of years to recuperate and work on it a bit more." At that, Ross said he thought it would be "a year or 18 months."

On November 13 came the CD/vinyl release of *Live at River Plate*—the day the band's snarly stand-off with digital

media eased a touch when, without fanfare, they suddenly threw their whole catalog up on iTunes.

After that, it all went quiet for a while. Until, in due course, social media took a firm grip on the wrong end of the stick.

⚡ ⚡ ⚡

"AC/DC are finished." Who said? Twitter said . . . In April 2014, somebody told ABC Radio Malcolm was "unable to perform." Then others piled in, expanding the rumor.

The band had to respond. Their statement broadly confirmed Malcolm's ill health, suggested he was "taking a break," and asked for "his family's privacy to be respected." Nonetheless, AC/DC affirmed, "The band will continue to make music."

That turned out to be true almost immediately, in fact. Williams said he got the call that January; there was to be a new album and the band wanted to record in Vancouver in May. Producer Brendan O'Brien's invitation went out oddly late—April, he told Fricke—considering that, from the outset, Malcolm had advised Angus to go back to him for the recording. Even so, he leapt at it.

They reconvened at Bryan Adams' Warehouse studio around May 1 (fans spotted Malcolm and Angus's nephew Stevie Young around town and drew the correct conclusion). Then . . . the band waited. Rudd arrived ten days late. When he finally did show, Angus told Fricke the drummer "did his job," but "it wasn't the Phil we'd known. He'd let himself go."

As for the recording, they went at it hard and fast. Stevie,

Malcolm Young, Cliff Williams, Angus Young, and Brian Johnson attend the Exclusive World Premiere of AC/DC *Live at River Plate* at the HMV Hammersmith Apollo on May 6, 2011, in London, England. *Jorge Herrera/WireImage/Getty Images*

born November 12, 1956—who'd played with his uncles while they grew up together in Sydney—stepped in at Malcolm's suggestion, just as he did when he played 120 shows in 1988. He'd spent the last many years playing pubs and clubs around his hometown Birmingham, England. But, after visiting Malcolm in Australia, he committed to doing "what I thought Malcolm would do" (Fricke).

Johnson told Christian O'Connell of *Absolute Radio*, UK, how he admired Stevie's dedication, "working every night in the hotel room getting the chops." Most important, Angus was soon saying he couldn't tell the difference, that Stevie had "that technique, that sound" (to

Benoît Guérin, *Kiosque*, France).

His brother's absence actually opened up Angus's relationships with the rest of the band, Johnson reckoned: "He shared more with the boys. He involved us" (Fricke). But O'Brien deliberately kept it pithy, always pulling Angus back to the question "Does an AC/DC fan want to hear that?" "You don't get a lot of explaining with those guys," the producer told Gary Graff for the *Oakland Press*. "To them, talking doesn't get anything done."

In about six weeks they finished recording. Soon after, said Angus, when one of the copious Young nephews played *Rock or Bust* to Malcolm, he smiled and laughed. By then he'd had to

move to a Sydney nursing home for full-time professional care—there, Angus told the *Guardian*, with his family around him, he enjoyed his Chuck Berry and Buddy Holly and went out for walks and a coffee . . . but "[i]t's a long way from what once was."

Despite it all, *Rock or Bust* finally came out in late November/early December. It promptly hit No. 1 in Australia and ten other countries, and top ten in thirteen more (United States and UK No. 3).

From reviewers, it needed no sympathetic excuses. In their interview round, Angus and Johnson explained how the album turned out to be their shortest ever, despite its eleven tracks; everything

Stevie Young (left) plays with the band at the AC/DC listening event in New York in 2014. *Madison McGaw/BFAnyc/Sipa USA*

Who's Drumming, Anyways?

If the late August surprise announcement of *Head Job*—Phil Rudd's solo album, a first for any AC/DC member—registered only among cognoscenti, the events of November 6—and beyond—made larger headlines.

Police dawn-raided his home, arrested him, and charged him with attempting to procure two murders, threatening to kill a man, and cannabis and methamphetamine possession. He denied all charges and Tauranga court released him on bail for trial in February 2015. Within two days, police dropped the hitman-hire charge. Subsequently, though, Rudd lurched through further court hearings (on one occasion having forgotten both his shoes and his teeth), a scrap in a local café, and a shit-storm of media stories about other alleged improprieties.

Recalling that Rudd's difficulties with the big time go back to late '70s on-the-road anxiety attacks, it may be significant that in one recent YouTube interview he declared the *Black Ice* tour made him richer than ever before and he'd "enjoy it till I die." Nearer to Christmas, talking with Graham Hartmann of *loudwire.com*, he told the world and AC/DC, "I want my job back, I want my reputation back and . . . I'm gonna fucking take it back!"

But at press time for this book, it remained uncertain who would occupy the drum stool on the *Rock or Bust* tour. Angus joked that he fell out of bed when the radio news reported Rudd's arrest. But his consistent, serious line on Rudd's future came down to what he told the *Oakland Press*: "If we're gonna do something, he's got to be reliable." The band firmly denied that Welsh veteran Bob Richards, who sat in for Rudd for the "Rock or Bust" and "Play Ball" video shoots, might become the if-necessary replacement.

Phil Rudd gestures to members of the media after leaving Tauranga District Court on November 26, 2014. *Joel Ford/Getty Images*

was deliberately short and punchy "like the songs of the '60s . . . excitement all the way through" and also "more bluesy," though they weren't going to attribute that to missing Malcolm—not even on "Rock the Blues Away." There was to be no succumbing to sentiment round their way, they insisted.

As so often in recent years, most critics understood AC/DC's intentions exactly and rejoiced in their dedication to the wonderful same-old, from the iron-ration riffs to the scruffy sex, cars, and booze-filled double-entendrous lyrics.

Kitty Empire in the *Observer* loved their "blue-collar grind" and the way "this band of cheerfully unreconstructed Neanderthals retain their scuffed knuckle-hold on the sublime." *NME*'s Gavin Haynes reckoned the producer had "taken a bit too much dirt out from under their fingernails" but gave it 7 out of 10 as "a testament to the often-derided power of formula: these guys have spent a lifetime figuring out where to turn the screws on a lick, where to swing the drumbeat."

Keith Cameron, for *Mojo* this time, called the title track, "a song so elementally perfect it can tell the time." Adrian Thrills of the *Daily Mail*, UK, hailed Angus for "face-melter" solos in "Play Ball" and "Rock the House." And while the odd writer did perceive a deficit which they reckoned could be attributed to Malcolm's absence, *Paste*'s Robert Ham reckoned all the publicity about his illness "has the potential to overshadow the simple fact that *Rock or Bust* is the best LP that AC/DC has produced in over 20 years."

And this writer? My inner grin lit up maybe two seconds into "Rock or Bust" with that silence the moment after the first feral four-note guitar grunt. It was George and Malcolm bloodline discipline, sustained in the Young hearts of kid brother and nephew—after that, for me, the relieved-sigh feeling, "Oh great, they've pulled it off," only subsided briefly with the hackneyed lyrics to "Dogs of War" (mercenary soldiers only ever worked as a rock 'n' roll theme in Warren Zevon's "Roland the Headless Thompson Gunner"

for me). The *Sticky Fingers* Keefness of "Play Ball," the southern boogieness of "Miss Adventure" developed, dare one say, subtly by Little Featy hints in "Got Some Rock & Roll Thunder" and ZZ Topped off by "Rock the House" . . . exactly. Always and again.

Happy and sad, AC/DC are off round the world again. At time of writing, the *Rock or Bust* tour's scheduled first night is the Coachella Festival, California, April 10, 2015—possibly via a public re-emergence at the Grammy Awards show on February 8—with twenty-five European dates booked, May to July, and more to follow.

As laughingly acknowledged in their November 2014, interview round, they know how lights and cameras will expose age's withering effects. "From 300 yards I'm covered," Angus told the *Wall Street Journal*'s John Jurgensen, "but get too close to the stage and you'll say, 'Wait a minute, what's Tutankhamen doing up there?'" Still, he stands by the status and identity

they've earned: "You spend those early years defining who you are. All of that time you wanted people to hear a song [you'd written] and go right away, 'Oh, that's AC/DC!'" (to Jon Dekel, *o.canada.com*). "My priority is to play really well. Malcolm said to me one day a long time ago to play perfectly above all things. The rest is bonus" (Guérin). "Even when we were younger, playing in a bar or club or something, you always went on with that attitude, 'We gotta make this. We gotta win those people.' We don't give up" (Graff).

Nobody knows how much longer this story of a mighty, massive working-man's band will last. But a Triple M Sydney radio *Rock or Bust* interview took Angus back to the start—just down the road, Burwood, the suburb where he grew up, 1963 onwards, right across the street Chequers Club where he played in 1972 with his first real band, Kantuckee. The memories made him smile. "I always said, make it big in Burwood and you'll make it big anywhere." ⚡

The Boxes
Backtracks

By Gary Graff

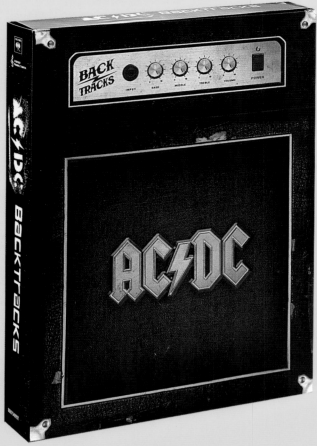

It wasn't particularly

surprising that AC/DC's "Rock 'N Roll Train" turned into a steaming locomotive when the group got back on the tracks in 2008. But that renewed interest spurred a demand for more music, and it wasn't like a group that took eight years between studio albums was going to turn another one out in short order.

Unlike the 1997 box set *Bonfire*, which held together as a tribute to the late Bon Scott, *Backtracks* is a kitchen-sink affair, opening the vaults and tossing together a batch of studio rarities and live tapes for a kind of AC/DC "experience." It did serve the purpose of pulling together a variety of loose ends within the group's catalog, and for new initiates to the highway to hell, *Backtracks* was a fair immersion into what they may have missed before the *Black Ice* album.

The big issue for most fans was which version of *Backtracks* to buy. The standard edition contained two CDs (one live, one studio) and a DVD affair, while the deluxe set, limited to 50,000 copies, came with three CDs, two DVDs, a vinyl LP, a 164-page coffee table-size book, and assorted *tzatchkes*—and was housed in a fully operational one-watt guitar amplifier that Angus, of course, would short out with one power chord but was an appropriately over-the-top touch.

The most important element of the set is the disc of studio rarities—twelve on the standard edition, eighteen on the deluxe—culled from nooks and crannies of AC/DC's discography but mostly from Australian releases that were different from their U.S. counterparts. Hence, we get different takes of "High Voltage," "It's a Long Way to the Top," "Rocker," "Dirty Deeds Done Dirt Cheap," and "Ain't No Fun (Waiting Round to Be a Millionaire)" along with an extended twelve-inch mix of "Who Made Who," "Big Gun" from the 1993 Arnold Schwarzenegger film *Last Action Hero*, and the B-sides "Borrowed Time" and "Cyberspace." Mixing the Bon Scott and Brian Johnson eras, it's not exactly a greatest hits disc but rather the rest of the story in one convenient piece.

The live material ranges from 1977 to 2000 and comes from B-sides, promotional releases, compilations, video soundtracks, and other sources. In both incarnations—the standard box's single CD and the deluxe's double—there are mini "sets" of songs from locales such as Landover, Maryland, Detroit, and Moscow, giving a greater sense of continuity than hodgepodge collections like this usually offer. The thirteen-plus minute version of "Jailbreak" from 1985 in Dallas, which appears on both versions, is a particular highlight.

The *Family Jewels Disc 3* DVD also appears on both editions as an addendum to the video collection AC/DC released in 2005, and it features latter-day clips, such as "Big Gun," which cuts in footage from *Last Action Hero*, and videos from the *Ballbreaker*, *Stiff Upper Lip*, and *Black Ice* albums. The disc is filled out with alternate versions of previously released videos for "Jailbreak," "Highway to Hell," "You Shook Me All Night Long," and others, as well as live footage of "Dirty Deeds Done Dirt Cheap" and "Highway to Hell," and "making of" featurettes about the videos for "Hard as a Rock" and "Rock 'N Roll Train."

The deluxe version's second DVD is a live show from the Circus Krone in Munich, Germany, in 2003, the same year AC/DC was inducted into the Rock and Roll Hall of Fame. The mania of the rare small-venue gig is heightened by a twenty-song set list heavy with early and seldom performed fare, and the quintet is visibly aware that this is a little more special than one of its arena- or stadium-sized spectacles.

Backtracks is, clearly, one for the aficionados, but AC/DC is one band whose converts usually become enthusiastic enough to want as much as the group can give them. A whole lotta AC/DC is a rosy prospect, indeed. ⚡

They Are Among the Great Rock Bands

By Joe Elliott, Def Leppard

Above all, AC/DC are about pure, unadulterated energy. They haven't changed, and we haven't wanted them to . . .

The first time I came across them it was in an advert in the U.K. music weekly *Sounds* for the single "Jailbreak" (released August 1976). I thought they were covering Thin Lizzy! I remember thinking it was a cool name; I didn't even know about the double meaning then.

After Def Leppard started playing the Sheffield pubs in 1977, we did "Whole Lotta Rosie," "Problem Child," and "Sin City." We didn't do more than one cover of any other band. When we played *T.N.T.* and *Powerage*, I remember us realizing they used the same chords all the time—"Hell Ain't a Bad Place to Be" has the same chords as about five other songs on the first three albums. But nobody could play them like they did—that's the point.

The first time we saw them live was Sheffield Polytechnic in 1978. Down the back, shirts off, bouncing all over the place. And then a year on we were supporting them on a U.K. tour.

They didn't even check us out the first couple of nights, and I was moving into that moment of thinking my heroes were going to turn out to be arseholes. But in Manchester (October 29 and 30, 1979), we were in the bar, and Bon comes stumbling in, a girl on each arm, takes the room over. He peels this wad of tenners out of his pocket. He gives a big smile and says, "Can I buy you guys a drink?" We ask for pints, and he comes back

and slams a bottle of whiskey on the table. So I get drunk and I say, "I'd buy you a drink but I haven't got any money." So he gives me a tenner—which I still owe him . . .

Bon sang from the heart about situations he knew and had lived through. "It's a Long Way to the Top (If You Wanna Rock 'n' Roll)" sums it up for everyone who's been in a band and not made it. I see him in a van with everyone sleeping and farting in the back and him up front jotting down those lyrics.

The early albums, sometimes they were out of tune, but it didn't matter. Until they started working with Mutt (Lange, on *Highway to Hell*, 1979). It's a very small difference between a Vanda and Young recording and a Mutt recording. It's about the frequencies that get records on radio. So they grew up. I don't mean that in a bad way. Mutt pushed them there. From the naturalness, they had to, being challenged to up their game. We got a tape of *Back in Black* before it came out (summer 1980) and played it on our tour bus on the way to New York, and it was, "You're shitting me! Silence in the room!"

After that, maybe they got a bit overproduced, and when they stopped working with Mutt, I understood why. Working with Mutt can be very hard. And they wanted to play what they'd always played. "Fuck this shit, let's bang an album out."

Sometimes in the '80s you'd wonder what were they thinking when they made

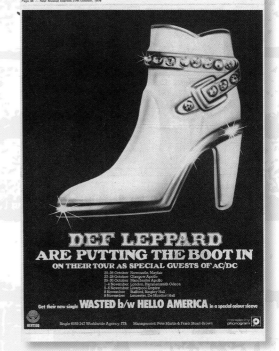

that record. But now, seeing *Black Ice*, you think, "That's more like it." It's OK to be older. Bands of a certain age have a value; there's so much history, and you don't know how much future there is, so you have to grab them now.

AC/DC and Def Leppard have both had the experience of losing band members. Bon dies. Steve (Clark) dies. But what you're born to do doesn't go away. Not even when someone dies. That restlessness, it can't be helped. We are very weak in some areas of life, but this is what we want to do. I've put myself through more pain. . . . AC/DC are like that—they push themselves to the limit. We want AC/DC out there. They are among the great rock bands, like the Beatles, the Stones, the Kinks, the Who. They've rarely let me down. ⚡

211

Selected Discography and More (Also Selective)

By Phil Sutcliffe

Albums

This annotated listing does its best to cope with the particular problem of any AC/DC discography: How do you deal with the confusing titles and contents of those early albums where they'd have an LP out in Australia and then what appeared in Europe or America under the same name a year or so later would be something rather different? Well . . . grab your machete and hack your way through the info-jungle. We've included Australia-Anglo-American studio, live, and compilation albums in order of appearance. Of course, unless you're a collector, what you'll probably want to buy if you're digging back into the AC/DC catalog—as so many unpredicted millions have since the millennium—is the epic remaster of whichever title you're after. Because AC/DC has never been a "singles band," our choices of "notable" 45s (!) follow each album (interesting B-sides shown where known). Read this start to finish in one go, and it could well have the same effect on your brain as standing with your head in a bass bin at the Marquee back in 1976.

HIGH VOLTAGE

Recorded: November 1974, Albert Studios, Sydney
Released: February 1975, Australia only (Albert label)
Chart position: Australia No. 7
Producers: Harry Vanda and George Young
Line-up: Bon Scott (vocals), Angus Young (guitar), Malcolm Young (guitar). George Young and short-term AC/DC member Rob Bailey (bass), while Sydney session man Tony Currenti (sometimes spelled Kerrante) played most of the drum parts except on "She's Got Balls" (temporary AC/DC member Peter Clack) and "Little Lover" (John Proud from Vanda and Young's Marcus Hook Roll Band).
Songwriters: A. Young/M. Young/Scott, except where noted "Baby, Please Don't Go" (J. Williams); "She's Got Balls"; "Little Lover"; "Stick Around"; "Soul Stripper" (Young/Young); "You Ain't Got a Hold on Me"; "Love Song"; "Show Business"
Notes: The debut album was recorded while the line-up was in a state of flux, but by the time it came out, the band had taken on a new manager (Michael Browning), moved to Melbourne, and acquired a new rhythm section in drummer Phil Rudd and bassist Mark Evans.
The original Australian sleeve featured a cartoon dog peeing on an electrical substation. Albert's designer Chris Gilbey called it "naff" but "confrontational."
Scott said he wrote the "Little Lover" lyric about Angus because he was "the most prominent littlest lover that I know."
NOTABLE SINGLES: "Can I Sit Next to You Girl" (Young/Young) b/w "Rockin' in the Parlour" (Australasia only, July 22, 1974, debut single); "Baby, Please Don't Go" b/w "Love Song" (Australia No. 10, 1975)

T.N.T.

Recorded: January 1974 ("Can I Sit Next to You Girl"); March–April, July 1975, Albert Studios, Sydney
Released: December 1975, Australia only (Albert)
Chart position: Australia No. 2
Producers: Vanda and Young
Line-up: Mark Evans (bass), Phil Rudd (drums), Scott, A. Young, M. Young
Songwriters: Young/Young/Scott except as shown "It's a Long Way to the Top (If You Wanna Rock 'n' Roll)"; "Rock 'N' Roll Singer"; "The Jack"; "Live Wire"; "T.N.T."; "Rocker"; "Can I Sit Next to You Girl" (Young/Young); "High Voltage"; "School Days" (C. Berry)
Notes: Underpants bearing the word "Dynamite" on the crotch were one promotional item conceived by manager Browning. On February 23, 1976, they boosted the "It's a Long Way to the Top . . ." single by playing it live on a flatbed truck driving around Melbourne's business district.
The success of hard-rockin' *T.N.T.* coincided with AC/DC being approached by musical super-sophisticate Frank Zappa in January 1976. Via his manager he offered to ship them over to Los Angeles, but they had other plans at the time. In 1993, Angus and Malcolm were rumored to have done some unreleased recording with Zappa's son, Dweezil.
NOTABLE SINGLES: "High Voltage" b/w "Soul Stripper" (Australia No. 6, 1975); "It's a Long Way to the Top (If You Wanna Rock 'n' Roll/Can I Sit Next to You Girl" (Australia No. 5, 1976); "T.N.T." b/w "Rocker" (Australia No. 11, 1976)

HIGH VOLTAGE

Recorded: January 1974, November 1974, March-April, July 1975, Albert Studios, Sydney

Released: April 1976, U.K./Europe; September 1976, U.S. (Atlantic)

Chart position: None (U.S. No. 146 when re-released 1981)

Producers: Vanda and Young

Line-up: Evans, Rudd, Scott, A. Young, M. Young (except for "Can I Sit Next to You Girl," "Little Lover," "She's Got Balls" as above)

Songwriters: Young/Young/Scott except as above
"It's a Long Way to the Top (If You Wanna Rock 'n' Roll)"; "Rock 'N' Roll Singer"; "The Jack"; "Live Wire"; "T.N.T."; "Can I Sit Next to You Girl"; "Little Lover"; "She's Got Balls"; "High Voltage"

Notes: For AC/DC's first international release, Atlantic took six tracks from *T.N.T.* and three earlier tracks, then named it after the band's first album—and *T.N.T.* track "High Voltage," which AC/DC had written too late for inclusion on the album of the same name. Confused? Potential fans actually weren't, of course, because they didn't know about the Australian releases.

Evans told Volker Janssen of *Daily Dirt* that "It's a Long Way to the Top (If You Wanna Rock 'n' Roll)" arrived as one long jam in the studio. George Young edited it into shape and got Scott to overdub the bagpipes, which he'd rarely if ever played before (he'd played side drum in the Perth/Fremantle pipe band).

NOTABLE SINGLES: "It's a Long Way to the Top (If You Wanna Rock 'n' Roll)/Can I Sit Next to You Girl" (U.K. debut single, April 1976; U.S. debut single, October 1976)

DIRTY DEEDS DONE DIRT CHEAP

Recorded: December 1975, late January-February 1976, Albert Studios, Sydney; September 1976, Vineyard Studios, London ("Love at First Feel")

Released: September 1976, Australia (Albert); November 1976, U.K./Europe; May 1981, U.S. (Atlantic rejected the album in 1976)

Chart positions: Australia No. 4 (1976), U.S. No. 3 (1981), Sweden No. 50 (AC/DC's first chart success outside Australia)

Producers: Vanda and Young

Line-up: Evans, Rudd, Scott, A. Young, M. Young

Songwriters: Young/Young/Scott
"Dirty Deeds Done Dirt Cheap"; "Love at First Feel"; "Big Balls"; "Rocker"; "Problem Child"; "There's Gonna Be Some Rockin'"; "Ain't No Fun (Waiting Round to Be a Millionaire)"; "Ride On"; "Squealer" (Australian version featured "R.I.P. [Rock in Peace]" and "Jailbreak" and lacked "Love at First Feel")

Notes: Hipgnosis designed the very un-AC/DC U.K. cover—it would have done nicely for their most famous clients, Pink Floyd.

Early in 1977, Atlantic in America considered dropping AC/DC because their sales were poor and their lyrics over-robust. A personal appeal from Atlantic U.K. boss Phil Carson to label founder Ahmet Ertegun saved their bacon.

NOTABLE SINGLES: "Jailbreak" b/w "Fling Thing" (Australia No. 5, 1976); "Dirty Deeds Done Dirt Cheap" b/w "R.I.P. (Rock in Peace)" (Australia No. 21, 1976); "Love at First Feel" b/w "Problem Child" (Australia No. 31, 1977)

LET THERE BE ROCK

Recorded: January-February 1977, Albert Studios, Sydney

Released: March 1977, Australia (Albert); June 1977, U.S. and U.K./Europe (Atlantic)

Chart positions: Australia No. 19, U.K. No. 17, U.S. No. 154

Producers: Vanda and Young

Line-up: Evans, Rudd, Scott, A. Young, M. Young

Songwriters: Young/Young/Scott
"Go Down"; "Dog Eat Dog"; "Let There Be Rock"; "Bad Boy Boogie"; "Overdose"; "Crabsody in Blue"; "Hell Ain't a Bad Place to Be"; "Whole Lotta Rosie" (U.S. version featured "Problem Child" from *Dirty Deeds Done Dirt Cheap*—then unreleased in America—instead of "Crabsody in Blue")

Notes: To get the phrasing right for "Let There Be Rock," Scott bought a Bible from a bookshop near the studio and studied Genesis.

In the studio, Angus and Malcolm used new Marshall amps obtained via a sponsorship deal Browning negotiated with the manufacturer in U.K.

The atmosphere at Albert's proved particularly convivial because they recorded on alternate shifts with Adelaide band The Angels, who had been recommended to Albert's label by Scott and Malcolm Young.

NOTABLE SINGLES: "Dog Eat Dog" b/w "Carry Me Home" (Australia, 1977)

POWERAGE

Recorded: February–March 1978, Albert Studios, Sydney

Released: May 1978, worldwide (Atlantic, though the Albert imprint remained on AC/DC albums for the duration regardless of their global deals)

Chart positions: Australia No. 22, U.K. No. 26, U.S. No. 133

Producers: Vanda and Young

Line-up: Rudd, Scott, Cliff Williams (bass), A. Young, M. Young

Songwriters: Young/Young/Scott
"Rock 'n' Roll Damnation"; "Down Payment Blues"; "Gimme a Bullet"; "Riff Raff"; "Sin City"; "What's Next to the Moon"; "Gone Shootin'"; "Up to My Neck in You"; "Kicked in the Teeth" (U.K./Europe edition had a different running order and an additional track, "Cold Hearted Man")

Notes: This was the first album Angus recorded with his cordless guitar—he found it as useful in the studio as on stage because he moved just as wildly wherever he played.

Backstairs discussion of Vanda and Young's role began; Malcolm told *Metal CD* why he was glad to stick with what they knew, musically: "We were happy to stay in the same area as *Let There Be Rock* because all that stuff was going down so well on stage."

Like other early albums, *Powerage* may well include some bass playing from George Young carried through from demo tapes.

NOTABLE SINGLES: "Rock 'n' Roll Damnation" (U.K. No. 24, 1978)

IF YOU WANT BLOOD YOU GOT IT

Recorded: probably Glasgow Apollo, April 30; Hammersmith Odeon, London, May 7; San Antonio Municipal Auditorium, Texas, July 8; New York Palladium, August 24, 1978 (possibly other shows that year)

Released: October 1978 (Atlantic)

Chart positions: Australia No. 37, U.K. No. 13, U.S. No. 113

Producer: Vanda and Young

Line-up: Rudd, Scott, Williams, A. Young, M. Young

Songwriters: Young/Young/Scott
"Riff Raff"; "Hell Ain't a Bad Place to Be"; "Bad Boy Boogie"; "The Jack"; "Problem Child"; "Whole Lotta Rosie"; "Rock 'n' Roll Damnation"; "High Voltage"; "Let There Be Rock"; "Rocker"

Notes: In October 1978, Scott told Edinburgh radio interviewer Jay Crawford he understood all the tracks actually came from the Glasgow show, which was also filmed for a thirty-

five-minute promo for European TV. But he could have been wrong or playing to the local crowd.

In different interviews, Angus has both claimed he came up with the album title in a TV interview and allowed that Scott at least inspired it when he replied to another journalist's question, "What can we expect from you?" with one word, "Blood!"

The previous year's *Live from the Atlantic Studios* (see *Backtracks* below) had been released only as a promotional run of 5,000 copies in America.

NOTABLE SINGLES: "Whole Lotta Rosie (Live)" (Netherlands No. 3, 1978)

HIGHWAY TO HELL

Recorded: March–April 1979, Roundhouse Studios, London

Released: July 1979 (Atlantic)

Chart positions: Australia No. 13, U.K. No. 8, U.S. No. 17

Producer: Robert John "Mutt" Lange

Line-up: Rudd, Scott, Williams, A. Young, M. Young

Songwriters: Young/Young/Scott
"Highway to Hell"; "Girls Got Rhythm"; "Walk All Over You"; "Touch Too Much"; "Beating Around the Bush"; "Shot Down in Flames"; "Get It Hot"; "If You Want Blood (You've Got It)"; "Love Hungry Man"; "Night Prowler"

Notes: AC/DC dumped all the material recorded at Criteria Studios, Miami, with Eddie Kramer, the first producer they worked with after deciding to move on from Vanda and Young. Kramer later generously told Murray Engleheart that Scott was "just bloody amazing" and AC/DC "a fundamental rock 'n' roll band."

The band resisted U.S. record company suggestions they should change the album title because of concerns about the Bible Belt market. But the album carried another unwitting time bomb in "Night Prowler," claimed by "Night Stalker" serial killer Richard Ramirez in 1985 as his inspiration.

The Australian edition used the same much-retouched Jim Houghton cover photograph as the worldwide edition but with added hellfire flames and a guitar neck bearing the album title. East Germany had a third, very plain sleeve, and a nasty, mustard-yellow-back vinyl edition came out in West Germany.

NOTABLE SINGLES: "Highway to Hell" (Australia No. 24, U.K. No. 56, U.S. No. 47, 1979); "Touch Too Much/Live Wire (Live)/Shot Down in Flames (Live)" (U.K. No. 29, Germany No. 13, 1980)

BACK IN BLACK

Recorded: April–May 1979, Compass
 Point Studios, Nassau, Bahamas
Released: July 1980 (Atlantic)
Chart positions: Australia No. 1, U.K.
 No. 1, U.S. No. 4, Canada No. 1,
 New Zealand No. 1
Producer: Lange
Line-up: B. Johnson (vocals), Rudd,
 Williams, A. Young, M. Young
Songwriters: Young/Young/Johnson
 "Hells Bells"; "Shoot to Thrill"; "What Do You Do for
 Money Honey"; "Givin' the Dog a Bone"; "Let Me Put My
 Love into You"; "Back in Black"; "You Shook Me All Night
 Long"; "Have a Drink on Me"; "Shake a Leg"; "Rock and
 Roll Ain't Noise Pollution"
Notes: AC/DC went into the studio within a week of appointing
 Johnson because the band got a sudden special offer from
 Compass Point when another band pulled out of its slot.
In the booklet accompanying the 1997 *Bonfire* compilation,
 Malcolm said that after Scott's death, "You're sort of in a
 limbo world and I think that came through in all the stuff
 . . . on that record. [Bon's] spirit was all over it."
The "hell's bell" was supposed to be the "Denison bell"
 (because it was founded by Edmund Denison) in the
 200-foot-high Loughborough (England) monument to local
 casualties of both World Wars, but sound engineer Tony
 Platt couldn't get a suitably solemn recording because of
 birds' incessant twittering.
NOTABLE SINGLES: "Dirty Deeds Done Dirt Cheap" (U.K. No.
 47, 1980), "High Voltage" (U.K. No. 48, 1980), "It's a Long
 Way to the Top (If You Wanna Rock 'n' Roll)" (U.K. No. 55,
 1980), "Whole Lotta Rosie" (U.K. No. 36, 1980), "You Shook
 Me All Night Long" (Australia No. 8, U.K. No. 38, U.S. No.
 35, 1980), "Rock and Roll Ain't Noise Pollution" (Australia
 No. 7, U.K. No. 15, 1980), "Back in Black" (U.S. No. 37, 1981)

FOR THOSE ABOUT TO ROCK
(WE SALUTE YOU)

Recorded: August–September 1981,
 on Mobile One at H.I.S. Studio
 and Family Studio, Paris
Released: November 1981 (U.S.,
 Europe), December 1981
 (Australia, Atlantic)
Chart positions: Australia No. 3, U.K.
 No. 3, U.S. No. 1, Canada No. 4
Producer: Lange
Line-up: Johnson, Rudd, Williams, A. Young, M. Young
Songwriters: Young/Young/Johnson
 "For Those About to Rock (We Salute You)"; "I Put the
 Finger on You"; "Let's Get It Up"; "Inject the Venom";

"Snowballed"; "Evil Walks"; "C.O.D."; "Breaking the Rules";
 "Night of the Long Knives"; "Spellbound"
Notes: They scrapped all material recorded in July 1981 at EMI
 Pathé-Marconi, Paris. H.I.S. was a former factory where
 they'd rehearsed, but Lange thought the sound was so
 good he recorded there on a hired-in mobile studio. They
 used Family for vocals.
Angus' Roman-history-referencing title idea had been used
 before—though there's no indication that AC/DC knew
 about it—by prog rockers Colosseum for their 1969 debut
 *Those Who Are About to Die Salute You—Morituri Te
 Salutant.*
Although AC/DC did break off from recording for the
 Donington Monsters of Rock festival, that summer they're
 said to have turned down a million dollars for one stadium
 show supporting the Rolling Stones.
NOTABLE SINGLES: "Let's Get It Up" (U.K. No. 13, U.S. No. 44,
 1982—b/w "Back in Black/T.N.T. (Live)" in Europe), "For
 Those About to Rock (We Salute You)/Let There Be Rock
 (Live)" (U.K. No. 15, 1982)

FLICK OF THE SWITCH

Recorded: April 1983, Compass Point
 Studios, Bahamas
Released: August 1983 (Atlantic)
Chart position: Australia No. 3, U.K.
 No. 4, U.S. No. 15, Norway No. 4
Producers: AC/DC
Line-up: Johnson, Rudd, Williams, A.
 Young, M. Young
Songwriters: Young/Young/Johnson
 "Rising Power"; "This House Is On Fire"; "Flick of the
 Switch"; "Nervous Shakedown"; "Landslide"; "Guns
 for Hire"; "Deep in the Hole"; "Bedlam in Belgium";
 "Badlands"; "Brain Shake"
Notes: Discussing the inspiration for his lyric writing,
 in a *Flick of the Switch* interview, Johnson told Youri
 Lenquette of French magazine *Best*, "It can come from
 anywhere. A conversation with a taxi driver or with a kid
 after a concert." Angus added, "And if he's short he goes to
 the nearest crapper and copies the graffiti!"
Looking for a new drummer to replace Rudd, who'd finished
 his work on *Flick of the Switch* just before Malcolm fired
 him, AC/DC advertised in UK music weekly *Sounds* for
 someone "hard-hitting"—that was the only requirement
 stated.
NOTABLE SINGLES: "Guns for Hire" (U.K. No. 37, U.S. No. 84,
 1983), "Nervous Shakedown" (U.K. No. 35, 1984)

'74 JAILBREAK EP

Recorded: 1974 and 1976
Released: August 1984 (Atlantic)
Chart position: U.S. No. 76
Producers: Vanda and Young
Line-up: Rob Bailey (bass), Peter
    Clack (drums), Tony Currenti
    (drums), Mark Evans (bass,
    "Jailbreak" only, probably), Scott,
    Rudd (drums, "Jailbreak" only), A. Young, G. Young (bass),
    M. Young
Songwriters: Young/Young/Scott except as shown
    "Jailbreak"; "You Ain't Got a Hold on Me"; "Show
    Business"; "Soul Stripper" (Young/Young); "Baby, Please
    Don't Go" (J. Williams)
Notes: Line-up uncertainties because of brisk personnel
    turnover in AC/DC's early days.
Some discographies list Phil Lynott as writer or co-writer of
    "Jailbreak," but it was an AC/DC original. The confusion
    derives from Thin Lizzy releasing an album of the same
    name in March 1976.
U.S. release only it seems. Probably. One source refers to
    it charting elsewhere, but it's not confirmed. The EP
    eventually sold a million in America.

FLY ON THE WALL

Recorded: October 1984–February
    1985, Mountain Studios,
    Montreux, Switzerland
Released: June 1985 worldwide
    (Atlantic), but Australia in
    August
Chart position: Australia No. 4, U.K.
    No. 7, U.S. No. 32
Producers: A. and M. Young
Line-up: Johnson, Williams, Simon Wright (drums), A. Young,
    M. Young
Songwriters: Young/Young/Johnson
    "Fly on the Wall"; "Shake Your Foundations"; "First
    Blood"; "Danger"; "Sink the Pink"; "Playing with Girls";
    "Stand Up"; "Hell or High Water"; "Back in Business";
    "Send for the Man"
Notes: Recording went slowly by AC/DC's standards, and
    not just because of the Rock in Rio interruption during
    January. New boy Simon Wright noted, "Most of the
    recording I had done before was always rushed and
    chaotic, we had lots of time to get things right" (*Bonfire*
    website).
Unusually, Angus and Malcolm took the tapes back to Sydney
    for mixing.
Despite their relative sloth, Malcolm recalled to *Guitar World*'s
    Richard Bienstock in 2008 that with *Fly on the Wall* they'd
    just "knocked out ten tracks," and it was "stripped down"
because they were "trying to become a simple little band
    again."
NOTABLE SINGLES: "Danger" (U.K. No. 48, 1985)

WHO MADE WHO

New tracks recorded: December
    1985, Compass Point Studios,
    Bahamas (others as above)
Released: May 1986
Chart position: Australia No. 4, U.K.
    No. 11, U.S. No. 33
Producers: Vanda and Young except
    "You Shook Me All Night Long,"
    "Hells Bells," and "For Those About to Rock (We Salute
    You)" (produced by Lange) and "Sink the Pink" (produced
    by A. Young and M. Young)
Line-up: Johnson (except "Ride On"), Rudd (except "Shake Your
    Foundations," "Sink the Pink"), Scott ("Ride On" only),
    Williams, Wright ("Shake Your Foundations," "Sink the
    Pink" only), A. Young, M. Young
Songwriters: Young/Young/Johnson except as shown
    "Who Made Who"; "You Shook Me All Night Long"; "D.T."
    (Young/Young); "Sink the Pink"; "Ride On" (Young/Young/
    Scott); "Hells Bells"; "Shake Your Foundations"; "Chase
    the Ace" (Young/Young); "For Those About to Rock (We
    Salute You)"
Notes: *Maximum Overdrive* movie soundtrack excerpts "D.T."
    and "Chase the Ace" were the first instrumentals AC/DC
    had released since "Fling Thing" in 1976.
Angus recorded a lot of guitar-led instrumentals for the movie
    that have never appeared on record.
NOTABLE SINGLES: "Shake Your Foundations/Jailbreak
    (Live)" (U.K. No. 24, 1986), "Who Made Who/Guns for Hire
    (Live)" (U.K. No. 16, 1986), "You Shook Me All Night Long/
    She's Got Balls (Live)/You Shook Me All Night Long (Live)"
    (U.K. No. 46, 1986)

BLOW UP YOUR VIDEO

Recorded: August–September 1987,
    Miraval Studios, Le Val, France
Released: February 1988 (Atlantic)
Chart position: Australia No. 2, U.K.
    No. 2, U.S. No. 12, Norway No. 3,
    Sweden No. 4, Switzerland No. 4
Producers: Vanda and Young
Line-up: Johnson, Williams, Wright,
    A. Young, M. Young
Songwriters: Young/Young/Johnson
    "Heatseeker"; "That's the Way I Wanna Rock 'n' Roll";
    "Meanstreak"; "Go Zone"; "Kissin' Dynamite"; "Nick of
    Time"; "Some Sin for Nuthin'"; "Ruff Stuff"; "Two's Up";
    "This Means War"

Notes: Miraval had been created by *Play Bach* jazz pianist Jacques Lousier in 1977.

AC/DC imported two New York engineers, Tom Swift and Roy Cicala, who'd worked on *Who Made Who*, to co-operate with Frenchman Jean-Jacques Lemoine.

That summer Johnson repeatedly had to deny rumors that he'd joined a consortium endeavoring to buy his favorite soccer team, Newcastle United FC. But he did tell French magazine *Hard Rock* that "Meanstreak" might have taken over from Bon Scott's "Down Payment Blues" as his favorite AC/DC song.

NOTABLE SINGLES: "Heatseeker" (Australia No. 5, U.K. No. 12, 1988), "That's the Way I Wanna Rock 'n' Roll/Go Zone/Snake Eye" (U.K. No. 22, U.S. No. 28, 1988–"Snake Eye," Europe only, by Young/Young/Scott, see *Backtracks* below)

THE RAZORS EDGE

Recorded: March–May 1990, Little Mountain Studios, Vancouver, Canada

Released: September 1990 (ATCO)

Chart position: Australia No. 3, U.K. No. 4, U.S. No. 2, Canada No. 1, Norway No. 2, Switzerland No. 2

Producer: Bruce Fairbairn

Line-up: Johnson, Chris Slade (drums), Williams, A. Young, M. Young

Songwriters: Young/Young
"Thunderstruck"; "Fire Your Guns"; "Moneytalks"; "The Razors Edge"; "Mistress for Christmas"; "Rock Your Heart Out"; "Are You Ready"; "Got You by the Balls"; "Shot of Love"; "Let's Make It"; "Goodbye and Good Riddance to Bad Luck"; "If You Dare"

Notes: AC/DC emerged from their worst personal difficulties since Scott's death–Malcolm's recovery from alcoholism and Johnson's from a fierce divorce–with a substantial commercial revival.

Chris Slade got his AC/DC introduction via guitarist Gary Moore, who shared a manager with the band (Stewart Young).

Angus told Martin Aston of the *Auckland Star* he liked *The Razors Edge* as a title because it "sounded tough" and because "that's what we are in our music, though not as people. We aren't Mike Tysons!"

NOTABLE SINGLES: "Thunderstruck" (Australia No. 4, U.K. No. 13, Germany No. 2, 1990), "Moneytalks" (Australia No. 21, U.K. No. 36, U.S. No. 24, 1990–b/w "Borrowed Time," Europe only, see *Backtracks* below), "Are You Ready" (Australia No. 18, U.K. No. 34, 1991–b/w "Down on the Borderline," Australia only, see *Backtracks* below)

LIVE

Recorded: Mostly April 20, 1991, Glasgow SECC; June 21-22, Edmonton ALB Northlands Coliseum, Canada; August 17, Castle Donington, England; September 28, Moscow Tushino Airfield, Moscow

Released: October 1992 (ATCO)

Chart position: Australia No. 1, U.K. No. 5, U.S. No. 15 (the two-CD Collector's Edition charted separately in Australia at No. 44 and in the U.S. at No. 34–Canada No. 7, Germany No. 5)

Producer: Bruce Fairbairn

Line-up: Johnson, Slade, Williams, A. Young, M. Young

Songwriters: As shown
"Thunderstruck" (Young/Young); "Shoot to Thrill" (Young/Young/Johnson); "Back in Black" (Young/Young/Johnson); "Who Made Who" (Young/Young/Johnson); "Heatseeker" (Young/Young/Johnson); "The Jack" (Young/Young/Scott); "Moneytalks" (Young/Young); "Hells Bells" (Young/Young/Johnson); "Dirty Deeds Done Dirt Cheap" (Young/Young/Scott); "Whole Lotta Rosie" (Young/Young/Scott); "You Shook Me All Night Long" (Young/Young/Johnson); "Highway to Hell" (Young/Young/Scott); "T.N.T." (Young/Young/Scott); "For Those About to Rock (We Salute You)" (Young/Young/Johnson)

Notes: It was said that, before the Moscow gig, the Russian air force "seeded" the clouds to prevent rain.

The single-CD edition had nine fewer tracks. Between them, the two versions sold 3 million copies in the U.S. and 600,000 in France, the latter a great comeback there.

"Bonny" is "Fling Thing" reworked by Angus as a homage to Scott when they played Glasgow (nearest tour stop to Scott's hometown, Kirriemuir).

NOTABLE SINGLES: "Highway to Hell" (U.K. No. 14, 1992), "Bonny (Live)" (Australia No. 29, 1992), "Dirty Deeds Done Dirt Cheap (Live)" (U.K. No. 68, 1993), "Big Gun" (Australia No. 19, U.K. No. 23, U.S. No. 65, 1993–from *The Last Action Hero* soundtrack)

BALLBREAKER

Recorded: January–March 1995, Ocean Way Studios, Los Angeles

Released: September 1995 (East West)

Chart position: Australia No. 1, U.K. No. 6, U.S. No. 4, Sweden and Switzerland No. 1, New Zealand and Norway No. 2

Producers: Rick Rubin, co-producer Mike Fraser

Line-up: Johnson, Rudd, Williams, A. Young, M. Young

Songwriters: Young/Young

"Hard as a Rock"; "Cover You in Oil"; "The Furor"; "Boogie Man"; "The Honey Roll"; "Burnin' Alive"; "Hail Caesar"; "Love Bomb"; "Caught with Your Pants Down"; "Whiskey on the Rocks"; "Ballbreaker"

Notes: A few months before Rudd's return to the line-up, *Let There Be Light* French fanzine asked George Young whether their errant friend was AC/DC's ideal drummer. He hesitated, then said, "Possibly . . . probably, because the key for AC/DC is raw power. And Phil sounds crude."

While AC/DC recorded, Phil Spector worked in the next room. Malcolm told Sylvie Simmons for *Mojo*: "I don't know what it was but it sounded great, like his old girl-group sound. I'd have gone in but no one fancies a gun to their head."

Australian cartoonist Dave Devris persuaded Marvel Comics to do sleeve artwork for *Ballbreaker* and wrote part of the storyline himself.

NOTABLE SINGLES: "Hard as a Rock" (Australia No. 14, U.K. No. 33, Germany No. 4, 1995), "Hail Caesar" (U.K. No. 56, 1996)

BONFIRE

Recorded: CD 1, December 7, 1977, live at Atlantic Studios, New York; CDs 2 and 3, December 9, 1979, live at Pavillon de Paris; CD 4, November 1974–April 1979, mostly Albert Studios, Sydney, though also Roundhouse Studios, London, and various live venues; CD 5, *Back in Black* as above

Released: November 1997 (Albert/Atlantic/East West)

Chart position: Australia No. 21, U.S. No. 90

Producers: Vanda and Young except CD 1 (no producer credit but engineered by Jimmy Douglas) and CD 5 (produced by Lange)

Line-up: Johnson (*Back in Black* only), Rudd, Scott (except *Back in Black* CD), Williams, A. Young, M. Young (and various others on *Volts* early tracks)

Songwriters: Young/Young/Scott except where shown, and *Back in Black* all Young/Young/Johnson.

DISC 1: *Live from the Atlantic Studios*

"Live Wire"; "Problem Child"; "High Voltage"; "Hell Ain't a Bad Place to Be"; "Dog Eat Dog"; "The Jack"; "Whole Lotta Rosie"; "Rocker"

DISC 2: *Let There Be Rock: The Movie—Live in Paris, Part 1* (soundtrack)

"Live Wire"; "Shot Down in Flames"; "Hell Ain't a Bad Place to Be"; "Sin City"; "Walk All Over You"; "Bad Boy Boogie"

DISC 3: *Let There Be Rock: The Movie—Live in Paris, Part 2* (soundtrack)

"The Jack"; "Highway to Hell"; "Girls Got Rhythm"; "High

Voltage"; "Whole Lotta Rosie"; "Rocker"; "T.N.T."; "Let There Be Rock"

DISC 4: *Volts*

"Dirty Eyes"; "Touch Too Much"; "If You Want Blood (You've Got It)"; "Backseat Confidential"; "Get It Hot"; "Sin City"; "She's Got Balls"; "School Days" (C. Berry); "It's a Long Way to the Top (If You Wanna Rock 'n' Roll)"; "Ride On"; (interview snippets)

DISC 5: *Back in Black* (remastered): as above

Notes: On *Volts*, "Dirty Eyes" is an early version of "Whole Lotta Rosie," and "Backseat Confidential" is a precursor of "Beating Around the Bush." "She's Got Balls" comes from the Bondi Lifesaver shows in July 1977 when Cliff Williams made his illicit debut with The Seedies, or Dirty Deeds.

STIFF UPPER LIP

Recorded: July–October 1999, Warehouse Studios, Vancouver, Canada

Released: February 2000 (Elektra)

Chart position: Australia No. 3, U.K. No. 12, U.S. No. 7, Austria, Germany, and Sweden No. 1)

Producer: George Young

Line-up: Johnson, Rudd, Williams, A. Young, M. Young

Songwriters: Young/Young

"Stiff Upper Lip"; "Meltdown"; "House of Jazz"; "Hold Me Back"; "Safe in New York City"; "Can't Stand Still"; "Can't Stop Rock 'n' Roll"; "Satellite Blues"; "Damned"; "Come and Get It"; "All Screwed Up"; "Give It Up"

Notes: Angus told Richard Bienstock of *Guitar World* (2008) they really had to "twist George's arm" to persuade him to produce them again (and without Vanda): "The poor guy has spent most of his life in studios. He said, 'For anyone else, no, but for you two guys, yes.'"

Johnson told Linda Lacoste of *Le Mag* (2000) that he observed George getting Angus cranked up to record a solo: "George said to him, 'So Angus, are you ready to play a little guitar?' Angus replied, 'Oh yes, yes.'" And George kept him back for an hour, very eager, and then he told him, 'Now you can go to it!'"

The Clash's Joe Strummer paid a surprise visit to one of the sessions.

NOTABLE SINGLES: "Stiff Upper Lip" (U.K. No. 65, 2000), "Safe in New York City/Cyberspace/Back in Black (Live)" (Europe, 2000—"Cyberspace" was recorded for *Stiff Upper Lip*, then omitted)

BLACK ICE

Recorded: March–April 2008, Warehouse Studios, Vancouver, Canada

Released: October 2008 (Columbia)

Chart position: Australia No. 1, U.K. No. 1, U.S. No. 1, Canada, Germany, Japan, Norway, New Zealand, and Sweden No. 1—and another 20 countries

Producer: Brendan O'Brien

Line-up: Johnson, Rudd, Williams, A. Young, M. Young

Songwriters: Young/Young

"Rock 'N Roll Train"; "Skies On Fire"; "Big Jack"; "Anything Goes"; "War Machine"; "Smash 'N Grab"; "Spoilin' for a Fight"; "Wheels"; "Decibel"; "Stormy May Day"; "She Likes Rock 'N Roll"; "Money Made"; "Rock 'N Roll Dream"; "Rocking All the Way"; "Black Ice"

Notes: One of the biggest, fastest-selling rock albums of all time, it spun off no significant hit singles, although "Rock 'N Roll Train," "Big Jack," and "Anything Goes" were released in various territories.

An unknown number of copies of the vinyl album were mistakenly pressed with *The Clash: Live at Shea Stadium* on side 2.

Wal-Mart backed up its exclusive deal on store sales of *Black Ice* by launching "AC/DC Rock Band Stores" in New York and Los Angeles, big cities where they had no shops.

BACKTRACKS

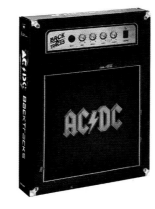

Recorded: 1975-2008

Released: November 2009 (Columbia/Albert)

Chart position: Australia No. 16, U.S. No. 39

Music producers: Vanda and Young, Robert John "Mutt" Lange, AC/DC, Bruce Fairbairn, Rick Rubin, George Young (tracks as above, except most of CD 2's *Live Rarities* carry no production credit)

Line-up: Evans, Johnson, Rudd, Scott, Slade, Williams, Wright, A. Young, M. Young (as above with other early contributors)

Songwriters: Young/Young/Scott, Young/Young/Johnson, Young/Young (as above, except where shown)

DISC 1: *Studio Rarities*

"High Voltage"; "Stick Around"; "Love Song"; "It's a Long Way to the Top (If You Wanna Rock 'n' Roll)"; "Rocker"; "Fling Thing"; "Dirty Deeds Done Dirt Cheap"; "Ain't No Fun (Waitin' Round to Be a Millionaire)"; "R.I.P. (Rock in Peace)"; "Carry Me Home"; "Crabsody in Blue"; "Cold Hearted Man"; "Who Made Who"; "Snake Eye"; "Borrowed Time"; "Down on the Borderline"; "Big Gun"; "Cyberspace"

DISC 2: *Live Rarities*

"Dirty Deeds Done Dirt Cheap"; "Dog Eat Dog"; "Live Wire"; "Shot Down in Flames"; "Back in Black"; "T.N.T."; "Let There Be Rock"; "Guns for Hire"; "Sin City"; "Rock and Roll Ain't Noise Pollution"; "This House Is On Fire"; "You Shook Me All Night Long"; "Jailbreak"; "Shoot to Thrill"; "Hell Ain't a Bad Place to Be"

DISC 3: *Live Rarities*

"High Voltage"; "Hells Bells"; "Whole Lotta Rosie"; "Dirty Deeds Done Dirt Cheap"; "Highway to Hell"; "Back in Black"; "For Those About to Rock (We Salute You)"; "Ballbreaker"; "Hard as a Rock"; "Dog Eat Dog"; "Hail Caesar"; "Whole Lotta Rosie"; "You Shook Me All Night Long"; "Safe in New York City"

DVD 1: *Family Jewels* Disc 3

"Big Gun"; "Hard as a Rock"; "Hail Caesar"; "Cover You in Oil"; "Stiff Upper Lip"; "Satellite Blues"; "Safe in New York City"; "Rock 'N Roll Train"; "Anything Goes" (bonus videos "Jailbreak"); "It's a Long Way to the Top (If You Wanna Rock 'n' Roll)"; "Highway to Hell"; "You Shook Me All Night Long"; "Guns for Hire"; "Dirty Deeds Done Dirt Cheap"; "Highway to Hell" (bonus features "The Making of 'Hard as a Rock'" and "The Making of 'Rock 'N Roll Train'")

DVD 2: *Live at the Circus Krone (June 17, 2003)*

"Introduction"; "Hell Ain't a Bad Place to Be"; "Back in Black"; "Stiff Upper Lip"; "Shoot to Thrill; "Thunderstruck"; "Rock 'n' Roll Damnation"; "What's Next to the Moon"; "Hard as a Rock"; "Bad Boy Boogie"; "The Jack"; "If You Want Blood (You've Got It)"; "Hells Bells"; "Dirty Deeds Done Dirt Cheap"; "Rock and Roll Ain't Noise Pollution"; "T.N.T."; "Let There Be Rock"; "Highway to Hell"; "For Those About to Rock (We Salute You)"; "Whole Lotta Rosie"

180-gram LP: *Rarities*

"Stick Around"; "Love Song"; "Fling Thing"; "R.I.P. (Rock in Peace)"; "Carry Me Home"; "Crabsody in Blue":"Cold Hearted Man"; "Snake Eye"; "Borrowed Time"; "Down on the Borderline"; "Big Gun"; "Cyberspace"

Notes: The listing above is for the Deluxe Edition, which also comes in a "guitar amplifier" case with a 164-page booklet and selection of memorabilia reproductions. The Standard Edition has two CDs plus the *Family Jewels* Disc 3 DVD.

Family Jewels Disc 3 picks up the compilation of AC/DC videos from where 2005's two-DVD *Family Jewels* left off in 1991 (see below for details).

The *Studio* and *Live Rarities* CDs do what they claim and hoover up loads of material that has appeared only in obscure corners of the AC/DC catalog, such as on B-sides.

AC/DC: IRON MAN 2

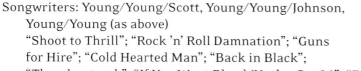

Recorded: 1976–2008
Released: April 2010 (Columbia/Sony)
Producers: Vanda and Young, Lange, AC/DC, Fairbairn, O'Brien (as above)
Line-up: Evans, Johnson, Rudd, Scott, Williams, A. Young, M. Young (as above)
Songwriters: Young/Young/Scott, Young/Young/Johnson, Young/Young (as above)
"Shoot to Thrill"; "Rock 'n' Roll Damnation"; "Guns for Hire"; "Cold Hearted Man"; "Back in Black"; "Thunderstruck"; "If You Want Blood (You've Got It)"; "Evil Walks"; "T.N.T."; "Hell Ain't a Bad Place to Be"; "Have a Drink on Me"; "The Razors Edge"; "Let There Be Rock"; "War Machine"; "Highway to Hell"
Notes: The career-spanning best-of they thought they'd never do? Arising as the soundtrack for the sequel to $600-million-grossing *Iron Man*.

A deluxe version carried a bonus DVD, and for vinyl devotees the music came out on double-LP, too.

Marvel Studios, who made the movie, excitingly revealed that "the band is delivering fans supercharged *Iron Man* branded music through all our combined consumer touch points;" Wal-Mart and Amazon got the retail exclusives again.

LIVE AT RIVER PLATE

Recorded: December 2, 4, and 6, 2009, Buenos Aires River Plate Stadium, Argentina
Released: November 13, 2012 (Columbia/Sony)
Chart position: Australia No. 11, U.K. No. 14, U.S. No. 66, Germany No. 2, Austria No. 3, Switzerland No. 4, New Zealand No. 23
Producer: "Recorded and mixed" Mike Fraser
Line-up: Johnson, Rudd, Williams, A. Young, M. Young
Songwriters: As shown
"Rock 'N Roll Train" (Young/Young); "Hell Ain't a Bad Place to Be" (Young/Young/Scott); "Back In Black" (Young/Young/Johnson); "Big Jack" (Young/Young); "Dirty Deeds Done Dirt Cheap" (Young/Young/Scott); "Shot Down In Flames" (Young/Young); "Thunderstruck" (Young/Young); "Black Ice" (Young/Young); "The Jack" (Young/Young/Scott); "Hells Bells" (Young/Young/Johnson); "Shoot To Thrill" (Young/Young/Johnson); "War Machine" (Young/Young); "Dog Eat Dog", "T.N.T.", "Whole Lotta Rosie", "Let There

Be Rock", "Highway To Hell" (all Young/Young/Scott); "For Those About To Rock (We Salute You)" (Young/Young/Johnson)
Notes: Released seven months after the DVD and Blu-ray version.

The double-CD (or triple red vinyl) version was augmented in Germany by a third disc featuring three songs recorded on June 17, 2003, Munich Circus Krone: "Rock And Roll Ain't Noise Pollution" (Young/Young/Johnson), "If You Want Blood (You've Got It), "What's Next To The Moon" (both Young/Young/Scott).

The set list (order as under "Songwriters" above) hardly changed throughout the tour. Nobody seems to have asked why, but the reason may now be inferred.

The album release coincided with AC/DC releasing their whole catalogue on iTunes for the first time, resulting in the U.K. Rock & Metal Singles Chart Top 10 becoming all-AC/DC for a week–studio and live tracks included.

NOTABLE SINGLES: "Shoot To Thrill (U.K. No. 98, 2011) . . . and that's it.

ROCK OR BUST

Recorded: May–June 2014, Warehouse Studios, Vancouver, Canada
Released: November 28 (Australia), December 2 (rest of world), 2014 (Columbia; Albert/Columbia in Australia)
Chart position: Australia No. 1, U.K. No. 3, U.S. No. 3, Austria, Belgium-Flemish, Belgium-Walloon, Canada, Denmark, Finland, France, Germany, Norway, Sweden, Switzerland No. 1 and Top Ten in Croatia, Czech Republic, Hungary, Ireland, Italy, Netherlands, New Zealand, Poland, South Korea, Spain
Producer: Brendan O'Brien
Line-up: Johnson, Rudd, Williams, A. Young, S. Young (rhythm guitar)
Songwriters: A. Young/M. Young
"Rock or Bust"; "Play Ball"; "Rock the Blues Away"; "Miss Adventure"; "Dogs of War"; "Got Some Rock & Roll Thunder"; "Hard Times"; "Baptism By Fire"; "Rock The House"; "Sweet Candy"; "Emission Control"
Notes: After 41 years, *Rock or Bust* is the first AC/DC album without Malcolm Young.

Stevie Young came to AC/DC from Birmingham pub gigs with bands called Blue Murda and 1Eye. His son Angus (known as "Gus") played rhythm guitar with Blue Murda from 2011 onwards.

Despite its eleven tracks, at 34:55 *Rock or Bust* is the shortest AC/DC album, undercutting *Flick of the Switch*'s 37:02.

NOTABLE SINGLES: "Play Ball" (Australia No. 53 U.S. No. 5–used as theme track for Major League Baseball play-offs; Switzerland No. 19, all 2014), "Rock Or Bust" (U.S. No. 17, Denmark No. 47)

AC/DC before AC/DC

Although the Young brothers never deviated from the true path in terms of recording before they formed AC/DC (aside from the odd session for Vanda and Young), their longtime bandmates did, and here are the original albums they made in those ancient times, most of them still obtainable in one form or another (main members only, in alphabetical order).

BON SCOTT

Band: Fraternity
Line-up (when Scott joined in 1970): John Bissett (keyboards), Tony Buettel (drums), Bruce Howe (bass), Mick Jurd (guitar), Bon Scott (vocals, recorder); Scott also played with Same See (guitar), John Freeman (drums), John Ayers (harmonica)

Albums: *Livestock*, 1971 (Sweet Peach); *Flaming Galah*, 1972 (RCA)

Notes: The two albums are combined on the 1997 double-CD *Bon Scott & Fraternity: The Complete Sessions* (Raven). Fraternity changed its name to Fang while floundering in the U.K. in 1973 but didn't record then. Scott's early bands didn't make any albums, but their recordings may still be found on *Bon Scott with The Valentines: The Early Years* (1991, C5), *The Legendary Bon Scott with The Spektors & The Valentines* (1992, See for Miles), and *Bon Scott: The Early Years, 1967–1972* (1988, See for Miles). The Mount Lofty Rangers, whom he joined after Fraternity, may be hard to find, though they did record a three-track single in 1973—possibly credited to Bon Scott rather than the band.

PHIL RUDD

Band: Buster Brown
Line-up: Gary "Angry" Anderson (vocals), Paul Grant (guitar), Geordie Leach (bass), Phil Rudd (drums)
Album: *Something to Say*, 1974 (Mushroom)

Notes: Rudd also played with Buster Brown on two live tracks of the festival album *Highlights from Sunbury '74*. He left the band before *Something to Say* was released. An extended CD version of *Something to Say*, including the Sunbury material, came out in 2005.

CLIFF WILLIAMS

Band: Home
Line-up: Mick Cook (drums), Clive John (keyboards), Mick Stubbs (vocals), Cliff Williams (bass), Laurie Wisefield (guitar); Williams also played with Jim Anderson (keyboards)

Albums: *Pause for a Hoarse Horse*, 1971 (Epic); *Home*, 1972 (CBS); *The Alchemist*, 1973 (CBS)

Band: Bandit
Line-up: Graham Broad (drums), Jim Diamond (vocals), James Litherland (guitar), Danny McIntosh (guitar), Cliff Williams (bass)

Album: *Bandit*, 1977 (Arista)

Notes: Home ranked fifth on *NME*'s 1973 Most Promising New Name readers' poll, and *Disc*'s reviewer called *The Alchemist* "a work of genius." The band had a small hit with *Home* (U.K. No. 41). In Home days, Williams was given to playing bass with a violin bow. They say he even did it on the night in November 1971 when Home supported Led Zeppelin! In 1977, the entire line-up of Bandit backed Alexis Korner on what was eventually released as *The Lost Album* (1995, Thunderbolt).

BRIAN JOHNSON

Band: Geordie
Line-up: Brian Gibson (drums), Tom Hill (bass), Brian Johnson (vocals), Vic Malcolm (guitar)

Albums: *Hope You Like It*, 1973 (Regal Zonophone); *Don't Be Fooled by the Name*, 1974 (Regal Zonophone); *Save the World*, 1976 (Regal Zonophone)

Notes: The three original albums are out there, as are several compilations, the handiest of which is probably *Geordie: The Singles Collection* on 7T (2001). Johnson sang on three tracks of an album called *No Good Woman* (1978) after he'd left the band and had no involvement at all in a further album, *No Sweat* (1983). Johnson's Geordie II (1978–1980) didn't release anything at the time, but the 2001 reunion line-up did contribute folk songs "Byker Hill" and "Wor Geordie's Lost His Liggie" (that would be a marble) to a boxed set called *Northumbria Anthology*.

DVD-ography
(still, with a bit of video)

The following list is selective, not comprehensive, although given their discomfort with the video medium— at least, until they ran into director David Mallet in 1986— AC/DC hasn't exactly flooded the market. Collectors can also seek promo videos for *Fly on the Wall, Who Made Who,* the Australian collection of nine early clips called *AC/DC,* DVDs like *Clipped* (a 1999 video collection from *Blow Up Your Video* and *The Razors Edge,* augmented when reformatted in 2002), and maybe "event" films like *For Those About to Rock* (the 1991 Moscow Monsters show with four AC/DC songs and performances by several other bands).

AC/DC: LET THERE BE ROCK, THE MOVIE
Recorded: December 9, 1979, Pavillon de Paris, France
Released: 1980 (Warner Bros.)
Director: Eric Dionysius
"Live Wire"; "Shot Down in Flames"; "Hell Ain't a Bad Place to Be"; "Sin City"; "Walk All Over You"; "Bad Boy Boogie"; "The Jack"; "Highway to Hell"; "Girls Got Rhythm"; "High Voltage"; "Whole Lotta Rosie"; "Rocker"; "T.N.T."; "Let There Be Rock"
Notes: Originally released to movie theaters, then sold on video, and not yet a DVD! A rare lapse in the re-release program of the past decade. Come on, guys, it's only ancient geezers like this author who still have the means to play this thing. Extended double-CD audio version included in *Bonfire* boxed set (see above).
Features interviews with the band.

AC/DC: LIVE AT DONINGTON
Recorded: August 17, 1991, Donington Park, England
Released: 1992 (VHS), 2003 (DVD), 2007 (Blu-ray) (Warner Bros., now Sony BMG)
Director: David Mallet
"Thunderstruck"; "Shoot to Kill"; "Back in Black"; "Hell Ain't a Bad Place to Be"; "Heatseeker"; "Fire Your Guns"; "Jailbreak"; "The Jack"; "Dirty Deeds Done Dirt Cheap"; "Moneytalks"; "Hells Bells"; "High Voltage"; "Whole Lotta Rosie"; "You Shook Me All Night Long"; "T.N.T."; "Let There Be Rock" "Highway to Hell", "For Those About to Rock (We Salute You)"
Notes: AC/DC's third Donington Monsters of Rock appearance, more than 70,000 attending, more than twenty cameras filming (one in a helicopter).
Special features include commentary from band members, 5.1 surround sound, and "Iso-cam versions of certain songs for different band members"—you could practically be Cliff Williams on "Dirty Deeds Done Dirt Cheap"! The concert is also available on *Rock Band.*

Aficionados complain that the audio was tarted up when transferred from video to DVD—except in Brazil, apparently.

NO BULL
Recorded: July 10, 1996, Plaza de Toros de Las Ventas, Madrid, Spain
Released: 1996 (VHS), 2000 (DVD) (East West)
Director: David Mallet
"Intro"; "Back in Black"; "Shot Down in Flames"; "Thunderstruck"; "Girls Got Rhythm"; "Hard as a Rock"; "Shoot to Thrill"; "Boogie Man"; "Hail Caesar"; "Hells Bells"; "Dog Eat Dog"; "The Jack"; "Ballbreaker"; "Rock and Roll Ain't Noise Pollution"; "Dirty Deeds Done Dirt Cheap"; "You Shook Me All Night Long"; "Whole Lotta Rosie"; "T.N.T."; "Let There Be Rock"; "Highway to Hell"; "For Those About to Rock (We Salute You)"
Notes: Inflatable Rosie and cannon fire full-on. Interwoven interviews with Angus and Johnson.
DVD "Director's Cut," out in 2008, was newly mastered and mixed, with special features including four songs on "Angus-cam" and bonus tracks "Cover You in Oil" and "Down Payment Blues" from other shows.

STIFF UPPER LIP LIVE
Recorded: June 14, 2001, Olympiastadion, Munich, Germany
Released: 2001 (Warner Music Vision)
Director: Nick Morris
"Newsflash"; "Stiff Upper Lip"; "You Shook Me All Night Long"; "Problem Child"; "Thunderstruck"; "Hell Ain't a Bad Place to Be"; "Hard as a Rock"; "Shoot to Thrill"; "Rock and Roll Ain't Noise Pollution"; "What Do You Do for Money Honey"; "Bad Boy Boogie"; "Hells Bells"; "Up to My Neck in You"; "The Jack"; "Back in Black"; "Dirty Deeds Done Dirt Cheap"; "Highway to Hell"; "Whole Lotta Rosie"; "Let There Be Rock"; "T.N.T."; "For Those About to Rock (We Salute You)"; "Shot Down in Flames"
Notes: Another hot concert film, no expense spared, up there with *Live at Donington.* The opening "Newsflash" got changed for the video after 9/11 occurred, to avoid causing offense—the reason for that can be discovered via close examination of *Plug Me In* (see page 223).

FAMILY JEWELS
Recorded: 1975-1991
Released: 2005 (Sony Entertainment)
DISC 1
"Baby, Please Don't Go"; "Show Business"; "High Voltage"; "It's a Long Way to the Top (If You Wanna Rock 'n' Roll)"; "T.N.T."; "Jailbreak"; "Dirty Deeds Done Dirt Cheap"; "Dog

Eat Dog"; "Let There Be Rock"; "Rock 'n' Roll Damnation"; "Sin City"; "Riff Raff"; "Fling Thing/Rocker"; "Whole Lotta Rosie"; "Shot Down in Flames"; "Walk All Over You"; "Touch Too Much"; "If You Want Blood (You've Got It)"; "Girls Got Rhythm"; "Highway to Hell"

DISC 2

"Hells Bells"; "Back in Black"; "What Do You Do for Money Honey"; "Rock and Roll Ain't Noise Pollution"; "Let's Get It Up"; "For Those About to Rock (We Salute You)"; "Flick of the Switch"; "Nervous Shakedown"; "Fly on the Wall"; "Danger"; "Sink the Pink"; "Stand Up"; "Shake Your Foundations"; "Who Made Who"; "You Shook Me All Night Long"; "Heatseeker"; "That's the Way I Wanna Rock 'n' Roll; "Thunderstruck"; "Moneytalks"; "Are You Ready"

Notes: It's a mixture of promos and historic live clips. Disc 1 is especially salty, of course, being ancient and little seen. It got U.K. music monthly *Classic Rock*'s DVD of the Year award.

Disc 1 covers the Scott era (including a TV film from just before he died), Disc 2 covers 1980 and onward with Johnson.

For Disc 3 see the *Backtracks* box set, page 219.

PLUG ME IN

Recorded: 1975-2003
Released: 2007 (Sony Entertainment)

DISC 1: BON SCOTT ERA

"High Voltage"; "It's a Long Way to the Top (If You Wanna Rock 'n' Roll)"; "School Days"; "T.N.T."; "Live Wire"; "Can I Sit Next to You Girl"; "Baby, Please Don't Go"; "Hell Ain't a Bad Place to Be"; "Rocker"; "Rock 'n' Roll Damnation"; "Dog Eat Dog"; "Let There Be Rock"; "Sin City"; "Bad Boy Boogie"; "Highway to Hell"; "The Jack"; "Whole Lotta Rosie"–bonus features include "Interview at Sydney Airport, April 1976"; "Interview in Covent Garden, London, August 1976"; "Baby, Please Don't Go"; "Interview/Dirty Deeds Done Dirt Cheap, Melbourne Radio, 1976"; "Bon Scott Interview, *Countdown*, 1977"; "Rock 'n' Roll Damnation"; "Live performance and interview, Atlanta, Georgia, 1978"; "Live Super 8 bootleg film, Theatre de Verdure, Nice, France, 1979"

DISC 2: BRIAN JOHNSON ERA

"Shot Down in Flames"; "What Do You Do for Money Honey"; "You Shook Me All Night Long"; "Let There Be Rock"; "Back in Black"; "T.N.T."; "Shoot to Thrill"; "Guns for Hire"; "Dirty Deeds Done Dirt Cheap"; "Flick of the Switch"; "Bedlam in Belgium"; "Back in Black"; "Highway to Hell"; "Whole Lotta Rosie"; "For Those About to Rock (We Salute You)"; "Gone Shootin'"; "Hail Caesar"; "Ballbreaker"; "Rock and Roll Ain't Noise Pollution"; "Hard as a Rock"; "Hells Bells"; "Ride On"; "Stiff Upper Lip"; "Thunderstruck"; "If You Want Blood (You've Got It)"; "The

Jack"; "You Shook Me All Night Long"–bonus features include "Beavis and Butthead Ballbreaker tour intro film, 1996"; "Hells Bells interview and live performance, *Countdown*, 1981"; "Interview at Monsters of Rock, Donington, 1984"; "Gone Shootin' rehearsal 1996"; "Rock Me Baby, Angus and Malcolm with The Rolling Stones, Germany, 2003"

DISC THREE: BETWEEN THE CRACKS

"She's Got Balls"; "It's a Long Way to the Top (If You Wanna Rock 'n' Roll)"; "Let There Be Rock"; "Bad Boy Boogie"; "Girls Got Rhythm"; "Guns for Hire"; "This House Is On Fire"; "Guns for Hire"; "Shoot to Thrill"; "Highway to Hell"; "Girls Got Rhythm"; "Let There Be Rock"; "Angus 'Statue Intro', Stiff Upper Lip Tour film intro, 2001"–and *Live at the Summit*, Houston, 1983: "Guns for Hire"; "Shoot to Thrill"; "Sin City"; "This House Is On Fire"; "Back in Black"; "Bad Boy Boogie"; "Rock and Roll Ain't Noise Pollution"; "Flick of the Switch"; "Hells Bells"

Notes: The "standard edition" has only the first two discs; the "Collector's Edition" has all three. Maybe the ultimate audio-visual digest of what AC/DC has been all about, from Disc 1's "School Days"–celebrating those Chuck Berry roots at St. Alban's High School, Melbourne, in March 1976–to closing Disc 2 with three songs from Downsview Park, Toronto, in 2003, performed to an audience of 490,000.

Oddly, all sorts of slightly different versions of *Plug Me In* exist because of special retail exclusives offered to different chain outlets.

It sold massively, another confirmation of AC/DC's ascent to rock 'n' roll immortality.

LIVE AT RIVER PLATE

Recorded: December 2, 4, and 6, 2009, Buenos Aires River Plate Stadium, Argentina
Released: May 10, 2011 (DVD/Blu-Ray)
Director: David Mallett

"Rock 'N Roll Train"; "Hell Ain't a Bad Place to Be"; "Back In Black"; "Big Jack"; "Dirty Deeds Done Dirt Cheap"; "Shot Down In Flames"; "Thunderstruck"; "Black Ice"; "The Jack"; "Hells Bells"; "Shoot To Thrill"; "War Machine"; "Dog Eat Dog"; "T.N.T."; "Whole Lotta Rosie"; "Let There Be Rock"; "Highway To Hell"; "For Those About To Rock (We Salute You)"

Notes: Its first public showing took place in Buenos Aires to an audience of a thousand on April 13, 2011, a month before the official world premiere in London.

Director Mallett first worked with AC/DC in 1986 on the "You Shook Me All Night Long" promo.

Live at River Plate, which hit No. 1 on seventeen countries' DVD charts, includes a documentary element-interviews with band, roadies and fans.

Acknowledgments

To AC/DC. I loved them when they had nothing and played scruffy London pubs. Who'd have thought *the world* would love them more than ever right now as they roar on through their late fifties (OK, older in Brian Johnson's case) on their biggest tour ever, demonstrating the eternal verities of hard rock 'n' roll across the globe and down the generations of man?

To all the ace brother and sister writers who've made this such a frankly high-voltage, headbanging tome (find out more about these ace scribes in the "Contributors" section), as well as to Joe Elliott, who was there and was kind enough to share his memories and thoughts.

To Dennis Pernu, the Voyageur editor who peered quizzically at every syllable and every semicolon and ensured that they behaved themselves, then peered quizzically at thousands of photographs and pieces of memorabilia. And stayed calm and civil at all times.

To those people and parties who came through with stunning visual materials, including Motor City institution Robert Alford (the prolific Motor City Lens Man whose images grace the cover and inside of this book), Corbis, Robert Ellis (whose imagery not only transcends photography but amazingly documents so many of *the* key moments in the band's history), Robert Francos and Jenny Lens (both of whom were on the scene, cameras in hand, at those legendary '77 "wish I was there" gigs at CBGB and the Whisky A Go Go, respectively), Getty Images, Nathaniel Gorman at Australia Post, Bob King and Philip Morris (both had the foresight to document those antipodean/ante-fame days), Newspix, Graeme Plenter (whose up-to-the-minute imagery of the 2010 Australia tour grace the last chapter), Retna, Jay Allen Sanford at Re-Visionary Press/Revolution Comics, Joel Schnell in the CPi photo studio, Brannon Tommey (check out his collection at photosets.net), and last but certainly not least, Acca Dacca historian and collector extraordinaire Bill Voccia.

On the design side, special thanks to Voyageur Press creative director Becky Pagel and to design manager LeAnn Kuhlmann for championing the spinner.

Now, if you AC/DC fans find any mistakes sneaking through all the sweated endeavor of this diligent yet rather less-than-perfect team, don't just smile smugly and keep it to yourselves— let us know, and we'll put it right next time. Unless what you tell us is wrong, in which case we'll put it wrong next time. (No, we'll check, honest.)

Finally, to my wife, Gaylee, who again read the whole thing before it went off to Minneapolis and made improving suggestions, many of them polite. And she was there back in the '70s, melting at the Marquee with me.

All the best,
Phil Sutcliffe

Sources

A remarkably private bunch, considering all the bedlam and arse-baring they get up to onstage, AC/DC would nonetheless give the most forthright answers to any question they didn't consider intrusive—and that covered a lot of ground, from girls and guitars to God. Most of the quotes herein are attributed and noted in the text, but here's the official honor roll:

Martin Aston (*Auckland Star*); François Barras (*www.24heures.ch*); Richard Bienstock (*Guitar World*); Mark Blake (*Metal CD*); Dante Bonuto (*Kerrang!*); Keith Cameron (*Q & Mojo*); Paul Cashmere (*undercover. com*); Thierry Chatain (*Rock & Folk*); Caroline Coon (*Melody Maker*); Jon Dekel *(o.canada.com);* Tom Doyle (*Q*); Arnaud Durieux (*Hard Force*); Charlie Eliezer (*Juke*); Murray Engleheart (*Bonfire* boxed set booklet); Angus Fontayne (*Sydney Daily Telegraph*); Cathy Free (*People*); David Fricke (*Rolling Stone*); Gary Graff (the *Oakland Press); Benoît Guérin (Kiosque);* Michael Hann (the *Guardian); Graham Hartmann (loudwire. com);* Volker Janssen (*Daily Dirt*); Howard Johnson (*Kerrang!*); John Jurgensen (*Wall Street Journal*); Howie Klein (*New York Rocker*); Lynda Lacoste (*Le Mag*); Phil Lageat (highwaytoacdc.com, *Hard Rock*, *Rock Hard, Let There Be Light*); Youri Lenquette (*Best*); Robert Levine (*New York Times*); Dave Lewis (*Sounds*); Vince Lovegrove (*RAM*, adelaidenow.com. au); Eric Mackinnon (*Stornoway Gazette); James McNair (Mojo*); Maggie Montalbano (*Metal Hammer & Classic Rock* AC/DC special); Christian O'Connell (*Absolute Radio); Jan Olbrecht (Guitar Player*); Anthony O'Grady (*RAM*); Michel Rémy (*Let There Be Light*); Sylvie Simmons (*Mojo*, *Creem*, *Metal Creem,* interview transcript); David Sinclair (*Q*); Robin Smith (*Record Mirror*); Jacqui Swift (the *Sun*); Adrian Thrills (*Daily Mail*); and Charles M. Young (*Musician*).

Some quotes in this narrative are unattributed, usually because they come from the web jungle of fan sites. However, many of these anonymous web sources are written in French, which I retranslated, but you may miss that distinctive Aussie flavor in those instances. Same applies to quotes from the French journalists among the fine interviewers and writers listed below, whose work was much enjoyed and appreciated while researching. Special thanks to my colleague Sylvie Simmons for her articles but also for the interview transcript she sent me. And special admiration to Phil Lageat; I don't know him, but he has been a wondrously indefatigable chronicler of all things AC/DC down the decades in all manner of publications.

INTERVIEW SOURCES FOUND ON THE WEB WITH NO AUTHOR CREDITED:
Best, Bonfire, Classic Rock, crabsodyinblue, cyberdrum, Guitare Et Clavier, Hard Rock, Hot Press, Juke, KNAC.com, *Let There Be Light, Metal Attack, Metal CD, RAM*, and *Rock Hard.*

AMONG NUMEROUS AC/DC BOOKS AVAILABLE, THE DADDIES IN TERMS OF DEPTH, WINGSPAN, AND THOROUGHLY RESEARCHED ACCURACY ARE:

Engleheart, Murray, with Arnaud Durieux. *AC/DC: Maximum Rock & Roll.* Sydney: HarperCollins Australia, 2006.

Evans, Mark. *Dirty Deeds: My Life Inside/Outside of AC/DC.* New York: Bazillion Points, 2011.

Fink, Jesse. *The Youngs: The Brothers Who Built AC/DC.* Sydney: Random House Australia, 2013.

Johnson, Brian. *Rockers and Rollers: A Full-Throttle Memoir.* New York: IT Books, 2012.

Walker, Clinton. *Highway to Hell: The Life and Death of AC/DC Legend Bon Scott.* Portland, Ore.: Verse Chorus Press, 2007.

OTHER BOOK SOURCES OF BACKGROUND INFORMATION OR QUOTES:

Bunton, Richard. *AC/DC: Hell Ain't No Bad Place to Be!* London: Omnibus, 1982.

Dome, Malcolm. *AC/DC.* London: Proteus, 1982.

Dome, Malcolm, editor. *AC/DC: The Kerrang! Files.* London: Virgin, 1995.

Dome, Malcolm, and Jerry Ewing. *AC/DC: The Encyclopaedia.* New Malden, U.K.: Chrome Dreams, 2008.

Huxley, Martin. *AC/DC: The World's Heaviest Rock.* London: Boxtree, 1996.

Johnson, Brian. *Rockers and Rollers: An Automotive Autobiography.* London: Michael Joseph, 2009.

Johnson, Howard. *Get Your Jumbo Jet Out of My Airport: Random Notes for AC/DC Obsessives.* Pewsey, U.K.: Black Book, 1999.

Masino, Susan. *The Story of AC/DC: Let There Be Rock.* New York: Omnibus, 2006.

Putterford, Mark. *AC/DC: Shock to the System.* London: Omnibus, 1992.

Stenning, Paul. *AC/DC: Two Sides to Every Glory.* New Malden, U.K.: Chrome Dreams, 2005.

Taylor, Barry, with Dan Wooding. *Singing in the Dark: A Rock 'n' Roll Roadie Comes Clean.* Eastbourne, U.K.: Kingsway, 1990.

WEBSITE SOURCES OF REFERENCE AND COMPARATIVE DATA:

en.wikipedia.org/wiki/AC/DC (no, really—massive and accurate . . . as far as I can tell)

acdc.com (official site)

ac-dc.net

acdccollector.com

allmusic.com

crabsodyinblue.com

gogomag.com

highwaytoacdc.com

rocklineradio.com

songkick.com

youtube.com

Contributors

Robert Alford is a veteran rock 'n' roll photographer of thirty-five-plus years. The list of the more than five hundred acts he has photographed range from AC/DC to ZZ Top. His work has featured prominently in magazines (*Creem*, *People*, *Rolling Stone*, and more), on album covers, in liner notes, on television, and in documentaries.

Joe Bonomo is the author of *Sweat: The Story of the Fleshtones, America's Garage Band*; *Installations*, a collection of prose poems; *Jerry Lee Lewis: Lost and Found*; and *AC/DC's Highway to Hell*. He teaches in the English department at Northern Illinois University.

Anthony Bozza is a New York City–based author and journalist best known for his bestselling biographies of Mötley Crüe drummer Tommy Lee (*Tommyland*), Guns N' Roses guitarist Slash, comedian Artie Lange (*Too Fat to Fish*), and Tracy Morgan (*I Am the New Black*), as well as *Why AC/DC Matters*, his analysis of the legendary Australian rockers.

Jen Jewel Brown was *Rolling Stone*'s first Australian reporter and has since become a widely published, freewheeling writer Down Under for publications including *RAM*, *The Age*, *The Australian*, and *Mediaweek*. The author of the Australian bestseller *Skyhooks Million Dollar Riff*, Jen also worked at MCA and Mushroom and helped sign INXS, The Church, and Yothu Yindi.

Daniel Bukszpan is the author of *The Encyclopedia of Heavy Metal*. He has been a freelance writer since 1994, and he has written for such publications as the *New York Post*, *Pop Smear*, *Guitar World*, *The Pit Report*, and *Hails and Horns*. He lives in Brooklyn with his wife, Asia, and his son, Roman.

New Zealand–born, London-based **Garth Cartwright** is an award-winning journalist and critic who regularly contributes to *The Guardian*, *The Sunday Times*, *fRoots*, and the BBC's website. He is the author of *Princes Amongst Men: Journeys with Gypsy Musicians* and *More Miles Than Money: Journeys through American Music*.

Ian Christe (*soundofthebeast.com*) is the author of *Sound of the Beast: The Complete Headbanging History of Heavy Metal* and *Everybody Wants Some: The Van Halen Saga*. He is also host of the weekly *Bloody Roots* metal history show on Sirius XM and publisher of Bazillion Points Books (*bazillionpoints.com*). His articles have appeared in *Spin*, *CMJ*, *Metal Maniacs*, and *The Trouser Press Guide to '90s Rock*.

David Dunlap Jr. is a contributing writer for the *Washington City Paper*. His work has appeared in other books, including *Whole Lotta Led Zeppelin: The Illustrated History of the Heaviest Band of All Time* and *Queen: The Ultimate Illustrated History of the Crown Kings of Rock*.

Andrew Earles has contributed to *Spin*, *Paste*, *Magnet*, *Memphis Flyer*, and other publications. Additionally, his writing can be found in several books, including *Whole Lotta Led Zeppelin: The Illustrated History of the Heaviest Band of All Time* and *Queen: The Ultimate Illustrated History of the Crown Kings of Rock*. He lives in Memphis, Tennessee.

Robert Ellis (*repfoto.com*) began his career as a music photographer in the late 1960s, working a folk club in the back room of a pub in the English Midlands. Ellis moved to London in 1971 and worked for *New Musical Express* for four years before moving on to *Melody Maker*. His tenure with *NME*'s rival didn't last long due to Ellis' in-demand status as a touring photographer with bands like Genesis, Wings, and Status Quo. By the early 1980s, other photographers were asking if Ellis could place their photographs in the same magazines he was supplying, and Repfoto was born.

From 1977 to 1988, **Robert Francos** published *FFanzeen* in New York City, covering the wide-ranging indie music scene of the period. Today, Francos resides in Saskatoon, Saskatchewan.

Gary Graff is a regular contributor to the *New York Times* Features Syndicate, *Billboard*, and *Revolver*. He is the editor of *The Ties That Bind: Bruce Springsteen A to E to Z* and the series editor of the *MusicHound Essential Album Guide* series, as well as the co-author (with Tom Wechsler) of *Travelin' Man: On the Road and Behind the Scenes With Bob Seger* and (with Daniel Durchholz) of *Neil Young: Long May You Run: The Illustrated History*.

Dave Hunter is an author, musician, and journalist. He is the presenter and co-author of the *Totally Interactive Guitar Bible* and its two follow-ups, *Interactive Fender Bible* and *Interactive Gibson Bible*. Among his other books are the popular *The Guitar Amp Handbook*, *Guitar Rigs*, *Guitar Effects Pedals*, and *Star Guitars: 101 Guitars That Rocked the World*. He contributes regularly to *Guitar Player* and *Vintage Guitar* magazines.

Bob King (*bobking.com.au*) began his career as an entertainment photographer in 1964 when he captured images of the Beatles at Sydney Stadium. Over the decades, he has shot virtually every visiting concert act of consequence and a dramatically wide spectrum of Australian entertainers.

From 1976 to 1980, **Jenny Lens** (*jennylens.com*) captured a major cultural revolution from a decidedly L.A. female perspective. Classic photos of the Ramones, the Clash, Blondie, Patti Smith, X, Devo, Chuck Berry, and dozens of others made her the most published West Coast photographer of the early punk era. Her work has appeared internationally for more than thirty-four years in liner notes, magazines, documentary films, and books, including her own *Punk Pioneers*. As of this writing, she's still pulling up photos she's never seen.

James McNair is a Glasgow-born music journalist who lives in London. A regular contributor to *Mojo* and the U.K. broadsheet *The Independent*, he counts Keith Richards, Björk, Brian Wilson, and the late James Brown among his favorite interviewees.

Inimitable Australian rock photographer **Philip Morris** (*rockphotograph.com*) boasts one of the most extensive photo archives of Australian rock. Morris started his career in Sydney at the age of fifteen. In the 1970s he was a contributor to all the major Australian music magazines, shooting the Easybeats on their last national tour, as well as almost every international band touring the country, including the Rolling Stones, Led Zeppelin, and Paul McCartney, among others. Morris is still the only photographer to document AC/DC at Albert Studios.

Graeme Plenter (*rockvizion.com.au*) has been photographing live music Down Under since 1983. He lives in New South Wales.

Martin Popoff (*martinpopoff.com*) is the author of twenty-eight books on hard rock and heavy metal. Additionally, he has written more record reviews than anyone living or dead. His band bios include works on Black Sabbath, Deep Purple, Judas Priest, UFO, Rainbow, Dio, Rush, and the mighty Blue Öyster Cult.

Rock 'n' Roll Comics was launched in 1989 by Todd Loren to spin illustrated (and unlicensed) biographies of rock stars. Some were supportive, while others sued. Loren was convinced the First Amendment to the U.S. Constitution protected his "illustrated articles," and the California Supreme Court agreed. In June 1992, Loren was found murdered in his San Diego condo. The comics continued for two more years, with Jay Allen Sanford serving as managing editor. In 2005, BulletProof Film released the documentary *Unauthorized and Proud of It: Todd Loren's Rock 'N' Roll Comics*, featuring interviews with Loren's family, friends, and adversaries. Loren's murder remains unsolved.

Sylvie Simmons (*sylviesimmons.com*) was born in London and lives in San Francisco. She's been writing about rock since 1977, first as L.A. correspondent for U.K. weekly *Sounds* and then for *Kerrang!*, legendary U.S. magazine *Creem*, and *Mojo*. Her writing has also appeared in *Q*, *Rolling Stone*, and *Blender*, as well as the *Guardian* and the *San Francisco Chronicle*. Her own books include the cult fiction of *Too Weird for Ziggy* and biographies of Neil Young and Serge Gainsbourg.

Bill Voccia is a New York music journalist who has published articles about AC/DC in *Record Collector*, *Goldmine*, and *Daily-Dirt*. He has interviewed former members of AC/DC, Fraternity, The Valentines, and others, and has one of the world's largest AC/DC collections. An expert in the band's history, collectibles, and autograph authentication, he was hired to promote *Black Ice* in 2008, and was also involved in promotion of *Backtracks* in 2009. He performs and tours around the world in his AC/DC tribute band, Live Wire (*www.acdctributeband.com*).

Index

We can't just sit on our arses and say the world owes us
a livin' because we've paid our dues.
Me, I think if I fluff a note I'm robbin' the kids.
You're gonna pour it all on until you drop.

—Angus Young, *Sounds*, 1979